TEACHERS IN TROUBLE: AN EXPLORATION OF THE NORMATIVE CHARACTER OF TEACHING

Stuart Piddocke, Romulo Magsino, and Michael Manley-Casimir

D0949395

The teacher who has an affair with a student. The teacher who is a transvestite. The teacher who advocates personal beliefs. These are 'teachers in trouble.' Their behaviour, whether it occurs in the classroom or off the job, offends the community and brings down censure from the school board.

At root, schools are cultural institutions and teaching, a cultural activity. Teachers are expected to shape students according to accepted community norms. They interpret and apply curricula – and can divert curricula from their intended purpose. Teachers are at the eye of the vortex in the struggle for control over education, buffeted by the forces of social change and conflicting public expectations. The authors of this book examine how teacher conduct is monitored and what types of misconduct can produce 'social dramas.' Boards of reference have been established to arbitrate disputes between school boards and teachers who are dismissed. Drawing on the decisions of these boards of reference across Canada, the authors identify normative issues and propose a classification scheme for contentious behaviours.

Teachers in Trouble poses fundamental questions about the role of teachers in society. It is an invaluable guide for teachers and professional organizations, education administrators, and members of the community who are concerned about ethics in our schools.

STUART PIDDOCKE is research associate at the Centre for Education, Law and Society, Faculty of Education, Simon Fraser University.

ROMULO MAGSINO is dean of the Faculty of Education, University of Manitoba.

MICHAEL MANLEY-CASIMIR is professor in the Faculty of Education, Simon Fraser University.

STUART PIDDOCKE
ROMULO MAGSINO
MICHAEL MANLEY-CASIMIR

Teachers in Trouble: An Exploration of the Normative Character of Teaching

UNIVERSITY OF TORONTO PRESS
Toronto Buffalo London

© University of Toronto Press Incorporated 1997
Toronto Buffalo London
Printed in Canada

ISBN 0-8020-2979-5 (cloth)
ISBN 0-8020-7436-7 (paper)

Printed on acid-free paper

Canadian Cataloguing in Publication Data

Piddocke, Stuart, 1936–
  Teachers in trouble : an exploration of the normative
  character of teaching

  Includes bibliographical references and index.
  ISBN 0-8020-2979-5 (bound)   ISBN 0-8020-7436-7 (pbk.)

  1. Teachers – Professional ethics – Case studies.
  2. Teachers and community – Case studies.   3. Teaching –
  Social aspects – Case studies.   I. Magsino, Romulo F.
  (Romulo Fernandez), 1941–   .   II. Manley-Casimir,
  Michael E.   III. Title.

  LB1775.P52 1997   371.1   C97-931399-6

University of Toronto Press acknowledges the financial assistance to its
publishing program of the Canada Council for the Arts and the Ontario
Arts Council.

The publication of this book was assisted by the Centre for Education, Law and
Society, Simon Fraser University.

Contents

Acknowledgments

This book is one outcome of a national study into community values and the unconventional teacher, conducted under the direction of Dr Michael Manley-Casimir of the Faculty of Education at Simon Fraser University, Burnaby, B.C. The study was funded during 1988–91 by a grant from the Social Sciences and Humanities Research Council of Canada, whose financial help rendered this research possible.

Research such as this inevitably depends upon the help of a good many people. We would like to thank the several organizations and individuals whose assistance made this study possible. In many cases, individuals have changed their roles and affiliations; we acknowledge these individuals in the roles they held at the time the study was conducted.

Research Funding

Social Sciences and Humanities Research Council, small grant, December 1987–February 1988, for a pilot study; and major three-year research grant, April 1988–April 1991, for the national study.

Access to Ministry of Education Records

Hon. Anthony Brummet, Minister of Education, British Columbia, for permission to view ministry records (February 1988).

Hon. Lorne H. Hepworth, Minister of Education, Saskatchewan, for permission to view ministry records (June 1988).

Dr Bernard J. Shapiro, Deputy Minister of Education, Ontario, for permission to view ministry records (March 1989).

For Answers to Enquiries

Mr Earle McCabe, Deputy Executive Director, Ontario Separate School Trustees' Association (17 June 1988).

Mr John Jakub, Director, Legal and Personnel Services, Ontario Public School Trustees' Association (18 May 1988) – and for a collection of cases.

Mr David M. Eaton, General Secretary, Ontario Secondary School Teachers' Federation (20 May 1988).

Mr David J. Lennox, Secretary, Ontario Public School Teachers' Federation (26 May 1988).

Assistance to the Field Researcher, S. Piddocke

Stuart Piddocke would particularly like to thank the people who showed him their procedures, helped him to understand the administration of boards of reference in British Columbia, Alberta, Saskatchewan, and Ontario, and helped him in the compilation of an inventory of board of reference cases:

Mr Earl Cherrington, Director of Professional Relations, Ministry of Education, Victoria, B.C.

Dr Larry Rappel, Director, Teacher Certification and Development Branch, Alberta Education, Edmonton, Alberta.

Ms Kathleen Stewart, Acting Associate Director, Teacher Certification and Development Branch, Alberta Education, Edmonton, Alberta.

Mr Gary Johnson, Teacher Certification and Development Branch, Alberta Education, Edmonton, Alberta.

Mr Earl Hjelter, Alberta Teachers' Association, Edmonton, Alberta.

Ms Judith Anderson, Director of Legal Services, Alberta School Trustees' Association, Edmonton, Alberta.

Mr Gene Hodgson, Director, Board and Teacher Services Branch, Saskatchewan Education, Regina, Saskatchewan.

Mr Michael Littlewood, legal officer, Board and Teacher Services Branch, Saskatchewan Education, Regina, Saskatchewan.

Mr Terence McKague, Saskatchewan Teachers' Federation, Regina, Saskatchewan.

Ms LaVonne Beriault, legal counsel, Saskatchewan School Trustees' Association, Regina, Saskatchewan.

Ms Patricia Llewellyn, Information and Privacy Unit Coordinator, Ministry of Education, Toronto, Ontario.

Ms Hilary Roy, Records Manager, Ministry of Education, Toronto, Ontario.

Dr Jack Berryman, Education Officer, Legislation Branch, Ministry of Education, Toronto, Ontario.

Mr Earle McCabe, Deputy Executive Director, Ontario Separate School Trustees' Association, Toronto, Ontario.

Mr John Jakub, Director of Legal and Personnel Services, Ontario Public School Trustees' Association, Toronto, Ontario.

Over the course of this research, we have published a number of papers reporting various aspects of the study in the *Education and Law Journal*; we refer the reader to the various articles when we cite them in this volume. We do, however, wish to thank the editor of the *Education and Law Journal*, Dr Greg Dickinson, for his permission to use material from our various articles freely in this volume. In addition, we wish to thank Eileen Mallory for her unfailing competence and good humour in preparing this manuscript for submission, and Shannon Sheppard for editorial assistance.

Finally, we wish to emphasize that the conclusions of this book are our own, and do not reflect the opinions of the above persons or of anybody else. This kind of research also touches the public and private lives of a good many people. Access to records was given to us on the understanding that the privacy of the people concerned would be scrupulously respected. We have tried to adhere to this understanding.

STUART PIDDOCKE
ROMULO MAGSINO
MICHAEL MANLEY-CASIMIR

TEACHERS IN TROUBLE

1

Contentious Behaviours

Four Hypothetical Cases

In the province of New Cumbria, public school teachers on a permanent or continuing contract may be suspended from their jobs without pay or even dismissed if the school board has 'just and reasonable' cause to suspend or dismiss them. If the suspension is for more than ten days, or if they are dismissed, the teachers then have the right to appeal that suspension or dismissal to a special tribunal or 'board of reference.' This board of reference has the power to change, even to reverse, the school board's decision.

This month, there are four appeals before the board of reference. In each of them, the school board has dismissed the teacher for something the teacher did 'off the job' outside the school. These contentious acts have been labelled 'misconduct.'

Case A:[1] The Affair

Mr T. is a science teacher in his late forties. He has been under considerable stress the last two years. His marriage is 'on the rocks' and his eldest son has been charged with possession of narcotics. Thirteen months before the school board dismisses him, Mr T. begins an affair with Miss G., a grade 12 girl who was a student in Mr T.'s grade 11 science class the previous year. As a result of the affair, Miss G. becomes pregnant. Under pressure from her parents, Miss G. reveals that Mr T. is the man responsible for her pregnancy. Her parents wish her to have an abortion, but Miss G. does not want this. Nor does Mr T.

News of the affair soon spreads. The Cumberland City *Daily Intelligencer* reports the affair. Mr T.'s wife leaves him. Miss G.'s refusal to terminate the pregnancy, in spite of her parents' desire that she do so, attracts the support of the local anti-abortion cause. Many people censure Mr T. loudly for Miss G.'s pregnancy. Some point to the fact that she was a student in his school and had once been his student.

The school board suspends Mr T. (with pay) and subsequently dismisses him. The school board's reason is that Mr T.'s liaison with the student is incompatible with the professional conduct required of a teacher. By the time of the dismissal, however, Miss G. graduates and has reached the age of eighteen. Mr T.'s wife institutes divorce proceedings against him and claims maintenance payments. Miss G. leaves her parents' home and moves in with Mr T. Following his dismissal, Mr T. promptly appeals to the board of reference. The hearing begins eight months after the dismissal. Mr T. requests reinstatement, claiming that his affair with Miss G. does not reasonably warrant dismissal because she was not his student either when or after the affair began.

Mr T. is regarded as a good teacher. As a result of the stress that he has been under, however, his classroom teaching is not as good as it was. He is currently seeing a psychotherapist. His psychotherapist testifies that the new relationship with Miss G. is helping to stabilize Mr T.'s emotional state. Mr T. and Miss G. announce that they will marry after Mr T.'s divorce is complete.

Case B: The Bare Facts

The second case takes place in the suburban semi-rural community of Windermere. Windermere is divided into a previously established population noted for its adherence to fairly strict 'fundamentalist' churches and a more recent population overflowing from Cumberland City. This second population does not share the religious affiliations of the first, and relations between the two populations are sometimes acrimonious.

Ms S., the teacher in question, is the wife of Mr B., a bookseller with strong 'New Age' and ecological interests. Both Ms S. and Mr B. are members of a local and regional nudist or (as its members prefer to be called) 'Naturist' Society. Besides nudism, the society advocates ecology and the study of natural history in the usual meaning. This society has a secluded summer camp in the Windermere region. Mr B. is, and has been for some years, a leading member of the Naturist Society and is on its executive. Mr B. is known widely in the town as an advocate of 'Naturism.' Ms S. is not on the executive. Ms S. is a grade 7 teacher at the Windermere Consolidated Secondary School. She teaches English and social studies. Her competence is not at issue in this dispute.

Four months before the school board dismisses Ms S., there is a public demonstration by members of the Naturist Society during which members march on the Windermere town hall and picket it while the town council is in session. At one point in the demonstration, some members of the Naturist Society begin to disrobe. This seems to be provoked by rude comments from bystanders opposed to the Naturists. The police are called in to stop the demonstration. Tempers flare and the demonstration becomes a riot. The rioters, including the Naturists, are arrested for disorderly conduct.

The reasons for the demonstration are relevant. A majority on the town council are opposed to the nudist camp, which is on private property owned by a member of the Naturist Society. The town council defines the nudist camp as a business that requires a business licence. When the society applies for a business licence, the town council refuses to grant the licence on the grounds that the proposed business is indecent and therefore unacceptable. The society nevertheless continues to operate the camp, and the town council attempts to close it down by locking its gates and seizing its property. The matter comes before the courts. This is the occasion for the demonstration by the Naturist Society. Mr B. is fined in county court for his role in the demonstration. Ms S., also present in the demonstration, is given a conditional discharge. The affair is further complicated by the fact that someone with a hidden camera manages to take photographs of the camp and of some of the members in the nude. These pictures are subsequently circulated widely in the town. They include pictures of Mr B. and Ms S.

Subsequent to the demonstration, the school board dismisses Ms S. for misconduct. The school board alleges, among other matters, that the notoriety of the affair interferes with Ms S.'s ability to maintain order in her classes and derogates from the dignity and authority that a teacher ought to have. Ms S. appeals to the board of reference. Evidence presented to the board of reference indicates that most of the secondary school students approve of Ms S. for standing up for her beliefs. A few students (mostly male) use the photographs as excuses for salacious allusions.

Case C: World-Views in Collision

In another community some distance from Cumberland City, Ms C. is required by her principal to teach biology to grade 10. Ms C., however, belongs to a religious group which supports the theory of 'special creation' and opposes the theory of biological evolutionism. The textbook and course outlines are based on evolutionist ideas. Ms C. teaches the required course materials. She also introduces 'creationism' into her lessons and dwells heavily on the deficiencies of the evolutionary theory that she is required to teach.

Her pupils include the children of Mr H., who describes himself as a 'committed secular humanist.' The children tell their father what Ms C. is teaching. He is aghast. Mr H. protests to the school board. The school board does nothing. Mr H. takes his protest to the newspapers. The newspapers seize upon the story as an example of the school board's obscurantism or the school board's judiciousness, depending on the newspaper.

The school board reacts to this publicity by suspending Ms C. for departing from the curriculum. She is suspended for three weeks, with pay. Ms C. is upset and appeals the suspension on the grounds that she is obliged to teach what she believes to be true. She claims that the suspension offends against her freedom of religion.

The suspension engenders some criticism of the school board by members of the public, including the parents of many children at the school. Some are secular humanists like Mr H. They object to Ms C.'s teaching creationism. Others are creationists like Ms C. They object to Ms C. not being allowed to present the creationist view.

Case D: Crossing Boundaries

Mr M. teaches in the junior high school in Coniston. Coniston is a medium-sized town not far from Cumberland City. Mr M. is married and has two small children. Mr M., however, is also a transvestite. Once a month he goes to a private club in Cumberland City where he can indulge in his inclination. His wife knows of his disposition. Until this affair, however, his children do not.

The club is raided by the police, who think that they are entering a place where illegal narcotics are consumed and sold. As it turns out, there are no narcotics on the premises. The raid leads to newspaper publicity. Photographs of the members in female costumes appear in the newspapers. These photographs are seen by people in Coniston, including members of the school board. There is widespread gossip among the townspeople.

After some discussion, the school board dismisses Mr M. They give three reasons. The first is that Mr M.'s transvestism makes him unsuitable as a role model for adolescents. The second is that the debate over his behaviour casts the school board and the educational system into disrepute. The third is that Mr M. refuses the option of leave to enable him to take therapy to help him control his psychological deviation. Mr M. appeals to the board of reference.

Discussion

These four cases are, of course, imaginary. There is no province of New Cumbria. The details of each case are not precisely the same as any actual cases known to us. The kinds of issues they involve, however, have appeared in one form or another in all the Canadian provinces. Let us take a brief look at the issues in these cases.

In each of these cases, the board of reference must decide if the school board's decision is 'just and reasonable' in the circumstances. In three of the cases, that decision is based upon the conduct of the teacher 'off the job,' meaning 'outside the classroom' (or is a teacher ever 'off the job,' even outside school hours?). The other case (case C) involves the teacher bringing beliefs from outside the classroom to bear on what she does in the classroom.

Case A involves behaviour between a teacher and a student. The student is not the teacher's own student (although she had been his student *before* the affair began), and the relationship between the two is not exploitative. Had either of these features been present, the case would presumably have a different outcome – or would it? Should this behaviour be forbidden because it is inconsistent with a proper teacher-student relationship? Is it inconsistent?

In addition, the teacher is married. The affair with the student is, by some standards, an extramarital relationship, which some would say is adulterous and thus forbidden. Had the school been a denominational school, this fact alone might have been acceptable grounds for dismissal. The school, however, is not denominational and the question then becomes: Is an extramarital affair sufficient grounds for dismissing or disciplining the teacher?

Should off-the-job behaviour be relevant to the continued employment of the teacher? If so, *what* behaviour, and when? Suppose that the teacher is in the wrong and has really done something unacceptable. Is dismissal the right sanction for the offence? What should the sanction be? Why?

Case B mingles several concerns. The 'Naturists' are a legal group acting within their rights. They advocate values, however, that half the local community regards as questionable or even pernicious. The teacher is acting within her legal rights as a citizen, but the school board believes that her behaviour is casting the school board and the school system into disrepute. The school board decides, therefore, that she must be dismissed.

How can the teacher's off-the-job behaviour cast the school board into disrepute? Note that the school board also alleges that the teacher's behaviour affects her ability to teach. The evidence given does not wholly support this allegation. The teacher's husband is a notorious person in the community. Should this fact render her unfit to teach? In the foreground of this case, then, there is an apparent conflict between the rights of the teacher as a citizen and the teacher's duty to the school board that employs her.

Another question arises from the teacher receiving a conditional discharge for what can be construed as a criminal offence, albeit a minor one. Is the offence sufficient to render her unfit to teach? Is the fact of being charged and found to have done the deed alleged, sufficient? Note that with a conditional discharge, the teacher is formally deemed not to be convicted of the crime.

A further consideration arises from the behaviours – namely the teacher's participation in the nudist activities of the Naturists. These behaviours offend the standards of half the community, and the school board responds to this offence. Should they respond?

Case C also involves a conflict between the teacher's duties to the school board and the educational system, on the one side, and, on the other, the rights enjoyed by citizens. Specifically, the teacher's religious beliefs and loyalties collide with her duty as an employee of the school board to teach the specified curriculum.

This case, more openly than the other three, displays the school board's need to be seen to respond to the concern of the community that (presumably) elects it. A three-week suspension with pay is more of a symbolic than an economic penalty. Had the school board made the suspension only ten days or less, the teacher could not have appealed to the board of reference and we would have no story. The teacher appeals the decision because of the principle involved, with the result that both sides are monetarily 'out-of-pocket.'

The teacher does not refuse or neglect to teach the required curriculum. She adds to it and her additions upset a member of the community who sends his children to the school and he publicly protests. The story does not make clear, however, whether or not the school board expressly forbids her to teach the additions. Would (or should) the outcome be different if they had expressly forbidden her to depart from the established curriculum?

Another issue is the question of community control over curriculum. The teacher, in this instance, is an agent for two curricula – one set by the school system, the other by the religious group to which she belongs – and these two contradict each other. Whose will should prevail and why? Is compromise possible?

Case D introduces yet another concern. The teacher follows a pattern of sexual or gender identity that is not accepted as right or legitimate by noticeable segments of the community in whose school he teaches. On the job (namely, in the school and the local community), the teacher follows the accepted pattern. Off the job (namely, out of town, away from the school and the local community), he follows the unacceptable pattern and this fact is made public.

The behaviour in question concerns gender identity. Do the schools teach gender identity? Ought they to do so? If they ought to do so, what gender identities should they teach? Should teachers be expected to uphold such ideals? Gender is a concern which many people find emotionally disturbing. People are often upset when behaviour crosses or confuses the boundaries between one gender and another. Sometimes they are violently upset.

Does the teacher's off-the-job conduct contradict his on-the-job conduct? Will his off-the-job conduct adversely affect his ability to teach what he is required to teach? Should teachers be expected to be role models? What sort of roles should they model? Is off-the-job behaviour relevant to this modelling?

The board of reference has to consider all of the reasons given by the school board. They have to ask whether or not the school board is right in proposing psychotherapy for Mr M. and whether or not Mr M. is right to refuse this option. For psychotherapy, justified or not, upon which employment becomes conditional is a form of social control.

Each of these cases addresses some value or standard of the school board and of the community that the school board represents. The cases, even though imaginary, declare that a public school teacher's life cannot be neatly divided between on-the-job and off-the-job spheres. The role of public school teacher expands from the school to the whole life of the teacher. Why should this be so? Ought it to be so? We might also ask: Is the dichotomy between public life and private life the same as that between on-the-job and off-the-job? The cases also raise the questions: What is the 'community' involved in each case? How do we know when a given supposed community is really upset or outraged? Who defines the community? These and related questions are the concern of this book and served to focus the research upon which this book is based.

The Case of Trouble

The starting point for the research reported in this book is the recognition that at root schools are cultural institutions and teaching a cultural activity. Consequently, when teacher behaviour offends community norms there is often an eruption of rancorous and even violent conflict around the offending behaviour. Such conflict is akin to the 'case of trouble' characterized by Llewellyn and Hoebel:

The case of trouble, again, is the case of doubt, or is that in which discipline has failed, or is that in which unruly personality is breaking through into new paths of action or of leadership, or is that in which an ancient institution is being tried against emergent forces. It is the case of trouble which makes, breaks, twists, or flatly establishes a rule, an institution, an authority. Not all such cases do so. There are also petty rows, the routine of law-stuff which exists among primitives as well as among moderns. For all that, if there be a portion of a society's life in which tensions of the culture come to expression, in which the play of variant urges can be felt and seen, in which emergent power-patterns, ancient views of justice tangle in the open, that portion of the life will concentrate in the case of trouble or disturbance. Not only the making of new law and the effect of old, but the hold and the thrust of all other vital aspects of the culture, shine clear in the crucible of conflict. (Llewellyn and Hoebel 1941: 28–9)

Disputes such as these are not at all simple. They occur at the intersection of education and law, and involve questions of public policy, community standards, professional standards, civil rights, social change, and cultural conflict. These questions can be very acute. What starts as a disagreement between a teacher and someone else, such as a principal, a school trustee, or a parent, can become a bitter contention going from school board hearing to board of reference to trial court and even to appeal court and to the Supreme Court of Canada, drawing more and more people into its vortex and changing its character as it proceeds. The outcome may please no one, and may yield a legacy of seriously bruised lives and careers. One such case is that of Margaret Caldwell, a Catholic teacher in a Catholic high school in North Vancouver, who married a divorced Methodist in a civil ceremony. The school subsequently refused to renew her contract, and her – ultimately unsuccessful – challenge to this decision eventually reached the Canadian Supreme Court (Parker-Jenkins and Osborne 1985: 66).

Such disputes, of course, are inevitable in complex societies where there are persons, such as public school teachers, whose professions or jobs place them in positions of trust and high public visibility. They increase, however, when a high but uneven rate of social change generates further stresses and anxieties on the various actors of society, or when the presence in the society of different cultural traditions and religious values poses disagreements concerning basic values in human life. Canada today, never a monocultural society, is both changing increasingly rapidly and becoming more multicultural than ever. Moreover, as the several contributions in Manley-Casimir and Sussel 1986 explored, Canada's Charter of Rights and Freedoms (Constitution Act, 1982) not only provides a new resource on which disputants in such cases as these may now call, but it also raises the question as to what degree the Charter's underlying philosophy is at odds with the philosophy behind the traditional role of teachers in the public schools.

The Normative Base

Both law and education are cultural enterprises devoted to the maintenance and promotion of a normative order in society, that is, of an ideal order or vision of the desirable. If that order already widely exists in the society, law and education are conservative and 'traditional.' If that order is followed only by a minority (albeit a minority influential or powerful), then law and education become reformist or even revolutionary. But in either instance, law sets up a set of rules or prescriptions for behaviour and provides rewards for compliance with these and punishments for non-compliance; and education provides pupils with knowledge and ideals which those pupils are expected to learn and to follow, with rewards for successful learning and following, and penalties for failure to do so. Furthermore, both law and education are deliberate enterprises; legislation, for example, prescribes and sets out policy and regulations, while curriculum guides and codes of ethics respectively establish programs of education and normative standards of professional conduct. Law, of course, depends on the acceptance of authority, and part of education's concern is to instil basic attitudes to authority (whether uncritical or critical depends on the particular content of education). Both laws and law-abidingness must be inculcated, and education in part at least inculcates them – or is intended to do so.

Both law and education are supported by sanctions (Piddocke 1986: 261), or rewards and punishments for compliance and non-compliance. The criminal sanctions of fines and imprisonment are only the most dramatic of the many sanctions of the law; other sanctions are the protections offered to property and civil rights, and the enablements offered by the law's recognition of contracts and associations. Education's sanctions are no less pervasive. Beyond the rewards of grades and prizes given to students for good performance in school, as well as the sense of mastery and personal growth emanating from success in an academic discipline or in sports, come credentials that pave the way for better jobs and promotion up the social hierarchy.

Law and education, then, are concerned with the maintenance and inculcation, respectively, of 'collective representations' (to borrow the phrase of Durkheim 1964) that model ideal behaviour. These collective representations express the fundamental values or postulates of the society (Hoebel 1954), and some of these may be very deeply held indeed. When these values, or more precisely, standards of value, are deeply held, their breach calls forth strongly emotional reactions which seek to punish the offender, often in a dramatic manner. And, such is the complexity of human nature, when these same deeply held values are opposed in the same person by strongly repressed contrary motives, the breach of the ideal may call forth even more intense emotions, projected upon the offender but designed to defend the offended person's own character against his or her own contrary motives.

Law and education not only shape human behaviour, but also become resources that people try to control to advance their own purposes and to defend themselves against others (Nicholas 1968). People try to win cases at law, using the power of the legal system to attack or defend particular interests; they try to have favourable legislation enacted and unfavourable legislation repealed. Similarly, they try to have students in the schools, whether their own children or other people's children, taught ideas and ideals conforming to their own purposes (Arons 1986), and they try to censor ideas and ideals perceived as detrimental to those purposes (Dick 1982).

The interplay between law and education entails that the two institutional domains cannot be sealed off from one another. Hence, law and struggles in the legal order can be aimed at controlling the educational order. And conversely, though perhaps less easily, education and struggles over educational policies and curricula may be aimed at influencing the legal order. Note again that these selfsame struggles, aimed at preserving or advancing particular interests, necessarily threaten to change other interests, and so foster further social change.

The Teacher's Role

In a society in which formal and public education is as important as it is in Canada, the teacher's role becomes an arena where all these struggles focus. The teacher deals directly with the students and is expected to shape the students in a particular way – in a word, to socialize them into a particular normative order. The teacher interprets and applies curricula – and can divert curricula from their intended purposes. Consequently, those who would control education must control the behaviour of the teacher. The teacher is thus at the eye of the vortex, buffeted turbulently by the forces of social change and conflicting public expectations.

School administrators, the servants of a ministry of education, even the minister of education himself or herself, can be largely background and unknown figures to the parents, obscured by the institution of which they are a part. But the teacher is on the 'front line' of the institution, dealing directly with the students. If students complain to their parents and friends about their educational personnel, they will complain foremost about their teachers; and it will be the teachers whom the parents hear most about. The teachers, that is, will mediate the educational system not only to the pupils but to the pupils' parents.

Teachers, it seems fair to say, are in North America expected to be role models for their students (see Waller 1965: 42–66, for a classic discussion of this issue). In the United States, at least, this expectation has been so strong that the British anthropologist Geoffrey Gorer could propose that the public school teacher in the United States became both the prime authority figure for Americans and an ideal role model. The equivalent figure for the English as a whole, Gorer suggested, is not the school-teacher but the policeman (1956: 329). This expectation enhances the public position of the teacher and intensifies the scrutiny which the teacher's behaviour, inside and outside the classroom, must bear. Like Caesar's wife, the teacher must be above reproach.

Hoyle notes that a major difference between British and American teachers is that in Britain a teacher is considered a professional who is responsible primarily to the profession and the educational system,

whereas in the United States a teacher is considered very much a representative of the community (1969: 70). Not surprisingly, the behaviour of
teachers becomes the occasion for the eruption of conflicts concerning
the control of education, and consequently the law is brought in as a
means of fighting and sometimes resolving these conflicts.

The Social Drama

A conflict between people in a society is not merely a struggle, but
becomes an attempt by each party to enlist on its side the norms of the
society. These norms may be expressed in public opinion, the law, and
the sanctions of authority. The dispute therefore becomes an occasion
for the expression and affirmation of the norms. Awareness of this norm-
precipitating character of disputes marks the social science method
known as the study of 'social dramas' (Turner 1957: 91). This is a variant
of the 'extended-case method' and 'situational analysis' already long
familiar in social anthropology (Epstein 1967). Within the anthropology
of law, a similar approach has long been followed in the analysis of
'trouble-cases' (Hoebel 1954; Epstein 1967).

According to Turner, the 'social drama' is a recurrent social process
which takes place in four stages: (1) breach of some important rule or
norm governing the relationship between the persons who come into
conflict; (2) widening crisis threatening the breach of more relationships;
(3) redressive measures brought into action by leading members of the
relevant social groups, with the purpose of stopping the disturbance; and
(4) reintegration of the conflicting parties *or else* recognition of schism
between them. This drama occurs through time and displays, as alliances
form and shift, the values and interests of the various persons involved. A
series of such dramas, either recurrent in the same particular group or
more widely spread over a larger group, highlights the structure of the
group and reveals its mechanisms of integration and change (Turner
1957: 91).

Social dramas, of which hearings and trials are special varieties, reveal
also the symbolic nature of social interaction. The breach initiating a
drama marks a disruption in an agreed definition of the situation. The
cases and postures put forward by the disputants are attempts to impose,
or argue for the adoption of, new definitions of the situation from which
the fulfilment of the disputants' purposes logically follows. Hence the
social-drama approach both allows and invites the sociological approach
known as 'symbolic interactionism' (Blumer 1986).

Social dramas are interplays not only of meanings but of the sanctions which confirm or weaken those meanings. The sanctions are responses to a person's actions which encourage or inhibit the repetition of those actions; but those sanctions depend for their effect upon the person perceiving them as rewards or punishments (Piddocke 1986: 261).

Social Dramas and the Teacher

The role of the teacher, therefore, affords a critical place in society where social dramas may be identified and the conflicts of value in a changing society may be highlighted and described. These conflicts of value are not of merely academic interest. They affect concerns in educational policy and law reform, not to mention judicial interpretation of the Charter. Stephen Arons's study (1986) shows this well for the United States, which has two centuries of experience with its own Bill of Rights. Arons takes a number of notable cases involving schools, teachers, school boards, and local communities, and draws from these such distinct concerns as the struggle between state departments of education and parents to control the kind of education – including textbooks and curricula – to which children will be exposed; the conflict of interest between public schools and private home instruction; the question of teachers' lifestyles being in conflict with school boards' and parents' expectations (sometimes expressed under the rubric of community standards); conflicts between state requirements and the desires of minority or dissident groups to have a different education for their children; and a conflict between individualist assumptions in the U.S. Bill of Rights and the majoritarian assumptions (fearing dissent) institutionalized in the various public school systems.

The Canadian situation is substantially different from that of the United States (Manley-Casimir 1982; Pitsula and Manley-Casimir 1989). Denominational education, for instance, is constitutionally supported in Canada in contrast to the strict separation of church and state in the United States (Wilson and Lazerson 1981: 1); the Canadian Charter of Rights and Freedoms is much more recent than the U.S. Bill of Rights, and its selection of rights is not the same; Canadian jurisprudence on rights and the constitution has a different history and comes to somewhat different conclusions than U.S. jurisprudence; Canadians have different attitudes to authority (Friedenberg 1980); and so on. But nonetheless there are similarities; and work needs to be done to discover both the similarities and the differences, so that Canadian jurists, educators, and policy-makers can make wise and proper use of American precedents, either as sources of good ideas or as poor examples better not followed.

Although education in Canada is a provincial concern, and the particular educational traditions of each province differ from one another, the cultural conflicts which make teachers' behaviour an issue are national in scope. Beyond brief discussions in recent reviews of school law in Canada (Mackay 1984; Proudfoot and Hutchings 1988; Hurlbert and Hurlbert 1992; Brown and Zuker 1994), there are no national studies of the control of teacher behaviour. Czuboka's crisp and practical study of teacher tenure cases is precisely a study of Manitoba cases (1965–85) which passed beyond the board of arbitration level to reach the courts (Czuboka 1985). While the Charter provides both a national framework for 'rights' and a nationwide resource in the struggle to define and enforce those rights, only a nationwide review can distinguish what is peculiar to provincial traditions from what is common to them all. Finally, it is simply time to conduct some genuinely 'national' studies of educational policy and practice in Canada. The tradition is well established in the United States; if we in Canada are serious about being considered a 'nation,' we need to conduct research into one of the central cultural institutions that shapes our identity – schools and the practice of teaching.

A National Study

With such thoughts in mind, we began in 1987 a national study of the role of teachers as bearers of norms. In particular, we wanted to focus on the tension between community norms or values and the behaviour of teachers. We proposed to collect instances in which teachers in public or separate (e.g., denominational) schools were accused of misconduct, and to trace these instances from their beginnings to their ends, namely, to the resolution or acceptance of the social conflict represented by these disputes. And we wanted to do so from one side of Canada to the other. To get at these conflicts, we proposed to seek out and examine the decisions of boards of reference, or equivalent tribunals, set up by statute especially for the purpose of adjudicating disputes between school boards and teachers. This inquiry fell into four overlapping stages.

Stage One: Inventory Classification

The first stage was to locate and identify the board of reference cases for each province. We hoped to have a complete inventory for each province, so that we could assess the frequency of the sorts of cases in which we were particularly interested. The diversity of provincial statutes and procedures, and some other constraints, prevented a complete inventory, but we were able to come close to completeness for the decade 1977–87 for all provinces, and for many years previous to 1977 for British Columbia and Ontario.

Stage Two: Selection and Examination

This stage involved the selection of a number of cases that highlighted in interesting ways the ideals in conflict, as well as their investigation as social dramas. Stage two was to have relied extensively on the interviewing of the principal actors in the cases wherever possible, and the examination of archival material if necessary. We found, in several instances, that the principal actors refused to be interviewed, in some cases passionately asserting their wish to be left alone; clearly the interviews threatened to dredge up painful memories best, from their points of view, left undisturbed; as a result, we were reluctantly placed in the position of using more archival material and secondary sources than we had at first expected. Consequently, the intensive case studies of the social dramas came more to be studies of the social, cultural, and community backgrounds to the disputes as a means of trying to contextualize each dispute as fully as possible.

Stage Three: Analysis and Comparison

This stage involved the analysis and explication of the motifs and structures of the conflicts involved, and, as the data permitted, the development of a general model both of the conflicts and of the options open to the actors in such dramas; at the same time, an effort was made to illuminate and contrast these conflicts with similar occurrences in the United States. Stage three, of course, overlapped and arose within both stage one and stage two.

Stage Four: Interpretation and Conclusion

The final stage consisted of interpreting the results of the enquiry and reporting them, first in periodical form and now in this book-length work describing the interplay of law and education as these bear especially upon Canadian teachers (a special issue of the *Education and Law Journal* reported some of the findings of the study).[2] This book provides a more complete and integrated treatment of the study and its findings. (Details of the research method, statutory background for provincial boards of reference, and statistical summaries for selected provinces are appended as Appendices A, B, and C respectively.)

A Classification of Contentious Behaviours[3]

Having an affair with a student, joining a public demonstration, adding unauthorized materials to one's teaching, and being a transvestite are only some of the behaviours that, when performed by a public school teacher, threaten to outrage the community and persuade its school board to censure the teacher. Very early on in the research, then, we became aware of the need to develop an inclusive classification system for various contentious teacher behaviours – behaviours that were, in effect, cases of trouble. Summarized, the behaviours that lead teachers into trouble can be classified as follows:

1. Character-related Behaviours

These are flaws of character which render the teacher unfit or unable to teach. They include behaviours in which teachers fall short of being adequate exemplars of self-control and rationality. Subclasses of character-related behaviours include the following:

a) alcohol abuse and drug abuse (this includes not only drunkenness, alcoholism, and drug addiction but also the promotion of drunkenness and drug addiction in others, whether this is or is not defined as criminal behaviour)
b) insubordination or contrary-minded behaviour
c) personal grooming, including cleanliness, the wearing of beards, and attire
d) behaviour showing signs of cruelty (whether physical or mental)
e) use of obscene or vulgar language
f) dishonest behaviour
g) gambling

2. Sex-related Behaviours

For one cause or another, sexual behaviour emerges as a frequent concern in allegations of teachers' misconduct. The sexual behaviours may or may not involve students. Behaviours that have caused offence include the following:

a) paedophilia or sexual advances towards small children
b) seduction of, sexual advances towards, and dating students (this includes both voluntary and involuntary [or harassing] relationships)
c) cohabitation, common-law marriage, or live-in relationships other than legal marriage
d) heterosexual relationships outside marriage, including adultery and those resulting in pregnancy
e) sexual exhibition and lewdness
f) homosexual or lesbian relationships (both public and private)
g) transsexuality, including sex-change and transvestism
h) sexual harassment of, and by, colleagues (the recognition of sexual harassment as a cause is distinctly modern)

3. Unauthorized Teaching Activities

These include activities conducted outside the classroom, among which the following may be distinguished:

a) use of unauthorized material (e.g., sex- or religion-related books, magazines, and films)
b) use of unauthorized strategies or methods of teaching
c) unauthorized teaching of controversial topics, issues, or subject matter
d) ideological teaching, including partisan politicking and partisan support for candidates
e) religious teaching for proselytizing purposes

4. Contentious Conduct as Citizens

Such conduct includes political, religious, academic, and social-personal activities, and involves actions related to the following issues:

a) free expression (written, oral, or symbolic; e.g., public espousal of controversial ideas or lifestyle; wearing symbolic material and religious material; criticism of school policy, colleagues, or superiors)
b) affiliation or association (e.g., membership in controversial political, religious, or social groups such as the Communist Party of Canada, the

KKK, neo-Nazi organizations, and cultic societies; marriage to a notorious person)
c) public activities (e.g., partisan speeches for a party or its candidate;
refusal to take patriotic oaths or to participate in patriotic activities;
participation in activities, such as demonstrations and petitions, of
controversial groups)

5. Criminal Behaviour

Being accused of a crime may be enough to cause an enquiry by a school
board and a suspension while the matter is being rectified. However, if
the school board and the community do not consider the crime serious,
being convicted, as well as charged with the crime, might be regarded as
unimportant. A further complication arises when a teacher is found to
have committed the alleged crime but is given an absolute or conditional
discharge by the court; when this happens, the offender is deemed not to
have been convicted of the crime. The categories of criminal behaviour
are as wide and complex as the Criminal Code. Some overlap the four
categories above.

6. Denominational Cause

Where religious denominations operate public or semi-public schools
and provide education under supervision by provincial governments, a
teacher's behaviour which offends a tenet or practice of the religious
denomination may be grounds for dismissal, even if it does not fall into
any of the preceding categories. It usually does, however, fall into one or
more of the preceding categories as well. The rights of the teacher as a
citizen (category 4) may collide with denominational cause.

In the following chapters, we examine a variety of actual cases in which
teachers were accused of such contentious actions. In some of these cases,
the school board was concerned with upholding its reputation and the
reputation of the school in the esteem of the community that the school
served. In the other cases, reference to the community was not so clear
but is probably there. These cases reached a board of reference (or a
board of arbitration) and were the subject of the board's decision. Some
cases went beyond the board of reference to the courts. Some of these
cases are well known and others are not.

Chapter Organization

Chapter 1, 'Contentious Behaviours,' sets the stage by presenting four hypothetical cases and commenting briefly on the issues involved. Further, the chapter introduces the idea of the 'case of trouble' as the unit of analysis, characterizes law and education as normative enterprises, sketches the origin of the study, and includes a classification of contentious behaviours.

Chapter 2, 'A System of Control,' looks more generally at the ways that the conduct of school teachers is monitored and controlled and the ways that teachers can defend themselves against unfair accusations and dismissals. In particular, this chapter reviews briefly the idea of 'misconduct' in the common law and the role of boards of reference as tribunals to which teachers who have been improperly dismissed may appeal.

The next three chapters examine a number of actual cases in which the alleged conduct of teachers leads to dismissal or suspension by their school boards and subsequent appeals to a board of reference or board of arbitration. Some of these cases went beyond the board of reference to the courts. In most cases, the courts agreed that the teacher had done or said what he or she was alleged to have done or said, but they did not always agree with the school board's labelling of, or decision concerning, this conduct.

Chapter 3, 'Misconducts of "Character,"' deals with cases in which the cruelty, self-control, or insubordination of the teacher was an issue. There are suggestions of an ideal of the teacher as a self-controlled, rational, decent, kind, and courteous person who shows due deference to authority. Two qualities concern the school boards and the tribunals: cruelty or the absence of cruelty; and deference and obedience to duly constituted authorities.

Chapter 4, 'Sexual Misconducts,' deals with cases in which the sexual behaviour of the teacher is an issue. Here, especially, we need to distinguish between sexual misconducts such as paedophilia and sexual liaisons between teachers and their students that necessarily corrupt the teacher/student relationship and other sexual misconducts which do not. The latter class reveals the community value-standards that teachers may be expected to uphold.

Chapter 5, 'Unorthodox Teachings and Unquiet Citizens,' deals with cases in which the teacher has taught doctrines not authorized by the school board, whether in school or outside it, or has exercised his or her rights as a citizen in some way that upsets the community or the school board. This chapter includes a consideration of 'denominational cause' as a special ground for dismissing teachers. These cases also illustrate, in varying degrees, how the school board can become an agency enforcing the value-standards of the community or constituency of the school and how boards of reference and the courts both allow and limit this 'community control.'

Chapter 6, 'The Normative Character of Teaching,' examines the normative character of teaching and the role of public school teacher. Distinguishing between the 'inherent necessities' of teaching and the other 'extrinsic' values which teachers may be expected to uphold, the chapter focuses on the 'character' of teaching and derives a set of norms necessarily inherent in public school teaching. The chapter concludes by reviewing the cases in light of these ideal norms.

2

A System of Control

Controlling the Public School[1]

It is implicit in a system of public school education in which schools are tax-supported and subject to some sort of public control, whether by state or community, that the behaviour of teachers in the public school ought to be monitored and controlled in some way. This may seem too obvious to mention; sometimes, however, the implications of the obvious deserve to be examined. If teachers must be monitored and their 'misconduct' corrected *who* should monitor and correct? And *how* should they monitor and correct?

These questions are answered easily enough: school authorities monitor and correct by means of their powers of suspension (with or without pay) and dismissal. This answer raises yet another question: who are these authorities and to whom are *they* accountable? In other words, who controls the public schools and who controls the controllers?

Within the framework of public school education, all the answers to these questions culminate in the combination of two types of institutions. While we may describe these types as ideal types, actual institutions blend the characteristics of these ideal types in varying proportions.[2]

The first type of control is by a system of *centralized control*. In such a system, the schools are made into agencies of the state or the central government (in Canada this means the provincial governments), and the state (through legislation, regulation, and a ministry of education) sets curricula and working conditions, and appoints the local administrators who run the schools. The teachers are employees of the government and may be classed as civil servants. State laws and regulations prescribe proper behaviour for teachers and forbid improper behaviour. The state is not necessarily responsible to the local community or the constituency of parents.

If the state is democratic, with a legislature elected by the people, there is a limited form of accountability to the local community and the parents. The parents help to elect the legislative representative for their area, and their representative provides a means whereby they can bring their concerns to the legislature and the ministry. If the state is not democratic, this limited possibility of local control disappears. Unless the centralized system gives great discretion to its local administrators, allowing them to attend to local concerns, the centralized system has difficulty in coping with local variations.

The second type of control is to entrust the school to a group of trustees.[3] This decentralizes the control much more so than the first alternative. If the school is supported by a local community that the school serves, these trustees may be elected by the members of the community. Alternatively, the trustees may be elected by the parents and guardians of the children who attend the school. This constituency need not coincide with the community where the school is located. Trustees provide for the administration of the school and its teaching. They hire and fire the teachers. If there is collective bargaining between the school and the teachers, the trustees represent the school. In this alternative, the trustees would oversee and control the curriculum.

The trustee form also suits private schools that charge fees from parents or guardians who send, or wish to send, their children to the school. Such a school may also be supported by a society or association that elects or appoints the trustees.

A proprietary school, by contrast, is owned by an individual or a partnership or a corporate entity, and its services are sold to parents or guardians or even directly to the students. Either the owners themselves or a board of directors appointed by the owners run the school. If the school is unsatisfactory, the parents withdraw their children from the school. Such schools may be further regulated by legislation that prescribes the conditions under which they shall operate.

As far as the larger society is concerned, both the trustee kind and the proprietary kind of school comprise a decentralized system in which the schools are closely responsible to the local community or to the constituency that supplies the students.

North American public school systems are a compromise between these two alternatives. The provincial or state government sets the curriculum and certifies the teachers. Trustees elected by the people in the school district administer the schools, employ the teachers, and respond to the concerns of the parents and the communities that elect them. In some systems, the provincial or state government employs the teachers, but the local school board has the power to suspend or dismiss.

Schools run by religious organizations show the same contrast between centralization and decentralization. In the decentralized form, the school trustees are responsible to the local congregation that appoints them. In the centralized form, the head office of the church appoints the local administration and the teachers.

Where schools are run by religious organizations, there emerges the question of relationships between the state and religion. This question is part of the history of Canadian education. A partial compromise between the claims of state and religion is expressed in the notion of 'denominational cause.'

In all of these forms of control, the teachers appear as employees. They may be the employees of the board of school trustees or they may be the employees of the state but employees they remain. We must next consider, then, the law of employee discipline.

Public schools and private schools serving a public that controls them through trustees are not the only possible kinds of educational institutions. Private schools, especially proprietary schools, may be run as a business, selling their services on the market and controlled by nothing more than customer satisfaction. The teachers themselves might own and operate such a school, and we can imagine schools wherein the students themselves own the school and hire the teachers. None of these latter possibilities, however, easily fits the purposes of *public* education.

The Teacher as the Employee of the School Trustees

In Canada, for the most part, the public school teacher is actually or effectively the employee of the school trustees. The trustees have the power to hire and dismiss the teacher; to suspend the teacher with or without pay; or to reprimand the teacher and to inscribe these reprimands in the teacher's employment record. These disciplinary powers are governed by a variety of laws and regulations, which include the following:

1. the old common law of master and servant, which includes the law of contract applied to employer/employee relationships;
2. school acts and similar legislation governing public schools and modifying the common law;

3. labour legislation permitting collective agreements and regulating strikes and other job action (such legislation modifies the old common law and may override previous educational legislation);
4. collective agreements, made under the authority of labour and other legislation (a body of law has grown up concerning the interpretation and enforcement of such agreements).

At one time, teachers as employees were regulated according to the law of master and servant. This law allowed employers to dismiss employees with due notice for any reason at all or indeed for no reason at all. Dismissal without notice was allowed 'for cause.' Such cause included off-the-job behaviour by the employee that would likely damage the reputation of the employer. If the employee considered that he or she had been wrongfully dismissed, the employee could sue the employer for damages. The damages would be for wages remaining due. In some instances, when the employee had been grievously wronged by the employer, punitive damages might be obtained. The courts did not require the employer to re-employ the dismissed employee, as that was the employer's decision.

Behaviour by the employee justifying dismissal without notice was sometimes labelled 'misconduct.' This term was carried over into school acts[4] setting out the terms and conditions of employment for public school teachers. Whenever a school act allows a teacher to be dismissed for 'reasonable cause,' the old master-and-servant law provides examples and rules for deciding what is and is not 'reasonable.'

We need, therefore, to have some idea of what this older law of master and servant contained. In particular, what did this law imply concerning off-the-job misconduct by schoolteachers? For our account, we shall draw on three writers: Holdsworth, writing in 1907, Diamond, writing in 1931, and Avins, writing in 1968. While these sources may seem somewhat 'dated,' the principles of law they review are still the applicable principles here.

According to Diamond, the English common law of master and servant was created mainly during the hundred years after 1830, although the relationship of master and servant itself 'was well known before the close of the Middle Ages' (Diamond 1946: 1). In the English law of master and servant, according to Holdsworth, the terms 'master' and 'servant' are almost synonymous with 'employer' and 'employee,' including 'all persons between whom any contract exists for the render of service, or the fulfilment of duties on the one hand, and the payment of stipulated hire, wage, salary, or reward on the other, during a determinate or stated period or term, or until the expiration of a fixed notice to be given by either party' (Holdsworth 1907: 4). This relationship is 'purely one of contract, arising out of either an express or an implied mutual engagement, binding one party to employ and remunerate, and the other to serve for a determinate term or period, or until the expiration of a given notice ... Service in general implies obedience to orders and submission to the control of the master within limits either expressly fixed by contract or implied from what is customary in other cases of a like nature' (Holdsworth 1907: 5). Holdsworth, writing about the turn of the century, classified servants into (a) domestic servants and menials; (b) non-domestic servants, including managers, clerks, artisans, labourers, etc; and (c) apprentices.

Diamond, writing some quarter of a century later, defined the relation of master and servant as follows:

The relation of master and servant exists between two persons where by agreement between them, express or implied, the one (called 'the servant') is under the control of the other (called 'the master'). A person is under the control of another if he is bound to obey the orders of that other, not only as to the work which he shall execute, but also as to the details of the work and the manner of its execution. (Diamond 1946: 1)

However, 'a person employed for the substantial purpose of exercising his skill and an independent judgment and not of obeying the orders of another is not under the control of the other' (Diamond 1946: 8). By this test, for example, the consulting physicians and surgeons of a hospital would not be the hospital's servants and neither would the house physicians and surgeons. The nurses and other employees, however, such as the radiographers, would be servants of the hospital (Diamond 1946: 8). Agents, independent contractors, bailees, partners, and tenants are not servants (Diamond 1946: 13, 16, 19, 23, 18). Apprentices and domestic servants are distinguished by Diamond as special kinds of servants (Diamond 1946: 33).

A contract of service, according to Holdsworth (Holdsworth 1907: 117), ends when the agreed period of service ends or when the parties to the contract agree to end the contract. The death of the master or the compulsory 'winding-up' of a joint-stock company also bring the contract of service to an end. A contract of service may be ended by the master at any time without notice, however, if the servant is guilty of (a) wilful disobedience of his master's lawful orders; (b) gross moral misconduct; (c) negligence or conduct which may reasonably be expected to injure seriously his master's business; or (d) incompetence or permanent disability. Concerning gross moral misconduct, Holdsworth writes:

If a servant robs his master, embezzles his property, or falsifies his accounts, he may be forthwith dismissed. So unchastity while in the master's house or family will be sufficient to justify the dismissal of a female servant or governess; and the same may be said with respect to immoral conduct in the house on the part of a man-servant, tutor, or even a clerk, lodged and boarded in his employer's family. (Holdsworth 1907: 121)

By the time we come to Diamond, 'misconduct' is applied more broadly:

A master may dismiss without notice a servant who is guilty of misconduct, whether in the course of his duties or not, inconsistent with the fulfilment of the express or implied conditions of service. Such misconduct includes immorality, drunkenness, insolence, criminal conduct, and other conduct inconsistent with the relationship of master and servant. (Diamond 1946: 188)[5]

Other grounds for dismissal discussed by Diamond are disobedience, incompetence, permanent incapacity, breach of faith, and habitual or substantial neglect of duty.

In the mid-1960s, Alfred Avins gave a comprehensive and thorough survey of the law reports concerning employees' misconduct for the entire British Commonwealth. Reflecting on the results of his survey, Avins saw emerging a 'law of industrial discipline' with its own distinctive character:

The courts have generally thought of misconduct as a breach of contract of service. Yet, if there are two cardinal principles of contract law, they are that only such damages can be recovered as were actually suffered, with the corollary that no punitive damages can be recovered, and that liability attaches for breach of contract without fault. The law of industrial discipline is the exact opposite on both points. It can be repeatedly observed that no punishment can be inflicted without fault, regardless of the damage caused, and that fault may be punished although no damage actually occurs, if it creates a risk of damage. Even in tort law, punitive damages are reserved for a limited class of intentional torts.

It is believed that the law of industrial discipline is an independent body of law and not a branch of contract law, and is most akin to the penal law. It is a series of sanctions given to a unit of society commanding facilities for the production of goods or the rendition of services, and necessary to safeguard that unit of production. Without the law of industrial discipline, society's productive facilities could not function, just as without the penal law, society itself could not function. Employment is created by contract and its incidents can be modified by contract, but this is also true with many other forms of status in society, such as marriage. Even the operation of the penal law itself is sometimes influenced by the consent of the aggrieved party, for example, in cases of assault, rape, or theft. It is therefore not surprising that contract can modify the employer's disciplinary powers. However, if no such modification is made, the rules of discipline attach as an incident of the employment relationship itself. The uniformity of these rules in the various parts of the Commonwealth lends striking support to the universality of the problems they must cope with. Finally, the confusion as to whether industrial sanctions should duplicate criminal sanctions for the prevention of crime unrelated to employment ... shows how far industrial law is removed from ordinary contract principles, which would look no further than the harm caused to the employer by the breach of contract. All of this evidence points to the conclusion that industrial discipline is not part of ordinary contract law. (Avins 1968: 5)

Avins's table of contents is a thorough classification of employee misconduct. He groups misconducts under four main headings: 'Breach of Duty,' 'Breach of Discipline,' 'Moral Delinquency' and 'Disabling or Disgraceful Conduct.' 'Breach of Duty' is then divided into (1) being absent without leave; (2) failing to perform job duties; (3) failing to perform supervisory duties; and (4) disobeying orders. 'Breach of Discipline' is divided into (1) disrespect to and assaulting superiors; (2) other subversions of discipline (including usurpation of authority, obstruction to others, defiance of authority, complaints and criticism); (3) disrupting relations with co-employees (including acts done off-duty which disrupt relations with co-employees); and (4) collective action (including strikes). 'Moral Delinquency' is divided into (1) lying; (2) theft; (3) disloyalty and corruption; and (4) damage to property or goodwill. Finally, 'Disabling or Disgraceful Conduct' is divided into (1) disabling conduct (namely, drunkenness); (2) non-criminal disabling conduct (including pregnancy and illness); (3) arrest and detention for crime; and (4) disreputable outside conduct. 'Disreputable outside conduct' is further subdivided into (a) generally disreputable conduct (including sexual immorality, public drunkenness, and gambling); (b) untrustworthy conduct (especially lying, fraud, and theft); and (c) other acts (such as crimes and dishonourable failure to pay debts).

The misconduct of teachers on account of their 'lifestyles' (see cases 27 and 29 for examples) falls under the heading of disreputable outside conduct. Let us follow what Avins reports under this heading and particularly attend to any cases involving teachers.

He begins exploring the rationale for this category by reviewing a number of cases. A teacher at a denominational church school *supported by public funds and registered as a public school* may not be dismissed for misconduct even though he marries contrary to a rule of the church and subsequently leaves the church (a case from India, 1953).[6] A physician in a Roman Catholic hospital who publicly advocates euthanasia may not be dismissed, although this is contrary to Church morals (a Manitoba case, 1936).[7] A Scottish parochial schoolmaster who refuses to sign a document stating that he believes in the tenets and is a member of the Established Church of Scotland might, however, be dismissed (Scotland, 1834).[8] It is misconduct for a schoolteacher at a school founded on religious principles to refrain from public attendance at services of religion of the school (an English case, 1847).[9] He cites two further cases from Ceylon on similar concerns and with similar results.

The general principle behind these cases is that an employer is entitled to protection from an employee's outside conduct prejudicial against the business of the employer. If the employer's business depends on customers who are a distinct segment within the community and have their own special standards, the employee must not offend these individuals. If the employer's business is directed only towards the general community, the employee is obliged only to avoid violating the general community standards. Persons employed by religious institutions should, therefore, avoid offending the members of the religion or harming the institution by acting contrary to its tenets. This is not, says Avins, a question of religious freedom but of the right of the employer to demand that employees do not harm the employer's business.

Whether sexual immorality by employees is misconduct depends on whether it will injure the employer's reputation. Among the cases mentioned by Avins, it was held that any sexual immorality by someone in the position of a priest was likely to harm his employer (an English case, 1921).[10] A married university professor who seduces one of his female students is guilty of misconduct (an Australian case, 1956).[11] A constable of the RCMP who has sexual relations with a woman not his wife commits misconduct even though no one has public knowledge of it (Ontario, 1962).[12] Even if the employee's position is not a public one, sexual immorality may be punished if the publicity would likely harm the employer. Avins cites a 1961 Australian board of reference ruling that a butcher's apprentice whose arrest for rape draws unfavourable newspaper publicity and causes customers to change patronage may be dismissed if convicted but not if acquitted.[13]

Public drunkenness might be grounds for dismissal for misconduct if the behaviour reflects upon the employer. A clergyman, school principal, or a policeman who appeared publicly drunk were held to disgrace their positions and might, therefore, be dismissed.[14] Regard must be given to the special circumstances, however, and one should distinguish between habitual and gross intoxication directly interfering with the business of the employer and drunkenness in 'circumstances of festivity' unconnected with the employer's business.[15] Quebec courts have ruled that drunkenness at a convention is not misconduct when no one cares about it (a 1955 case)[16] and that a teacher cannot be dismissed for becoming drunk during a holiday (an 1861 case).[17]

Taking bets or gambling on the employer's premises, especially during working hours, is disreputable conduct.

Not only is an employer entitled to expect that his or her employee will safeguard the employer's reputation and goodwill, the employer is entitled to an assurance that the employee's outside conduct 'will not create any reasonable fear' that the employee will likely commit a misconduct in his or her employment. The employer, as Avins asserts (1968: 642), is entitled to peace of mind. The behaviours disturbing employers have included speculation on the stock exchange by a confidential clerk who advised his employers about stock market transactions;[18] speculation by a general manager who controlled large sums of his employer's money and whose speculations plunged himself deep into debt and made his own credit rating low;[19] and boasting by a servant with access to his employer's home and family while the employer is away that he had committed adultery with one woman and indecently fondled another.[20]

Similarly, if an employee lies outside his or her employment in such a way that reasonably causes the employer to fear the employee might lie to the employer, the employee would be guilty of misconduct. If the employee steals outside his or her employment, this shows the employee to be untrustworthy and renders the employee liable to dismissal.

Conviction for a crime that is likely to harm the employer's reputation would be grounds for dismissal. A teacher convicted of possessing undesirable and prohibited publications may thus be dismissed.[21] A New Zealand case held that a teacher who was, at his own request, registered as a conscientious objector and who was convicted for failing to report for non-combatant training, could be dismissed for misconduct.[22] Avins notes also that several rulings of the U.K. Education Ministry held that a teacher convicted for illegal possession of narcotics is guilty of misconduct in his employment (Avins 1968: 650). A schoolmaster who beats his wife publicly may be dismissed (an English case, 1847).[23] Mere accusation of a crime, however, is not grounds for dismissal, and acquittal of the crime following a successful appeal requires that the dismissed employee be reinstated (at least in India).[24]

If an employee fails to pay his or her debts honourably and this failure adversely affects the reputation or other interest of the employer, this is industrial misconduct. The expense imposed upon an employer as a result of an employee's wages being garnisheed could thus be grounds for holding the employee guilty of misconduct.[25] Association with disreputable friends or the expression of disreputable views may also be considered to be misconduct if it upsets the customers of the employer, injures the reputation of the employer, or gives grounds for the employer to regard the employee as untrustworthy.

These three writers show that the idea of employee misconduct has been legally recognized as part of the common law since the early nineteenth century, and they also indicate that off-the-job conduct has always been a relevant concern of employers. Avins particularly (and conveniently) reveals the existence of a law of industrial discipline common to the entire Commonwealth. This law is not entirely the product of the English common law. It strongly suggests that similar problems of industrial discipline precipitate similar legal solutions. For our purposes, however, these writers show the state of the common law concerning misconduct during those years when Canadian jurisdictions legislated public school systems and some began to provide special tribunals to handle disputes over the dismissal of public school teachers.

In Canada public schools and their teachers are controlled by provincial statutes which prescribe the powers and duties of school boards and teachers. These statutes constrain and modify the old law of master and servant, but do not necessarily abolish it. In particular, the statutes allow school boards to dismiss teachers for 'misconduct' or more generally for 'reasonable cause' (which includes misconduct). Of course, the statutes do not define these terms, and the courts therefore use the precedents established in the old law of master and servant to fill the gap.

Today public school teachers in Canada are frequently hired (and fired) according to the terms of collective agreements. These collective agreements may be made pursuant to special legislation empowering teachers to bargain collectively, or in accordance with general labour legislation. They also prescribe some sort of grievance procedure, including appeals against unfair dismissal. As a corollary, such collective agreements recognize the right of the employer to dismiss employees for reasonable and just causes. Such right of dismissal includes a power of summary dismissal for conduct detrimental to the employer's enterprise. As Krashinsky and Sack put it in their introduction to their summary of representative Canadian labour arbitration cases from 1978 to 1987, just cause

means ... that the employer must show that an employee's conduct warranted some discipline, and that the particular penalty imposed was appropriate having regard to all the circumstances including the nature of this misconduct, the employee's seniority and disciplinary record, and other relevant factors. (Krashinsky and Sack 1989: 6)

Krashinsky and Sack do not define 'misconduct,' but use the word to refer to any act which warrants some discipline (Krashinsky and Sack 1989: 7). They classified their cases as follows: (1) those concerning attendance at work; (2) insubordination; (3) disloyalty, conflict of interest, and improper public criticism of employer; (4) theft, vandalism, and dishonesty; (5) work performance problems; (6) abuse of fellow employees and others; (7) alcohol and drug offences; (8) union activity (such as unlawful strikes); and (9) off-duty conduct. Off-duty conduct was subdivided into (a) assault and weapons offences; (b) theft and possession of stolen property; (c) dishonesty and fraud; (d) vandalism; (e) drug and alcohol offences; and (f) other off-duty offences. Unlike Avins, Krashinsky and Sack cited no cases concerning schoolteachers.

The English common law of master and servant, which serves as the basis of the Canadian common law of same, has been modified by numerous statutes and regulations, and by the changes in industrial organization occurring in the twentieth century (see Hepple 1981; Anderman 1978). These changes prompted B.A. Hepple to comment:

There is little doubt that few other areas of case-law have so directly reflected the judges' views as to what was fit and proper behaviour on the part of 'servants' and their dealings with their 'masters.' Furthermore, whatever was the situation in the past, nowadays most people are employed by corporations, be they commercial companies, or public bodies. The typical employer is I.C.I. rather than plain Mr Jones. Because of this it is increasingly less relevant to refer to old cases on dismissal. (Hepple 1981: para. 251)

But 'less relevant' does not mean 'irrelevant.' The old law allowed an employer to dismiss, without notice, any employee whose words and deeds outside the place of work damaged the reputation of the employer in the community or among the employer's clientele. This principle still applies under the rubric of 'just and reasonable cause' for dismissal.

The School Board as Instrument of a Local Community

Under the common law, the decentralized version of school control allows the school trustees to dismiss the board's employees with due notice at any time and to dismiss them without notice for misconduct. This misconduct may include any off-the-job behaviour that in the view of the school board is likely to harm the reputation of the school in the community. The only recourse the employee has for unjust dismissal is monetary damages.

Who decides what will harm the reputation of the school? In the first instance, the school board itself decides. It has been elected by the community and is responsible to the community. Being thus duly regardful of the community's opinion, the school board becomes its agent or instrument for disciplining teachers, especially those teachers who upset influential sections of the community.

Under these conditions, the teacher's position can indeed be uncertain. Some telling examples are given in a study of teachers in the United States made by the American historian H.K. Beale in the early 1930s. This account shows what can happen when a teacher is expected by the community to be a paragon of virtue and the school board is the agent of the community. Writing after the First World War, Beale begins his discussion with this observation: 'Standards of conduct have changed rapidly since the War. Things unthinkable before the War are now accepted' (Beale 1936: 374). Nevertheless, schoolteachers were the last to be allowed to change. Teachers were expected to be examples of the older values long after most of the community had openly or secretly abandoned them. This expectation was strongest in small communities.

Beale first describes how communities judged the personal habits and amusements of teachers. Before the War, the theatre was forbidden to teachers in many small communities of the Middle West and South. 'Then came the War and the movies.' By 1930, the ban against theatre-going was largely gone. Card-playing and dancing were more stringently forbidden and objections to these faded more slowly. In 1929 a small town in Kansas fired eleven high-school teachers because they had gone to a dance at a local country club. Gambling and swearing, at least in public, were forbidden. There was the least objection to these in the North-eastern states, and the strongest in the South. In 1927 South Carolina passed a law revoking the certificates of teachers who swore. Gambling and swearing were also tolerated more in larger cities than in small towns.

Smoking was severely restricted. It was generally 'unusual' for men and 'impossible' for women to smoke on the school premises. Away from school, smoking was allowed but often censured. In small communities, women were expected not to smoke, even in private, and in larger com-munities, women who smoked often did so privately so that parents and school officials would not know it:

Teachers in the Oak Park High School near Chicago, for instance, smoke; but one of them whom the author met two thousand miles from Oak Park would not do so on a train or in a hotel, because, well, someone from Oak Park might see her, and the Principal would not like it if he knew. (Beale 1936: 377)

In the 1920s, several states and counties forbade smoking and refused to issue teaching certificates to smokers.

Drinking was also severely restricted. Before the coming of the temper-ance movement, drunkenness had been widespread among teachers. In Illinois in the 1820s, for instance, 'it was not uncommon for a school to be closed for a day while the teacher was "indisposed" from drinking too much' (Beale 1936: 379). The temperance movement changed this and people then went to the other extreme. Drinking teachers were promptly fired. With the First World War and the prohibition era, drinking by teachers became more common but was still forbidden. Drinking on the school grounds was generally (though not always) fobidden, while drink-ing away from school was often allowed, if it were done discreetly. Away from the larger cities, however, drinking was severely restricted and drunkenness nearly always led to dismissal. There was one exception: 'In some communities, on the other hand, even when drinking is officially tabooed, a teacher, especially a male teacher, cannot hold a position, or perhaps even obtain it initially unless he is a "good fellow" in drinking the liquor of the superintendent or a school board member' (Beale 1936: 381).

Sexual relations was another cause for concern. The label 'immorality' had so many meanings that it practically covered anything a school board official wanted to read into it in order to dismiss a teacher. Some of the more specific accusations made under this label were 'immoral relations with pupils,' 'making advances to girl pupils,' 'intimate relations with high school boys,' 'stepping out with married men,' and 'trying to cause X's wife to have an abortion' (Beale 1936: 382).

The most serious feature of an 'immorality' charge was that gossip alone was often sufficient to cause dismissal:

Where sex morality is involved gossip is usually sufficient cause for dismissal of a teacher without any proof of the charges. In the Northeast and the great cities about half of the teachers report that if charges are not proved they will not cause trouble, but in most communities an unproved charge, even though idle gossip, will bring dismissal. This, of course, lays the teacher open to malicious charges by anybody who wishes to injure him. Vague rumors of immoral conduct are a favorite means of attack against some one with unpopular ideas or against an opponent of the school administration. Furthermore, even where there is no malicious intent, town gossip is likely to magnify unconventional social habits or mere gaiety into insinuation of more serious offenses. Yet the courts have upheld dismissal on unproved charges of immorality, because teachers are unfit who do not have the *reputation* of good character. (Beale 1936: 382)

Divorce used to be a cause for dismissal. A few enlightened communities had allowed teachers to remain employed after divorce if the teacher were the injured party or had been cruelly treated ('mental cruelty' included), provided there was not too much publicity.

Getting married was one of the most frequent grounds for dismissing women. Often enough, women dismissed for marrying might be later rehired as substitute teachers at a lower rate of pay. A few cities welcomed married women as teachers. State laws neither required nor forbade dismissals because of marriage. The courts, for the most part, upheld the teacher's right to marry and avoided school boards' rules against marriage. Beale observes:

A number of reasons are advanced for not wishing married women to teach: neglect of the home, neglect of school duties for the home, a tendency of husbands to let teaching wives support them, problems of pregnancy. The basic reasons, however, are economic pressure of unmarried women who want the positions and the old spoils notion that a teaching position is a 'favor' to be given to those most deserving and that it is not fair to give it to one who has a husband to support her. The best opinion feels that marriage either makes no difference in the competence of a teacher or actually increases her value. Many feel that a wife or a mother has more poise and patience with children than a spinster or a young girl seeking matrimony. If teaching is ever to become a real profession there seems to be no good reason to force a woman who regards it as a profession to abandon it, because she marries, and to leave it only to those who never succeed in marrying and those who regard it as a stepping-stone to a husband. The recent return to barring married women from the schools because they have husbands to support them is a reversion to the spoils system, which tends to defeat professionalization of teaching. (Beale 1936: 386)

Taking time off for childbirth was frequently regarded as 'neglect of duty' warranting dismissal. The courts upheld the rights of school boards to dismiss on these grounds. In the late twenties and early thirties, some school boards in the Northeast made rules granting leave for childbirth.

Small communities especially restricted the friendships and social life of their teachers. A major restriction forbade friendships between Negroes and whites. This was rare in the Far West, in New England, and in some large cities of the North and more prevalent in the Middle West and the South.

Sex was another major restriction. Women teachers had to be very circumspect about the men they chose. Some contracts forbade women teachers to keep company with young men or allowed them to do so only with one man. Friendships between teachers of opposite sexes were frowned upon and were sometimes cause for dismissal. Friendships between teachers and pupils of the opposite sex often resulted in dismissal.

In some communities, the school board regulated the hours when teachers had to be 'home' at night. They also frequently decided where teachers might live. At one time, teachers had to 'board around' as part of their salary. Later, the school trustees might reward their friends by sending the teacher to board with them.

Dress was regulated. In 1924 the school board of Santa Clara, California, forbade bobbed hair and dismissed a teacher because she bobbed her hair. Cosmetics, short skirts, gaily coloured clothing, sleeveless dresses, and sheer stockings were among the items of dress forbidden by school boards.

Unconventional behaviour in small communities usually brought publicity, and bringing unfavourable publicity to the school was 'a mortal offense' (Beale 1936: 391). Unconventionality was regarded as showing indiscretion and lack of judgment. Popularity was often more important than competence.

There were further demands on the teacher. He or she was expected to engage in many extracurricular community activities. These included donating money to *all* worthy causes in the community. The teacher was often expected to attend church. This requirement could sometimes be extreme: 'A South Carolina teacher was recently taken to task for not attending the town churches. He did teach a Sunday-school class in the Baptist church, but the town thought he ought to show impartiality by attending all the churches *seriatim*' (Beale 1936: 394).

Though teachers were required to teach citizenship, in many communities they were not allowed to be active citizens. They were forbidden to take part in political campaigns because the school must be non-partisan. Teachers were also forbidden to engage in labour union activity. Administrators and businessmen did not wish teachers to unionize, as it would mean higher salaries for teachers and therefore higher taxes. Teachers themselves were often reluctant to unionize as this would emphasize their role as employees and detract from the dignity of teaching. Some teachers preferred to regard themselves as professionals and looked to medicine and law as examples. Some school boards forbade teachers to unionize, and teachers who tried to do so were dismissed. Some teachers, especially in the Northeast, did win the right to unionize, and this right was recognized by the courts and by state legislation. There was, however, a double standard: picketing *for* labour was generally opposed by school boards and administrators, but if teachers wished to demonstrate *against* labour they somehow were accommodated.

The organizations teachers might join were carefully supervised. Joining organizations not approved by the majority or the leaders of the community led to dismissal. Failing to join an approved organization also led to censure and dismissal. Beale's comment on these restrictions is instructive:

The result of all this restriction of conduct is that the life of an active and intelligent teacher is unbearable in small communities and not happy in larger ones. If the teacher teaches in his own town he probably is used to the community's attitudes and does not feel restricted. One solution, then, would be always to employ local teachers. But this merely accentuates provincialisms. Usually the teacher has been away for training; usually, too, he begins teaching when young. He is then doubly likely to have new ideas, at least when he enters the profession. Restrictions tend to drive the ambitious, the independent, and the unconventional away from teaching. Many an able person abandons teaching because of restrictions imposed on his personal life.

One reason that children and their parents do not have more respect for teachers is that they so meekly submit to dictation from every one who wishes to give it.

One does not respect a 'hired man.' That is all the teacher is in many communities. Much 'looser' conduct would win more respect than strict behavior now does, if pupils knew the teacher's behavior was voluntary. If education or intelligence means anything at all, the teacher should be actively interested, and his opinion should count in all community activities. But teachers rarely do count. It is this feeling of futility, this law against really mattering in the community, that frightens ambitious and able men and women out of teaching into other activities. (Beale 1936: 403)

Why did American communities restrict their schoolteachers in these ways? These restrictions went far beyond simple political or economic controls over labour unionizing and the like. Beale has an interesting suggestion:

One of the most restrictive forces is the determination of parents that their children be influenced by only the highest type of character. Parent pressure on teachers' conduct is powerful indeed. Parents feel that youth is plastic. They long to have their children better than their parents. Parents who smoke, swear, drink, commit adultery, hope their children will not. They want the teacher to help mold in their child virtues they lack. With great sincerity they believe a teacher should be a public servant who 'serves' the community through an upright, exemplary life and whose influence will give their children the characters they themselves aspired to and failed to attain. This parental aspiration for children makes understandable, even if still unfortunate, what otherwise would seem incomprehensible and arbitrary community attitudes toward teachers. (Beale 1936: 407)

The Teacher as a Servant of the State

The alternative method of administering schools and their teachers is by what we call 'bureaucratic centralism,' that is, through a ministry of education that is an agency of the state. Let us discover what this implies regarding controlling teachers' behaviours.

The schools, in this model, are 'people-processing institutions' whose purpose is to train children and juveniles to become good and proper members of the state or polity. 'Good and proper membership' may be defined in various ways, depending on the state: as educated and contributing 'citizens' of a democratic polity, as loyal 'subjects' of the Crown, as 'productive' members of society, and so on. To achieve this ideal, the state, through its educational ministry, must prescribe the curriculum of studies for the pupils and the means whereby this curriculum is to be taught. The state must also select and oversee the administrative and teaching personnel for the schools. Persons who cannot or, more seriously, will not teach the subjects and values to which the state is attached must be discouraged or even actively prevented from teaching. This censorship is inherent in the institution. The lessons the state seeks to inculcate in the pupils must not be deflected or subverted by contrary messages. The state sets up teachers' colleges (sometimes revealingly labelled 'normal schools') or educational faculties, where teachers are trained in the subjects, methods, and values they are supposed to teach. Properly trained teachers will then be provided with certificates or licences authorizing them to teach. If bureaucratic centralism is well advanced, the education ministry may go so far as assigning new teachers to positions it has selected for them.

Once the teacher is in the school teaching, some way must be established to observe and oversee teaching methods, to check for their adequacy and conformity to the state's ideals. Hence, inspectors are instituted to visit the teacher's classes, with or without notice, to observe the teacher's and the pupils' behaviours. Some type of authority is also delegated by the state to administrators whose job is to receive and investigate complaints from parents, students, other teachers, administrators, and members of the community and constituency of the school. For the most part, however, the teacher is to be left alone with the pupils in the classroom with no one else to observe him or her. Therefore, controls have to be instilled *in* the teacher. In other words, a 'conscience'[26] must be instilled in the teacher.

As outlined here, teachers are employees of the state. They are civil servants, and their employment may or may not be governed by contract. As state agents, however, teachers are expected to represent the authority of the state as an essential part of the state-employed teachers' mission. The teacher is, indeed, part of the state's 'mission to the people.' The authority of teachers is reinforced if the local community can be persuaded to respect them as bearers of knowledge, wisdom, and moral probity. In this role, teachers become similar to priests and ministers of religion who are part of centralized churches.[27]

If the image of the teacher as an authority figure in the local community is to be implemented and sustained, the teacher's 'off-the-job' conduct is highly relevant. That conduct must *both* maintain the values the state wishes to inculcate *and* gain the respect of the community. In this way, the teacher becomes a model character for the people in the community to imitate. As the teacher becomes accepted as a model, the authority of the state, as a carrier of the values the teacher demonstrates, is enhanced.

The community may have its own set of values distinct from those of the state, however, and may convert the teachers to these values. The teachers may gain respect in the community by departing from the values the state wants them to uphold.

This structure of bureaucratic centralism is, naturally, discordant with ideals of local initiative and decentralization. It is quite concordant, however, with ideals of representative democracy as well as with authoritarianism and even totalitarianism. The values may be those of a liberal education as well as those of servile training. Whatever set of values are taught, *respect for duly constituted authority* will be one of them. Without this, bureaucratic centralism cannot work.

In a system of bureaucratic centralism, school authorities are agents *of* the centre. In the pure form, they are appointed *by* the centre. If school authorities are elected locally, as in most school boards in Canada, their powers are specified by statute and subject to governmental overview. Local election of school 'trustees' under a regime of bureaucratic centralism is a concession to the interest of the community in its children's welfare. If the school is significantly supported by locally raised taxes, such a concession may be necessary.

Employment as a civil servant may increase the power of the teacher vis-à-vis the local community. No longer does the teacher depend on local approval for his or her income. Instead, the teacher depends on the approval of his or her superiors in the state administration. Much, therefore, depends on that administration's regard for the sensibilities of the local community.

Teachers' Organizations

Whether employed by a local community or the state, the teacher is still only one person against a group. In the small community, the teacher's own character may be such as to command respect, and the teacher's personal network may include persons influential in the community. This is more likely to be so if the teacher is well established in the community, with family connections and even another source of income. The teacher who is a servant of a state bureaucracy, by contrast, will be less likely to have such connections within the bureaucracy as it is so much bigger.

When the teacher does not have such connections in the local community or if the teacher is on the lowest level of a bureaucracy, how can he or she gain protection against exploitation and unjust treatment? The answer is that by oneself one cannot, but in combination one can. Teachers' combinations have taken two forms, namely the labour union and the professional association. These forms blend into one another.

The labour union is a combination of teachers who have agreed to bargain collectively with their employers (whether local community or state) and whose chief sanction is the strike or collective withdrawal of services. If union membership is made a precondition for employment, the union gains a certain sanction over its members. The union does not, as such, prescribe the off-the-job conduct of its members, nor set minimum standards of performance. It may do so but when it does, it moves towards becoming a professional association.[28]

A professional association of teachers sets standards for teachers. It supports teachers who meet those standards and may bargain on their behalf. It also penalizes teachers who do not meet those standards. Off-the-job conduct is part of its concern. The professional association, if well developed, controls admission into the profession, licensing or certifying teachers as fit to teach.

The teachers' role as employees, however, pushes professional associations closer to the labour union model. In its pure form, the professional association suits an occupation in which a number of independent practitioners offer services to non-practitioner clients who cannot judge the adequacy of the practitioners' preparation and knowledge, taking them largely on faith, but who can, and do, judge the results of the practitioners' work. The professional association best suits a decentralized market for the practitioners' services in which the practitioners have relatively strong bargaining positions as individuals or small firms. Too strong a position as individuals, however, is not desirable, as there would be less incentive to form a professional association.

This same independence of professionals makes it difficult for state agencies to control them. What the state can do, however, is partially *co-opt* them. It does so by (a) making the professional association responsible for certifying the professionals; and (b) making the association liable if professionals fall short of certain standards (which thereby become part of the professional standards). The professional association, thus gains a monopoly over the services its members offer but, in return, has to 'police' its members. This creates a symbiosis between the state and the professional association, encouraging the association to support the state.

Such co-optation occurs for public school teachers when legislation recognizes a professional council or organization, other than the ministry of education, who licenses or certifies teachers and may decertify them for 'professional misconduct.'

Of course, once a professional association has come into being with authority over its members, how are teachers to defend themselves against misuse of *this* authority? The same problem also arises in labour unions.

If the authorities in any organization abuse their authority over a member and there is no recognized grievance procedure, that member has then only four options: (a) suffer it; (b) leave the organization; (c) appeal to a higher authority outside the organization; or (d) organize a reform, or what is in effect a revolution, within the organization. If the grievance procedure has been exhausted without satisfying the member, then the member is also forced back on these four options.

For public school teachers, such higher authorities are provided by the courts and by tribunals of arbitration.

Boards of Reference and Arbitration

Each public school teacher is under pressure from three institutional interests, each trying to direct the teacher's behaviour in some way or another. These are (a) the community, represented by the elected school board;[29] (b) the state, that is, the provincial government, represented by the minister of education; and (c) the teaching profession itself, represented by professional associations and teachers' unions. Each of these interests is trying to influence the behaviour of the others, both directly and through the teacher. We can catch part of this complex by means of a diagram:

The teacher, the focus of all of this attention, is not at all passive but is trying to control,[30] in turn, state, community, and profession in those areas where he or she is affected by these institutions.

Faced by such uncertainties and pressures, Canadian public school teachers have sought to appeal to some sort of authority in order to mediate disputes between themselves as individuals and the school boards, governments, and professional councils to whom they are accountable. The basic authority provided by society for such disputes is, of course, the law and the courts. The common law had to be enlarged by additional legislation, and the courts were often time-consuming and increasingly expensive. Logically enough, teachers sought to institute some sort of alternative tribunal that could arbitrate such disputes.

Such an alternative was first sought with regard to school boards that employed teachers. In order to mitigate their insecure positions, often similar to those of the American schoolteachers whom we described above, teachers sought a quasi-judicial review through which they could appeal dismissals or suspensions by school boards and could get orders for reinstatement if the review tribunal found the school boards' reasons inadequate. Justice and job security were both at stake.

Sometimes these review boards were modelled after labour arbitration tribunals and came as the result of unionization and labour agitation. Just as often, however, they came as the result of pressure by teachers' professional associations and were part of an attempt to advance the status of teachers as professionals.

These review tribunals are known as 'boards of reference' or as 'boards of arbitration,' and the right to them has been established by legislation. The appearance of these boards has occurred at different times in the various provinces. In Ontario, Saskatchewan, and Alberta, for instance, they were instituted in the mid-1930s. In Manitoba (after some unsuccessful attempts), they finally arrived in 1963. In British Columbia, they did not come about until 1974. These tribunals govern the powers of school boards to dismiss and suspend teachers on 'continuing' contracts without pre-set terms.[31]

Boards of reference or boards of arbitration, as they are variously called, are special hearings set up, sometimes by the minister of education, sometimes by the parties themselves, to review the dismissals of *tenured* teachers and to confirm, reject, or vary the action of the school board, as may seem fair to the board of reference. The particular statutory provisions vary from province to province, as do the details of the administration of these boards. In Ontario, for instance, the setting-up of a board of reference is subject to the discretion of the minister of education and is not an automatic right of the person applying for the hearing. In British Columbia, Alberta, and Saskatchewan, on the other hand, the minister does not have the discretion to refuse to set up the board of reference, provided the applicant meets the other statutory preconditions.[32]

The procedures for setting up and holding boards of reference, or equivalent tribunals, fall into two types. Both types can be sorted into three maximal phases: before the hearing, the hearing itself, and after the hearing.[33]

The first type of procedure has the following general form:[34]

A. Before the Hearing:
1. The affair begins when the school board dismisses or suspends the teacher.
2. The teacher (very occasionally the school board) applies to the minister of education (whose ministry usually has the responsibility for adminstering this process) for a board of reference.
3. The ministry decides whether the application meets the statutory requirements.[35] If the ministry finds that it does, the ministry then sets out to arrange the hearing. Note that since boards of reference are set up pursuant to statute, they have no jurisdiction other than that conferred by the statute, and the ministry has no authority to set them up other than the authority conferred on the ministry by the statute. If the decision also involves ministerial discretion, then the minister exercises this discretion after the ministry has decided that the application meets the statutory requirements. If the minister then decides that the board of reference should be set up, the ministry proceeds to do so.
4. The ministry chooses[36] the persons who will comprise the board of reference and arranges the time(s) and place(s) of the hearing. This involves finding times suitable for all the persons involved in the hearing and is not always an easy task to accomplish.
5. Glitch time: there may be pre-hearings, arguments to be heard, papers to be exchanged, legal factums to be exchanged, and so on. Troubles may arise, and hearings may need to be postponed and rearranged.
B. The Hearing:
6. The hearing is convened. Both sides bring forth witnesses. The hearing may need to have several sessions. Delaying factors may emerge, such as the illness of important witnesses. Eventually the hearing is either adjourned (sometimes *sine die*) or concluded.

7. The board of reference gives its decision. It either confirms, rejects, or varies the school board's decision. What the board of reference may do depends on the powers given to it by the statutes. The board of reference usually gives reasons for its decision. These decisions may or may not subsequently be published.

C. After the Hearing:

8. The school board and the teacher consider the board of reference's decision. If either is not satisfied and cannot accept the decision, the teacher or the school board may appeal the decision to the courts. The grounds for the appeal depend in part on the statutes setting up the boards of reference.

9. The courts confirm or change the decision of the board of reference.

There is thus a progressively narrowing flow of cases through this procedure. Many applications are made but few eventually are chosen. Applications may be withdrawn before the board of reference is granted; they may be rejected and no board of reference granted; or applications may be withdrawn after a board of reference is granted but before the hearing commences. Even once the hearing has started, the parties may settle 'out of court,' and the hearing will then be ended without a decision being made. After the hearing has concluded and the decision rendered, the parties may decide that appeal to the courts is unnecessary or futile and so the case ends.

The second type of procedure, though governed by statute, does not require action by the minister. It has the following general form:[37]

A. Before the Hearing:

1. The school board dismisses or declines to re-employ the teacher.

2. Upon receiving reasons for the dismissal or non–re-engagement, the teacher notifies the school board that he or she wants a board of reference or board of arbitration.

3. The board of arbitration is set up pursuant to statute jointly by the school board and the teacher (or the teacher's representative) and in due course convenes. Since it is the teacher who is asking for the board to be set up, the teacher may also have the right to withdraw the request before the board actually convenes.

B. The Hearing:

4. The board of arbitration hears the parties to the dispute and makes its decision. This decision has the force of law but in one way or another may be appealed to the courts.

C. After the Hearing:
  5. The school board and the teacher consider the board's decision and decide whether or not to appeal to the courts.
  6. If there is an appeal to the courts, the courts review the board's decision and either confirm, vary, or reject it.

Again there is a filtering process, with the parties to the dispute having the options to withdraw from the arbitration and/or settle the dispute 'out of court.' In this second type of procedure, however, the opportunity to obtain statistics concerning the number of withdrawals and abandonments is much less than in the first type of procedure. The first type requires that application be made to the minister and thus requires the ministry to keep some record, whether or not the application is later withdrawn. The second type leaves the initiative entirely to the parties. Only those hearings that convene and produce a decision will be recorded, and these records may or may not (depending on statutory requirements) be sent to the ministry.

The institution of the board of reference is especially applied to the relationships among the teacher, the community, and the school board. It controls the action of the school board upon the teacher and may defend the teacher against unjust decisions by the school board or from community pressures to which the school board has succumbed. By doing so, of course, it may reduce and constrain the autonomy of the school board. However, the board of reference can also enhance the ability of the school board to resist pressures from the community, from the state, or even from the teaching profession itself. The school board can always state that it wishes to make a decision that will be upheld by the board of reference and the courts.

The effect of the board of reference is to make both the school board (and, through it, the community) and the teacher accountable to a wider and greater authority, namely the authority of the larger society as crystallized in the statutes and precedents of the law. This larger authority may itself be sound or unsound. Much depends upon what sort of law has been crystallized. Overall, the general thrust of accountability to law in the history of Western civilization has been towards standards of fairness, equity, and rationality, to say nothing of liberty.

The provision of boards of reference or boards of arbitration still left teachers at the mercy of provincial ministries of education. These ministries granted, suspended, and revoked teaching certificates and so controlled who entered and remained in the profession. Without a certificate, a teacher ordinarily could not teach, even if a school board wanted him or her.[38]

Who was to review the ministry's decision? Judicial review by the courts could decide only whether or not the minister had acted within proper jurisdiction with a due and fair attention to the relevant facts, and it was time-consuming and expensive. Some other review procedure would be distinctly helpful. This issue is still not settled in most Canadian jurisdictions.

In Alberta, however, the ministry of education has been trying to develop a procedure for reviewing certificates that is both fair and in accordance with well-established precedents in that province's tradition. In Alberta, teachers' behaviour or conduct is presently governed by three procedures. The first is the discipline procedure of the Alberta Teachers' Association concerning allegations of 'unprofessional conduct.' The A.T.A. gains this power under the Teaching Profession Act and has enjoyed it since 1935. The second procedure is the 'practice review procedure,' established by recent legislation and still largely untested. Administered by the ministry of education and the Council on Alberta Teaching Standards, it is concerned with allegations of incompetence. The third procedure is that of appeal to boards of reference, administered by the Teacher Certification and Qualification Branch of the ministry. These appeals may be made by teachers with respect to three acts by school boards: termination of the teacher's contract of employment; termination of the teacher's designation as principal or similar administrative functionary; and suspension of the teacher.

The Role of the Courts

In settling disputes between teachers and school boards (or, for that matter, between teachers and the state or the teachers' own professional organizations), a court first hears the parties to the dispute and then *imposes* a solution according to the court's own view of the right. This view is determined by three factors: (a) the statutes; (b) the tradition of the law; and (c) the judge's own sense of right and wrong. The judge's decision is constrained and partly directed by the statutes and by the legal tradition and must be reasonably anchored within requirements. If it is not so anchored, the judge's decision may be overruled by a higher court. However, accomplishing this anchoring may give the judge an opportunity for a good deal of creative thinking.

Boards of reference and of arbitration are set up as a stage between the disputing school boards and teachers, on the one side, and the courts, on the other, in order to reduce the number of disputes coming to the courts. Originally, these boards were supposed to be quicker and cheaper than the courts. In some jurisdictions, they include members from school trustees' associations and from teachers' associations who might be expected to know more than the courts do about what disputes between teachers and school boards entail.

Since one purpose of these tribunals has been to reduce the burden on the regular courts, the enabling statutes have sometimes provided that the decisions of the tribunals be final. Even if the tribunal is supposed to be the final trier of fact, the decision is usually appealable on the grounds that the board of reference has erred in law.

The ordinary court acts towards the board of reference as a court of appeal acts towards the ordinary trial courts. It reviews the evidence presented before the board and recorded in the transcript of the board hearing. It reviews the board's judicial or quasi-judicial reasoning and decides if the reasoning accords with the legal tradition. If the board has varied the decision of the school board (instead of merely affirming or reversing it), the court may review this variation and amend it. If the board's view of the law is unsatisfactory to the court or if the board's procedure is defective, the court may then replace the board's judgment with its own.

Sometimes the board of reference does more than the enabling statutes allow it to do. It has then exceeded its jurisdiction. If the court finds that the board has exceeded its jurisdiction, the court corrects the decision of the board.

If the board's procedure is highly defective, the court may require a new board to hear the dispute all over again. Or, depending on the case, it may not. In these ways, the courts act as a higher authority overseeing the procedures and decisions of boards of reference, just as boards of reference serve as higher authorities overseeing the procedures and decisions of the school trustees. This supervision encourages boards of reference to make their decisions as jurisprudentially sound as possible.

That jurisprudence is, of course, the jurisprudence of the common law (or, in Quebec, the equivalent civil law) as amended by statute. That common law includes, as we have discovered, the law of master and servant and the idea of employee misconduct. Within the law relating to misconduct is the notion that the employee should not act 'off the job' so as to damage the employer's reputation among the employer's customers or clientele. Hence, public school teachers should not act 'off the job' in ways that damage the reputation of the school or the educational system.

'Maintaining the reputation of the school or the educational system' can be (and sometimes is) rephrased as 'maintaining the confidence of the public in the school or the educational system.' Both of these formulas are rather elastic. They allow 'offending against community standards' to become 'damaging the reputation of the school in the community.'

'Misconduct' in the law of master and servant is, of course, *employee* misconduct. The public school teacher is the employee of the school board, representing the local community of the school board as an agent of the state; or sometimes the public school teacher is an employee of the state directly.

There is also the idea of *professional* misconduct in the law concerning professions. Here, such misconduct (logically enough) includes damaging the reputation of the profession or reducing the confidence of the public in the profession. In turn, offending against community standards may become damaging to the reputation of the profession. The results are much the same as for employee misconduct.

The law allows both boards of reference and the courts to require teachers to behave in accordance with community standards. This is especially so if the board or the court believes that these standards are standards to which teachers ought to conform.

When the board of reference or the court upholds community standards, we have the phenomenon of 'double institutionalization' (see Bohannan 1965).[39] This occurs when norms already established in, and sanctioned by, the local community are upheld by the courts representing the larger society and become norms sanctioned by the larger legal tradition.

3

Misconducts of 'Character'

Introduction

The cluster of misconducts that are grouped together under the label of 'misconducts of character' (see chapter 1, p. 18) include the following:

a) the abuse or misuse of alcohol and other 'drugs'
b) insubordination or contrary-minded behaviour
c) personal grooming and dress
d) behaviour showing signs of cruelty
e) use of obscene or vulgar language
f) dishonest behaviour
g) gambling

These classes are not logically exhaustive, so that we must allow for a further, residual class, namely (h): other.

What does personal grooming have in connection with behaviour showing signs of cruelty? Is drug abuse connected to dishonest behaviour or insubordination? Are the use of vulgar language and contrary-minded behaviour connected? When we ponder these proscribed behaviours, we *can* discern a connection. Behind these proscriptions there is an ideal. It is the ideal of the civilized, even cultivated, lady or gentleman in the Victorian or Edwardian meaning of the term: decent, courteous, thoughtful, self-controlled, cooperative, and rational.

Let us explore how these particular behaviours might relate to this ideal.

The Abuse or Misuse of Alcohol and Other 'Drugs'

The substances involved here usually include alcohol, marijuana, and narcotics or 'hard drugs' such as heroin, cocaine, and opium. They could include substitutes such as bay rum, vanilla extract, and glue and petroleum fumes. The proscriptions could also be extended to include LSD, psilocybin, mescalin, peyote, and other psychedelic 'drugs.' They do *not* usually include tobacco, coffee, tea, or other similar stimulants, but no doubt these substances could be proscribed if someone wanted them to be.[1]

The common concerns shown in the proscription of these substances are (1) that they induce changes in a person's emotional mood and mental set; (2) that if they are imbibed or consumed in a large enough quantity, the changes culminate in a loss of self-control by the user, hallucinations, unconsciousness, and sometimes even death; and (3) that they are addictive. There is some debate whether or not marijuana and the psychedelics really are addictive, but all of the substances named do alter moods and do change the user's experience away from the organized consensus of society.

The value that use of these substances offends is, therefore, the value of self-control or control by reason. They inhibit or disengage the long-range planning and control function in the mind which we name 'ego' or 'rational mind.' When these substances become addictive, furthermore, they enchain the ego to the necessity to acquire more of them, thereby reducing the person's real freedom and further distorting the long-range planning and control function. To proscribe drug abuse is, therefore, to support the values of rationality, ego-control, and of personal self-government.

In proper amounts, in proper circumstances, these substances have their place; particularly in medical and psychedelic uses. A rational approach to these substances, therefore, involves teaching when and how they may properly be used so that self-control is not endangered. A rational approach also includes knowing the addictive potentials of each substance, so that one knows which to avoid.

The possession and use of these substances is sometimes a concern for the criminal law. This adds a further complication. Conviction of a crime can be, in itself, sufficient grounds to warrant a teacher's dismissal. A criminal charge may be sufficient to warrant suspension until the charge is settled by acquittal or conviction. Whether or not the possession and use of addictive substance should be a criminal offence is another question and one that here we shall pass by.

Notice that these are behaviours that concern both education and law. The ideal of the 'reasonable person' is common to both, and the use of drugs that decrease rational self-control is a danger to this ideal in both domains. This is especially so if the substances are addictive.

Insubordination or Contrary-Minded Behaviour

In the context of public school teaching, insubordination and contrary-mindedness include failing to obey the directions of lawful authority and of properly appointed superiors, as when teachers ignore the principal's instructions. The label of 'insubordination' is applied to such conduct as criticizing the principal or the administration in public, verbally abusing the principal, assisting a boycott of the school by students, having a personality clash with the principal, or simply being a difficult person to work with. It is also extended to include being non-cooperative with colleagues as well as with administrative superiors.

The values which 'insubordination' offends might be described as proper respect for authority and cooperation in the common enterprise. The public schools certainly try to inculcate these values in their students and depend upon the predominance of these values in their day-to-day work. It seems only reasonable that teachers be expected to display these characteristics in their own behaviours.

Obedience to authority and cooperation with colleagues are not, however, the highest values. Docility can be overdone. Authorities and colleagues can command and enjoin shabby, even evil, acts. The good citizen is not the dutifully obedient one, but the one who also criticizes and sometimes disobeys laws and orders when they depart from and betray the purposes and values which the society, the institution, or the school have declared as their own. There are times when the principal, the administration, and the school board must be criticized in the best interests of school, students, education in general, and the rest of society. There is, therefore, a need to distinguish insubordination and mere contrariness from proper principled opposition in the service of higher values.

Insubordination and contrary-minded behaviour as misconduct are not usually complicated by criminal charges or convictions, unless they result in criminal behaviours such as assault.

Personal Grooming and Dress

Where there are 'dress codes' of one sort or another, conforming to the code signifies an acceptance of the social roles that the codes protect and of the authority associated with those roles. To break the code indicates a certain inattention to the role and perhaps some inattention to the authority as well; to break the code wittingly indicates a refusal to accept the role and the authority behind it.

Personal grooming and dress also express such dispositions as tidiness, cleanliness, and mental and bodily organization. The 'code,' therefore, implies a certain ideal about mental and bodily control, and opposition to, or neglect of, the 'code' implies opposition to, or neglect of, some or all of this ideal. There may, however, be more than one way of expressing the values involved, and the 'dress code' may be only one such way. A person *may* show his or her adherence to the values by deviating from the code or by following another code that also expresses those values. Misconduct of this sort is not usually complicated by criminal charges or convictions.

Behaviour Showing Signs of Cruelty

Such behaviour includes striking or otherwise treating students roughly, whether under the rubric of corporal punishment or otherwise. It also includes 'mental cruelty,' such as insulting or verbally abusing students so as to destroy their self-esteem and dignity.

The essence of cruelty is to treat another person as a thing and to take pleasure (often disguised as a sense of righteousness) in diminishing or destroying the other's being in some way. Inflicting pain is a common kind of cruelty, but so is making another person feel worthless. Cruelty destroys or disintegrates the body and mind of the other person, and from this the cruel person experiences enjoyment. Alas, we can also be unwittingly cruel when we do or say to other persons something that hurts or diminishes their being.

Now, clearly, persons who are cruel, or whose disposition for cruelty emerges frequently and dominantly, should not be teaching either younger or older children. If a public school teacher has any disposition to be cruel, he or she must at least control that disposition, so that it does not affect the children in his or her care.[2]

It has been said, 'A gentleman is never unintentionally cruel.'[3] This implies that courtesy is so much the gentleman's (or gentlewoman's) nature that he (or she) stops and thinks deliberately before acting in a cruel way – otherwise such a person will not act cruelly. It also implies that if those who are supposed to be, or claim to be, 'gentlemen' or 'ladies' do do something cruel, they are open to a presumption that they intend to be cruel. This notion of the gentleman still survives today in popular speech when someone is commended for being 'a scholar and a gentleman.' The idea that seems to go along with this now old-fashioned expression is that the person is being commended for their courtesy and kindness.

Insubordination or contrary-minded behaviour is sometimes complicated by criminal charges for assault or child abuse. When this happens, we have intimations of a character-failing in the person engaging in these behaviours.

Use of Obscene or Vulgar Language

Using obscene or vulgar language is similar to contravening a dress code. Language is labelled 'obscene' or 'vulgar' because it offends a code that certain matters are not spoken about in a certain way, if spoken about at all. Very often, the speech that is forbidden is that of 'lower' or 'uneducated' classes. Certain ideals of proper behaviour and decorum are encoded in the acceptance or rejection of certain words and speech forms. To break these codes signifies rejection or neglect of the attitudes thus encoded.[4]

Obscene language is not the same as verbal abuse. One can destroy another person's self-worth without swearing at them. Sometimes obscene language *is* verbal abuse as well. Refraining from verbal expressions that one knows will upset another person shows a kind of consideration for the other.

One positive value that the use of obscene language *may* contravene is courtesy or little deeds and words that show consideration and thoughtfulness for one's fellow human beings. Obscene or vulgar expressions may sometimes also reveal in the user a carelessness for language, though such carelessness is also revealed in a great many expressions found in academic and bureaucratic language. As well, there are situations in which a careful person might use obscene or vulgar language deliberately in order to produce a calculated effect.

The use of obscene or vulgar language is not usually complicated by criminal charges, but it could be by laws against obscenity. At one time, there were laws against blasphemy, and in some instances, language disrespectful to the flag constitutes a kind of secular blasphemy.

Language, in this sense, includes not only words but also gestures. Disrespectful gestures on some occasions arouse censure in bystanders.

Dishonest Behaviour

Lying, fraud, and similar behaviours are included in dishonest behaviour. Stealing, or taking what is not one's to take, is another kind of dishonesty. Honesty, the positive value, may be defined as a scrupulous attention and adherence to truth and to the rights of property. Both lying and theft create insecurity in social life and destroy trust between people. If a teacher is discovered to be a liar and/or a thief, the trustworthiness of that teacher is at once destroyed. It may or may not be regained.

Of these various failings of character, dishonesty, in particular, threatens teaching at its very root. The student has the right to expect that the teacher believes what the teacher is telling the student; that what the teacher offers as knowledge is, to the teacher's best judgment, true. This requirement is basic where 'facts' are taught. Skills are evident in their performance and so carry their own guarantee in a manner that facts do not.

Dishonesty, as a form of misconduct, is very often complicated by criminal charges for theft, fraud, embezzlement, and so forth. One could add civil suits for slander and libel as further complications.

Gambling

Gambling in moderation is not a defect of character. A certain amount of gambling, indeed, may be evidence of a degree of adventurousness and willingness to take risks. If it becomes habitual or extreme, however, it evidences a weakness of character that can lead to criminal involvement. Gambling can become addictive, and gambling debts can be a motive for theft, fraud, embezzlement, and even murder. When it becomes an addiction, gambling becomes an offence against self-control.

When we determine the values involved in proscribing these various misconducts, we find the following: self-control, rationality, proper respect for authority, cooperativeness, kindness, opposition to cruelty, consideration for others, and scrupulous honesty; or, in short, basic civilized *decency*. Such decency is not enough to maintain society nor achieve the good life,[5] but it is a basic minimum without which neither a good society nor the good life is possible.

There are hints that this decency is not as perfect as it might be. It may err towards too much docility with respect to administrative superiors. It may also be rather snobbish and uncaring towards persons whom it deems to be inferior in social status.

We can discover two 'value-centres,' as it were, appearing in this discussion. First is the set of ideas associated with the gentle-person: self control, decency, courtesy, and rationality. Second is the idea of due regard for social custom and authority. These are not the same. Sometimes they work together, and at other times they oppose one another.

Both have been ideals in Canadian teaching for over a century. In his recent history (and socio-political critique) of the development of educational policy and practice in pre-Confederation Ontario, Bruce Curtis describes the policy of Egerton Ryerson. Ryerson had been appointed assistant superintendent of common schools for Canada West, and during a year's leave, he had toured educational institutions in western Europe. In 1847, after his return, Ryerson published *A Report on a System of Public Elementary Instruction for Upper Canada*. Curtis describes this report and Ryerson's views on character development in the following words:

The *Report* presented a summary of the most progressive propositions of bourgeois political theory, with respect to both the social importance of education, and pedagogical method.

Ryerson was especially concerned with the elaboration of practices for the selective development of the forces of the self. Some of the potential forces of the self were to be developed in such a way that they would govern the others. The techniques of self-construction were the province of pedagogical practice. Underlying Ryerson's analysis was a typical bourgeois anatomy of the forces of the self – a 'psychology' – which both specified the order of development of the self, and ranked its parts. Education, if successful, would strengthen the individual's forces and structure them such that 'reason' and 'intelligence' rather than 'passion' would be dominant. Intellect and reason were to dominate the passions. The 'higher' tastes were to dominate the lower; the spiritual nature was to dominate the animal nature. The delicate senses were to be cultivated and the base impulses starved. The individual whose self was developed in this way was said to be in a state of 'self-government.'

Self-government as individual self-discipline, and self-government as representative democracy were seen to be sides of the same coin. With the French educational inspector M. Girardin, and with Archbishop Whately of Dublin – a Commissioner of Irish National Education – Ryerson argued that representative governments were imperilled by popular ignorance. The exercise of 'rights' in the absence of 'discernment' menaced the representative state; 'when a people know their rights, there is but one way to govern them, to educate them.' If people were to be 'governed as rational beings,' then 'the more rational they are made the better subjects they will be.'[6] Education was centrally concerned with the making of political subjects, with *subjectification*. But these political subjects were not seen as self-creating. They were to be made by their governors after the image of an easily governed population. This was a different version of what other writers called the creation of 'willing and cheerful' obedience. Self-government was social subordination. (Curtis 1988: 101–2)

In his last three sentences, Curtis, in effect, distinguishes between two forms of 'the rational intelligence.' One is 'self-creating'; the other is 'socially obedient.' Here are the two 'value-centres' whose appearance we noted above. We shall be required to return to them later.

Let us now examine a number of board of reference cases in which alleged misconducts against these values were debated and judged. These are board of reference cases[7] that occurred in various provinces of Canada, mostly between the years 1972 to 1987. To protect the privacy of the teachers and students involved in the cases, we have referred to people and places by letters which do *not* correspond to the initials of their actual names. Occasionally, when the case has reached the courts and names have been duly published, we have departed fron this anonymity.

The Abuse or Misuse of Alcohol and Other Drugs

Case 1: The Teacher Who Drank at Work

This first case occurred in British Columbia and involved alcohol abuse which led to frequent absences from work and eventually consuming alcohol secretively on the school premises, contrary to the school's regulations. It is a standard sort of situation that is normally settled before reaching a board of reference.

For ten years, Ms R. had a growing alcoholism problem with frequent absences from teaching. Finally, on 1 October 1986, the school board dismissed her under the rubric of 'misconduct.' This included bringing alcohol onto the school premises. This fact was apparently well established. She appealed the dismissal and at the board of reference hearing presented evidence that she was under curative treatment for alcoholism.

At the board of reference hearing (decision rendered 1986), the issue was whether the facts constitute misconduct or alcoholism. Misconduct is culpable; alcoholism, as an illness, is not. The board of reference decided that alcoholism was an illness and known as such to the school board.

Dismissal was inconsistent with the school board's own policy regarding alcoholism. Bringing alcohol onto the school premises was certainly misconduct, but since it was part of Ms R.'s illness, it did not justify dismissal. The board of reference ordered reinstatement under certain conditions that, if breached, would entail Ms R. ceasing to teach anywhere in British Columbia. (In effect, the board of reference said, 'Get better or stop teaching in B.C.')

Alcoholism affected this teacher both in school and out of school. It diminished her ability to do her job and led her to disobey school regulations. Both of these effects gave the school board, legally, good reasons to intervene. She was no longer doing her job properly. Suppose, however, that she had been able to manage her alcoholism outside school so that it did not interfere with her work in the school nor induce her to bring alcohol onto the school premises. Does the school board then have grounds to suspend or dismiss her?

Treating alcoholism as a disease and not as a moral failing deserving dismissal is found in Canadian jurisdictions other than British Columbia, as the next case indicates.

Case 2: Another Teacher Who Drank Too Much

A mathematics teacher in Nova Scotia drifted from social drinking to heavy drinking and finally to alcoholism over four years. Her problem had been recognized by her superiors, and she had followed their advice to undertake a rehabilitation program. Following an episode of being drunk in the classroom in October 1985, she was suspended for ten days without pay. After the school board deliberated further on the matter, they extended her suspension for the rest of the 1985–6 academic year. The teacher grieved the suspension to a board of appeal.

In resolving the dispute, the board of appeal noted that an alcohol and drug rehabilitation program had been established within the collective agreement. Policy statements made in connection with this program indicated that alcoholism and drug dependency were to be regarded as treatable illnesses, that the school board's concern with these illnesses was to be strictly limited to their effects on the teacher's performance on the job, and that no teacher with a problem of alcoholism or drug dependency would have either job security or promotion jeopardized by requests for diagnosis and treatment. The board of appeal, therefore, revoked the suspension (which was, remember, suspension without pay). The board held that the grievor's time spent in rehabilitation under an approved alcohol treatment program be regarded as time on sick-leave.

These cases suggest that misconduct performed under a condition of alcoholism will be regarded as a result of the influence of disease and therefore treated leniently, provided the offender undertakes treatment to cure the disease of alcoholism. There seems, however, to be two corollary implications: (1) if the teacher does not 'get better,' eventually the teacher will lose his or her job on the grounds that he or she cannot perform it; and (2) if the teacher refuses to take treatment, the teacher will also be dismissed on the grounds that he or she cannot perform the job.

The proscription against alcohol or drug abuse seems, therefore, to be modified by the notion that alcoholism and drug dependency are illnesses. The sufferer should be helped to be cured and not treated punitively.

In these two cases, the misconduct in question occurred on school premises or in the classroom. We encountered no cases, during the time period covered by our study, in which alcoholism or drunkenness outside the school as such led to suspension or dismissal.

Insubordination or Contrary-Minded Behaviour

Case 3: The Teacher Who Shouted at the Principal

Allegations of 'insubordination' normally arise from the teacher's conduct 'on the job,' that is, at school during school hours. We shall see from other cases, however, that they can also arise from conduct outside the school. Case 3, from British Columbia, shows the acts of alleged insubordination occurring in the school but entails a certain degree of community involvement.

In the spring of 1983, Mr H. (described in teacher reports of 1982 as experienced, dynamic, and professional) was placed by the school board of W— on probationary appointment. In the spring of 1984, this appointment was terminated by the school board. Mr H. was alleged to be an 'inappropriate role model' because of unacceptable language, 'putting-down' students, and grabbing some students by the ear. The news of this firing upset many people in W—, a multiracial community and newspaper reports alleged 'racism' (although Mr H. himself said that he thought this was only minor). The ministry of education sent a fact-finding commission. Subsequently, by the spring of 1985, the school board dropped the affair, for Mr H. was then still teaching in W—.

From 24 to 28 February 1986, Mr H. was suspended for altercations with the principal but was reinstated after he apologized. In May 1986 he was suspended for another altercation with the principal and shortly thereafter dismissed for misconduct, namely the use of loud and abusive language in spite of being previously warned. Mr H. appealed the dismissal.

The occasion for the second altercation seems to have been as follows: At a school party, Mr H. noticed two female students going off with men from outside. He stopped them and agreed with the girls not to tell their parents. He did, however, report later to the principal. The principal told one of the girl's parents. The parents reproved the girl, who later complained to Mr H. in a very upset manner. Mr H. took the girl from the classroom to the medical room and on the way met the principal. Mr H. and the principal argued, and Mr H. shouted, 'Leave her alone – go away – you have done enough damage.'

The board of reference (decision undated, but not filed with the ministry until February 1987; hearings held in November 1986) rejected Mr H.'s appeal. They held that Mr H.'s 'serious accusation against the principal in the proximity of others' was misconduct, and they further found that Mr H.'s previous history of unacceptable behaviour exacerbated this misconduct. The board of reference, in its four-page decision, made a particular point of quoting Mr H. as saying, 'My calling in life was to clean up School District W— because the School District really needed cleaning up.'

The board of reference also noted that the school board and the teacher's superiors had done many 'unacceptable' actions. Nevertheless, they did not excuse the teacher.

Mr H. appealed the decision of the board of reference to the B.C. Supreme Court but apparently lost this appeal.

Case 4: The Teacher Who Disagreed

The next case, from Alberta, shows allegations of insubordination arising partly from a frustrated teacher expressing his opinions of colleagues and administration in public. It also states that protesting a superior's action to higher authorities through recognized channels does not constitute insubordination.

In this case, Mr T., the teacher, disagreed with his principal on some matters of school discipline and administration that he found unsatisfactory. He tried to bring these matters to the attention of the principal, so

that the principal could rectify the problem. Dissatisfied with the principal's response, he tried to bring the matter to the attention of members
of the school board and the school district's administration. Finding
these persons also unresponsive, he next tried to take the matter to
higher authorities. On one occasion, however, that was a more or less
public occasion, he expressed his frustrations by criticizing the school
board and some of his fellow teachers. Shortly thereafter, the school
board sent him a notice of termination of contract. The letter of termination accused Mr T. of

continuous uncooperative and disrespectful behaviour toward superiors, providing inaccurate and exaggerated reports with respect to student and colleagues'
behaviour, creating a climate of tension and disharmony, failure to act in a reasonable manner with respect to suspensions, threatening to suspend and withhold credits, imposing unacceptable choices on students, inflexibility in dealing
with superiors, colleagues, and students.

At the board of reference hearing, the judge found for Mr T. and
ordered him reinstated. The judge said that there had been some misconduct by Mr T. in his criticizing the school board and other teachers at
a more or less public affair. Nevertheless, in trying to draw the attention
of higher authorities to the unsatisfactory conduct of the principal and
other administrators, Mr T. had followed a reasonable procedure and was
not guilty of the alleged misconduct.

Case 5: The Teacher Whose Action Was Rash and Uninformed

Another aspect of insubordination and its converse, proper respect for
and loyalty towards authority, is shown by a case from Newfoundland. It
was heard before a board of arbitration. In Newfoundland, all schools
belong to one or another of four denominational systems, Protestant,
Roman Catholic, Salvation Army, and Jewish.

Mr T. was a teacher and also head of the science department in the
school. Asked by two students for his opinion about dropping a religion
course, Mr T. discouraged the students from doing so. After the students
persisted in questioning him, however, he offered the view that they
could legally opt out of the course, provided they had the written consent
of their parents. After promising the students to ascertain the legalities
involved, Mr T. went to consult the principal. The discussion between Mr
T. and the principal became heated and Mr T. used some vulgar words.

The following day, Mr T. received a note asking him to meet with the superintendent of schools and the vice-chairman of the school board. When his request to be accompanied by a colleague was denied, Mr T. refused to continue the meeting. Nonetheless, three members of the school board convened and ordered that Mr T. be suspended for five months.

Mr T. appealed this suspension to a board of arbitration. In its judgment, the board agreed that a teacher may discuss school policies with students and even differ with a principal in the interpretation of school policy. The board also stated that it was the teacher's responsibility to familiarize himself with a policy before making pronouncements in class. The effect of Mr T. not doing so was to undermine the school board's religious education program and the authority of the principal. The board of arbitration discounted the other charges of insubordination (refusal to attend a meeting with school board representatives) and use of vulgar language. The board of arbitration did find, however, that as a department head, Mr T. had an obligation to support his principal in implementing approved policies. His 'rash and uninformed' action created a problem for the principal and could have caused strained relationships between the school and its public. Some disciplinary action was, therefore, warranted. The board revoked Mr T.'s suspension as teacher and reduced his supension as head of department to three months without pay.

Case 6: A Conflict of Values and Community Factions

In case 6, from Saskatchewan, we discover a conflict between the teacher and the principal arising out of differences in educational philosophy and ideas of proper classroom discipline. These differences were also generational. The resulting conflict divided the local community.

In this case, the teacher, Mr M., who was then fifty-one years old and had taught at the school in question for twenty-five years, had his contract terminated effective from 30 June 1983. The reasons given by the school board for terminating the contract were the following (we quote):

(1) Your failure to co-operate with the administration, and operating principles of the school and principal;
(2) Your failure to accept the goals of the school and community;
(3) Your relationships with and conduct towards pupils is not satisfactory to the Board;

(4) The philosophy and attitudes which you display towards teaching and pupils
    do not meet community expectations.

The present principal had been principal since 1980–1. All of the other
teachers at the school were much younger than Mr M. The chairman of
the board of reference, writing the majority opinion, described the conflict as follows:

The evidence clearly disclosed that over the years there has been a change in philosophy in the matter of student-teacher relationships. The emphasis is no longer
placed solely upon the so called '3 R's.' Equal emphasis is placed upon the social
and character development of the children. [The principal] described this as a
humanistic approach. Students are involved to a much greater degree in the decision making process, and the approach today seems to be to work things out with
the students, especially the older students, and explain reasons for certain actions
or matters of discipline, as opposed to simply imposing rules or punishment without explanation.
    There is no doubt that [Mr M.] is a very strict adherent to the 'old school' and
finds these new methods very difficult to accept. His approach is far more rigid
and moralistic. It is apparent that this rather inflexible attitude has led to difficulties in his relationships with the children and their parents. These relationships
played a very prominent role in the present difficulties, and also led to problems
for Mr M. sometime in 1977. At that time an incident occurred involving [Mr M.]
which led to a number of parents calling for his resignation. The Local Board at
that time even went so far as to purportedly put him on probation, although it
seems obvious that the Board had no power or authority to take such action.

No one took issue with Mr M.'s teaching ability. Differences had arisen,
however, between Mr M.'s approach and the new methods that the board
of education and the principal were attempting to introduce. One parent
wrote a letter complaining about the principal's conduct, and the principal felt that this complaint was 'engineered' by Mr M. The director of
education for the school division spoke to Mr M. but concluded that Mr
M. was unlikely to change his ways. A meeting of the local school board,
attended by forty to sixty parents in an apparent show of support for the
principal, discussed the issue. The director again met with Mr M. but concluded that Mr M. was not willing or able to adjust. A special meeting of
the local board requested that Mr M. be dismissed.
    The board of education contacted 80 per cent of the parents having
children in the school and ascertained that a 'majority of the parents con-

tacted, and in particular a majority of those having children in [Mr M.'s] class, responded by saying they did feel there was a problem and that [Mr M.] was the problem.' This was only one of the considerations affecting the school board's decision to terminate the contract.

Mr M., on an occasion significantly and adversely affecting the performance of a student, had gone contrary to an express instruction of the principal. On another occasion, Mr M. conducted Bible readings in his classroom without the local board's approval and in spite of the principal's instruction that he desist until such approval had been obtained.

The first reason given in the letter of termination was, therefore, supported by the evidence. It was not necessary to consider the other reasons. The majority of the board of reference avoided having to decide the relation of the teacher to the community. 'Apart from his other conduct, [Mr M.'s] disobedience of specific instructions constitutes a failure to co-operate with the principal and a breach of his duty under The Education Act.' Section 227(h) of that act required the teacher to 'participate, under the leadership of the principal, in developing co-operation and co-ordination of effort and activities of members of the staff in accomplishing the objectives of the school.'

The board of reference, however, agreed with counsel for the teacher that there really had not been sufficient warning to Mr M. that his actions were leading towards termination of his contract. Mr M.'s

... performance as a teacher, apart from his relationship with the students and staff, has been excellent. His attitudes are consistent with the so called 'old school,' and he is to some extent a victim of changing values in the education system. Under these circumstances I think that [Mr M.] was entitled to some extended consideration. In the absence of this, I think a longer Notice period should have been implemented. The length of this period must be determined after taking into consideration his length of employment, his age, his prospects of finding alternative employment and his loss of income including loss of pension benefits.

They awarded Mr M. a lump sum equal to his 1982–3 salary.

Two of the board of reference members concurred in this judgment without further ado, but one board member thought that some matters required further scrutiny. He thought that an award equal to two years' salary would have been more equitable. This member also drew attention to the role of the community in the debate, and his account is worth quoting:

There was an obvious rift in the community between people who liked the way the relatively new and young principal, [Mr P.], perceived the role of teacher, and those who felt more comfortable with the traditional manner of teaching as practiced by [Mr M.]. This rift was not simply one of preference for one method of teaching relative to another, it was a rift between those who simultaneously liked one method as exemplified by [Mr M.] and disliked the new methods as represented by [the principal], and *vice versa*. There were thus two opposing factions in the community at the beginning of 1983 when one of the members of the community supporting [Mr M.] wrote a letter to the local school board complaining of [Mr P.] and his activities as a teacher and principal. This letter was either produced or extensively quoted from at a public meeting of the Local Board on February 23, 1983. All of the witnesses appearing before the Board of Reference agreed that this meeting was unusually well-attended because there was general knowledge that it would likely be controversial. Those in attendance were apparently not disappointed in their expectations.

At that very same meeting [Mr Q.], at that time Superintendent of Education for the [district name] Rural School Division, announced to those in attendance that because of budgetary restraints the [—] school would have its staff complement of five teachers reduced to four.

If ever a stage had been set for a clash, surely this was one. A small community, sharply divided between two well-known teachers, each with their supporters, and an announcement that the teaching staff had to be reduced. Not surprisingly it was from that moment that events unfolded very rapidly.

On March 3, 1983, [Mr M.] was summoned to a meeting with [Mr P.] and [Mr Q.], the Superintendent, to which a S.T.F. Counsellor, [Mr C.], had also been invited. [Mr M.] was apparently told that he would have to change his approach, although from the evidence it is not clear as to precisely how [Mr M.] had to change.

In any event, within 5 days after this meeting in which [Mr M.] had apparently been told that he had to change his approach the local school board, on the recommendation of the Principal, [Mr P.], passed a resolution requesting the Division Board to dismiss [Mr M.]. While this was being debated and resolved by the local board a group of parents presented the same request to a meeting of the [district name] Rural Division Board.

It is difficult to escape the conclusion that one faction in the community stole a march on the other.

This member of the board of reference reviewed the evidence regarding the allegations in the letter of termination and found them all unsatisfactory. He described the board of education investigation as 'at best ... unprofessional.'

Since Mr M. no longer wanted to continue his employment with the board of education, this board of reference member agreed that the contract be terminated. He held that an award to Mr M. equal to two years' salary would be more equitable than the one-year equivalent ordered by the majority.

Case 7: The Teacher Who Supported a Student Strike

This case, from Ontario, and the next case, from Newfoundland, concern the degree to which teachers may support student boycotts without being insubordinate. A student boycott, organized by students and/or by parents, is one way that a section of a community may show its displeasure at the school board's actions.

Case 7 involves the school board's actions concerning French-language instruction in a bilingually divided community. It aroused a good deal of community concern and was reported in at least three Ontario newspapers. The teacher was dismissed in May 1973 for allegedly acting in an 'unprofessional manner' during demonstrations by some 750 francophone students who boycotted classes for two weeks in March of 1973 to back their demands for a French-language high school of their own.

The school where the teacher (whom we shall call Mr C.) taught was divided into two shifts. The morning shift was bilingual and the afternoon shift was French-speaking. Students tended to prefer the morning shift, not because it was bilingual but because it occurred in the morning. Consequently, more students attended the morning shift than attended the afternoon shift. This shift system was a consequence of overcrowding in the schools. The francophone students and their parents wanted a completely francophone school. The school board delayed moving on this possibility, rumours spread that the shift system would continue, and frustrated students took action.

The teacher taught in the French shift. The French Language Advisory Committee, composed of teachers from the French shift, made recommendations to the school board. The teacher was advisor to the student government of the French shift and sympathetic to the students' desires. The students prepared a march to a school board meeting and presented their demands for a fully francophone school and the relocation of the bilingual shift. The school board had decided in January to build a new high school and at its March meeting (when the students presented their demands) accepted a tender for the new school. The school board declined to accede to the students' demands. (It may be worth noting that all members of the school board but one spoke French and that the school board conducted its business in French, with the chairman translating for the benefit of the single English-speaking-only member.) The students were angry. They held meetings and stayed away from classes for a period of time totalling about two weeks. Some persons accused the teacher of aiding and abetting the student strike (he certainly spoke in support of the students) and even of organizing it (but this was denied by the student leaders).

Members of the community were aroused. Demonstrations – peaceful enough, in fact – were made by various persons. The matter was discussed on a radio 'hot-line' (where the teacher sometimes spoke) and in letters in the newspapers. Allegations were hastily and hotly made back and forth.

In May the school board decided to ask for Mr C.'s resignation and, failing this, to terminate his contract effective 31 August 1973. He was sent a letter, dated 30 May 1973, informing him of this decision, requesting his resignation by the 31st of May, and terminating his contract on the 31st of August if the school board did not receive his resignation by the 31st of May. The school board gave as its reason Mr C.'s having 'acted in an unprofessional manner in the current school year.' It gave no particulars concerning the unprofessional conduct.

Mr C. appealed for a board of reference, which was duly granted. The judge first appointed as chairman of the board of reference declined the position on the grounds that he lived in the community in question and thought it better that this difficult matter, which was emotionally dividing the community, be dealt with by a board of reference chaired by a judge from outside the community. A judge from outside was duly appointed chairman. This chairman finally held hearings (after some preliminary meetings) in January and February of 1974. He asked for two special court constables to be appointed to stand by just in case there were demonstrations and disturbances in the courtroom. The disturbances did *not* occur. The hearings were reported in the local newspaper.

In March 1974 the board of reference made its report. The chairman decided that the termination be upheld. The school board's appointee on the board of reference agreed. The teacher's appointee disagreed and held that the contract should be continued.

The chairman held that where the testimony of the witnesses conflicted with that of the teacher, he accepted the former. The chairman described Mr C.'s demeanour as lacking candour. He considered that the evidence showed that the teacher had been at meetings of the striking students, had joined in marches with the students, had advised students on how to pressure the school board (and striking was the only effective tactic available to them), had supported students on the 'hot-line' show, and (though the teacher denied this) had threatened a student with a libel suit for allegations in a letter (published in the local newspaper) about French teachers supporting the strike.

The chairman considered the statutory duties of teachers and students, including the requirement that students below the age of sixteen attend school. Mr C.'s actions, the chairman held, were incompatible with the duties of a teacher, as a servant of the school board, to give unbiased and unfettered advice to his master. *A teacher is a servant of his employer and is not a public officer.* The Board of Reference Act recognized that the relationship between school board and teacher was that of master and servant. Misconduct, that is conduct in any way inconsistent with the faithful discharge of the servant's duties, justifies the master's dismissing the servant.

The school board could quite properly dismiss the teacher, provided it gave him due notice and a reason for dismissal. It had done so. The notice was in accordance with the contract of employment. The teacher's only right was to apply for a board of reference.

Notwithstanding the unusual conditions in the town, the board of reference concerned itself only with the issue of the continuation or termination of the contract. In the judge's view, the reasons for termination were adequate.

The teacher's nominee dissented. He held that the school board had not followed its own required procedures in dismissing Mr C. The majority report, he said, de-emphasized the facts about the causes of tension in the community and the school board's own contribution to that tension. He reviewed Mr C.'s actions and found them neither improper nor irresponsible nor unprofessional. The school board, he said, had gone beyond the actions of its own administrators (who merely reprimanded Mr C. for one or two incidents) and based its decision on reports that were not authenticated.

This case could also be included under the label of the teacher exercising his or her rights as a citizen.

Case 8: The Teacher Who Encouraged a Boycott

In a Newfoundland case, Ms W., after being suspended by her school board for alleged unsatisfactory performance, encouraged the picketing of the school by parents and a boycott of classes. The school board then sent Ms W. a notice terminating her contract. Ms W. grieved the dismissal to a board of arbitration.

Having established that Ms W. knew of the picketing and the boycott and had encouraged the participants, the board of arbitration enquired whether her action could be considered as gross misconduct. The board concluded that, insofar as such misconduct involved a marked departure from the standards by which responsible and competent teachers habitually conducted themselves (note the formulaic phraseology), Ms W. had indeed done such. Responsible teachers (said the board) do not encourage parents to use their children as a lever against school boards in resolving personal grievances; nor do they espouse picketing as a form of social action, much less the doctrine that the end justifies the means. The board, therefore, denied the grievance. The board changed the dismissal, however, to suspension for five months.

Personal Grooming and Dress

During the years 1972–87, variations in personal grooming and dress do not seem to have given rise to disputes between teachers and school boards that led to board of reference hearings. There may have been labour arbitration hearings under collective agreements in which such matters were at issue, but we have not searched the labour arbitration cases.

Behaviour Showing Signs of Cruelty

Case 9: The Teacher Who Beat His Children

In this case, from British Columbia, the teacher's out-of-school conduct showed evidence of a disposition that threatened the welfare of children placed under his care in school.

In 1984 Mr A.'s marriage broke down and it came to the attention of the Ministry of Human Resources that Mr A. had assaulted his son, S. In early 1985, Mr A. was tried in provincial court for this offence and was placed on probation. It was determined that he had a history of beating his children when they reached five to seven years of age and that he was required to leave previous teaching positions because of allegations of child abuse. The school board dismissed him because of this abuse of his children, which, in the board's judgment, rendered him a distinct risk to the well-being of the children placed in his care as a teacher.

The board of reference upheld the school board. The board of reference noted that Mr A. was less than frank and honest in his testimony, that the breakdown of his family meant that Mr A. would no longer be able to work out his problems with his family, and that there was a danger to students in his care as a result of his inability to control his temper. He showed, in the view of the board of reference, no insight into what he had done nor did he seek to correct it.

This conduct amounted to misconduct.

Case 10: The Teacher Who Seemed to Be Too Rough

In case 10, also from British Columbia, the decision of the board of reference was based on ascertaining exactly *what* happened and then *categorizing* what had happened.

Mr B. was accused of misconduct consisting of 'the kneeing and/or kicking of certain students and tickling and/or touching various parts of the bodies of certain students, including the genital areas of certain male students.' This allegation was based on statements made by children and parents to a member of the school board. The school board suspended Mr B. on 20 November 1980 and dismissed him on 27 November. Mr B. appealed and a board of reference heard the appeal in May and in August of 1981.

The board of reference (decision dated 9 October 1981) allowed the teacher's appeal. They examined the alleged incidents and concluded that while physical contact had taken place in the alleged incidents, there had been no intent either to inflict corporal punishment and cause harm to the boys or to do anything indecent. The board of reference viewed the kind of physical contact involved as unwise and undesirable but not as misconduct within the meaning of section 122(1)(a) of the Public Schools Act.

Mr B. was duly reinstated.

Case 11: The Teacher Who Lost His Temper

In case 11, the Nova Scotia Board of Appeal affirmed the value of self-control even though it reduced the teacher's penalty from dismissal to nine months' suspension.

The grievor, Mr R., appealed his suspension and subsequent dismissal following an incident in October 1985 involving a student whom he mis-treated with a frightening, physical outburst. Before this incident, Mr R. had been suspended and dismissed following three separate incidents involving his use of physical force on students, despite his awareness of school board policy banning its use. He had also been warned of the con-sequences of his insubordination. Mr R. had successfully challenged the dismissal, although the suspension had been confirmed.

The present incident involved one of the more difficult students in Mr R.'s class. Having been interrupted by the student several times, Mr R. lifted her desk, which fell on the floor, slammed the door against her, and called her a bitch.

The board of appeal found that, although the last incident would not by itself have justified suspension or dismissal, it was nevertheless a seri-ous one, indicating lack of self-control or lack of recognition by Mr R. that his behaviour was aggressive, temperamental, and inappropriate. The board did not see the incident as serious enough to warrant dis-missal. Mr R. was suspended, however, from 29 October 1985 to 31 July 1986.

Case 12: The Teacher Who Didn't 'Fit'

This particular case from Ontario involves the question of 'physical and verbal abuse' of children in classroom discipline. The teacher is described as a 'misfit' out of accord with the values of his colleagues and of the community. The minority report refers expressly to the involve-ment of the community in setting standards for education in the school district, which in this case was rural.

The teacher, whom we will call Mr M., had been employed by the county board of education since 1972. During that time, he had taught grades 5 through 8 (at different times) in two small rural community schools. In 1980 the schools had, respectively, student populations of 355 and about 240. In September 1980, Mr M. joined the staff of the smaller school.

During 1977–9, a number of parents and students at the larger school complained that Mr M. had shaken a student, kicked a student, belittled various children, described one student as a 'mama's boy,' and called some students 'stupid.' In April 1980, the principal of the larger school heard that Mr M. had called a student an 'ass.' Mr M. admitted to the director of education of the school board that some of these incidents had happened but defended his actions on the grounds that some students needed punitive discipline. The director warned him to change his behaviour.

In September 1980 parents at the smaller school complained that Mr M. had pulled the hair of one student, twisted the ear of one, kicked one in the seat, and thrown a brush at another.[8] The principal did not investigate these complaints, although he noted them, because (as he said at the board of reference hearing some months later) he did not want to start the children spying against Mr M., and because parents had asked him not to reveal their names to the teacher.

In November 1980, Mr M. was again in trouble, this time for allegedly threatening a student with demotion in grade level. The principal wrote a letter, dated 20 November 1980, stating his disapproval of such behaviour and recommending an 'urgent' change in Mr M.'s behaviour. Two paragraphs from this letter seem worth quoting, as they reveal the principal's approach:[9]

... a very concerned parent ... stated that you have threatened weak students with a demotion in grade level. I assured her that only the principal is allowed to determine changes in grade level, and that then it is subject to the approval of the Director and the Board. I thought that I had made it abundantly clear to you as teacher that statements of this type are not to be made in this school. You are not to embarrass or insult any students regardless of their relative abilities. Instead, you are to provide for their individual differences to the fullest of your ability. I recommend positive encouragements, instead of criticism. I do not want to hear of another incident involving a student or class being ridiculed or compared unfavourably, either with other students in this school and/or elsewhere.

Last evening the parent was concerned with her child being compelled to write lines repeatedly at home. Again, this form of punishment is a negative approach ...

On 15 December 1980, Mr M. apparently lifted a student up by the hair while the student was turned around talking in class to a student in the seat behind him. Mr M. turned the student around to face front and set him down again. On the 17th of December, the principal asked the school board to terminate Mr M.'s contract.

On 13 January 1981 the school board summarily terminated Mr M.'s contract. The board did so under section 228 (now sec. 235) of the Education Act and thought that they had the minister's consent, but in fact they did not.

Mr M. applied for a board of reference. The ministerial inquiry concluded that the board of reference be granted because the termination was not in accordance with either Mr M.'s contract or the Education Act, and the board of reference was the proper forum to decide whether or not Mr M.'s actions merited the termination of his contract. The minister granted the board of reference.

The board of reference was held on 4 May 1981. It set aside the termination of contract on the grounds that the termination had not been procedurally correct.

On 13 May 1981 the school board again terminated Mr M.'s contract, effective 31 August. This termination was procedurally correct. The letter of termination gave the reason as Mr M.'s 'physical and verbal abuse' of children in his care. Mr M. denied these allegations and applied for a board of reference.

The ministerial inquiry concluded that the documentation provided was not sufficient to justify refusing a board of reference and that the board of reference was the proper forum to decide whether the abuse claimed was sufficiently severe to justify termination. The minister granted the board of reference.

The board of reference duly met and heard the school board's evidence. As the chairman of the board of reference explicitly noted, Mr M. did not himself testify nor present witnesses on his behalf. The chairman stated in the written decision that this did entitle a court to draw conclusions adverse to Mr M. On 4 December 1981 the majority rendered its decision. (The minority dissent was dated 26 November 1981.)

According to the chairman, the issue was whether the school board's evidence against Mr M. met the appropriate standard of proof. This standard was that appropriate to civil proceedings, namely the balance of probabilities on a preponderance of evidence. Because the effects of the finding on the teacher's employment were grave, however, the proof should be 'clear, cogent and convincing evidence.'

The chairman reviewed the duties of principal and teacher and various definitions of 'corporal punishment' and 'abuse.' He reviewed the allegations and complaints made against Mr M. On the basis of the evidence, the chairman clearly held that Mr M. had been at fault:

On the evidence before me, [Mr M.] was clearly aware of the policy in both the schools in question regarding the form of discipline he could use when dealing with his students, yet he chose to act contrary to the policy. His actions, as revealed by the evidence, lacked self-discipline. An inability to control his own temper was clearly shown by his unnecessary and improper outburst in the courtroom ... His concern over the failure of some of his students, who were not performing up to their potential, can be appreciated but his methods of dealing with the problem were out-of-date and unacceptable to the community and his superiors ...

[Mr M.] would appear to be a 'misfit,' not being able to work within the guidelines set by his superiors in the school administration and frustrated by his conflict with the acceptable standards ...

The acts of [Mr M.], from the evidence, would appear to be acts of insubordination in an employer-employee relationship and certainly unprofessional as a teacher. His actions are contrary to the standards as validly set by the administration and not in the best interest of the children involved in the particular area.

The future in teaching with this particular Board and community does not appear promising unless a drastic change in attitude and performance by [Mr M.] takes place.

Nonetheless, the chairman went on to conclude that the evidence presented was not 'clear, cogent and convincing' enough to warrant Mr M.'s dismissal:

I conclude on the totality of the evidence there is not clear, cogent and convincing evidence of physical and verbal abuse of children by [Mr M.] in the course of his employment to form the basis for termination of his contract of employment. The respondent Board has not satisfied me that its reasons for termination of the particular contract were well-founded on physical and verbal abuse of children. The grounds provided by the respondent Board have not been established.

He therefore ordered continuation of the contract.

The minority dissent, by the representative on behalf of the school board, was brief:

I have read the majority decision in this matter and unfortunately I cannot concur with the conclusion of Judge — and Dr —. I concur with the findings of fact in the majority decision to the extent that they relate to the suitablity of [Mr M.] as a public school teacher. There is no question that this man was a 'misfit' and is not suited to teach young children in — County. His conduct, as proven by the Board of Education during this hearing, is totally unacceptable in — County. The evidence clearly established that there is a great deal of community involvement in establishing standards of teaching and discipline at the schools in this County. As such the standards which teacher's [sic] are to maintain should not be those which are acceptable in a large metropolitan area such as Toronto but rather those which are acceptable to the small rural communities in — County.

I would have held that the Board of Education had clearly established and proven the reasons for terminating [Mr M.'s] teacher's contract and I would have held that the Board was perfectly justified in doing so.

Accordingly, I would have terminated [Mr M.'s] contract.

On 1 February 1982 the school board gave notice of an application for judicial review.

A year later, in January or February of 1983, the school board's appeal was heard by the Divisional Court. The appeal was allowed and the decision of the board of reference was set aside.

Case 13: The Teacher Who 'Slapped'

This case, also from Ontario, is particularly interesting because of comments made by members of the second board of reference about changing values concerning physical punishment in Canada, the growth of a taboo against touching, and the effect of the affair on the community.

In this case, the teacher, Ms F., who was a special education teacher employed by the school board on permanent contract since 1974, was given notice by the school board on 29 January 1981 that her contract would be terminated on 31 August 1981. The letter stated that the reasons for termination were the following:

1. You have not fulfilled your duties as a teacher under The Education Act, section 229 (c) 'to inculcate by precept and example respect for religion and the principles of Judaeo-Christian morality and the highest regard for truth, justice, loyalty, love of country, humanity, benevolence, sobriety, industry, frugality, purity, temperance and all other virtues'; in that from time to time your behaviour has appeared to be contrary to the foregoing precepts and principles.
2. You have not fulfilled your duty as a teacher under The Education Act, section 229 (a) 'to teach diligently and faithfully the classes or subjects assigned to him by the principal'; or under The Education Act, section 229 (b) 'to encourage the pupils in the pursuit of learning'; in that slapping a child for incorrect responses is not an acceptable teaching practice.
3. You have not fulfilled your duties as a teacher under Ontario Regulation 704/78, section 21 (a) to 'be responsible for effective instruction, training and evaluation of the progress of pupils in the subjects assigned to him and for the

management of his classes'; in that effective instruction must provide for emotional and social development as well as intellectual and physical development.
4. You have not fulfilled your duties as a teacher under Ontario Regulation 704/78, section 21 (c) to 'carry out the supervisory duties assigned to him by his principal'; in that the Principal on previous occasions had instructed you that no corporal punishment was to be administered without the permission of the Principal and that corporal punishment was to be administered by the Principal.

Ms F. applied for a board of reference, denying the allegations. The ministry held its inquiry and received submissions from both sides. The school board's submission was particularly detailed, giving a long history of occasions when Ms F. had allegedly struck children. This list was based chiefly on the evidence of the children involved. The school board's submission also included a transcript of an in-camera hearing with Ms F. In this interview, Ms F. denied slapping or hitting children but did say that she practised a technique of 'loving strokes' that she had been taught in her training as a special education teacher. (This technique was not discussed, as such, in the board of reference decision, but the importance of touching was.) In the view of the ministerial inquirer, the issue was whether or not Ms F. had actually slapped or struck children in violation of the school's rules concerning corporal punishment. The question was the credibility of the witnesses against Ms F. versus Ms F.'s own statements. The inquirer recommended a board of reference, and one was granted.

The board of reference convened in August 1981. Before the end of the presentation of the school board's testimony, however, the chairman of the board of reference tried to encourage the parties to settle the dispute in accordance with 'what was then the Board's view.'[10] A settlement was reached between the parties' legal counsel, accepted by Ms F., but rejected by the school board. The chairman, with both counsel present, informed Ms F. of the options open to her and adjourned the board of reference for the time being. Ms F. subsequently decided to pursue the matter. Reconvening the board of reference hearing was delayed, however, by the chairman's ill health and other commitments. In September 1982 the chairman, opining that the board of reference had been adversely tainted by his unsuccessful attempt to promote a settlement, withdrew.

Ms F. applied (as she was entitled to) for a new board of reference. The ministerial inquirer noted that the teacher had not begun to present her side of the story in the original hearing and recommended that a new board of reference be granted. The minister granted one.

On 31 January 1983 the new board of reference convened. Testimony was heard over the next several days, and the board of reference delivered its judgment orally on 10 February 1983. This hearing, including the testimony before it and the board's judgment, was reported in some detail in local and regional newspapers.

The chairman reduced the reasons given in the notice of termination of contract

... to the simple complaint that [Ms F.'s] behaviour in the application of corporal punishment was detrimental to learning, counter productive to the proper emotional and social development of the children and contrary to the declared Board policy that there can be no corporal punishment other than that administered by and with the permission of the school principal.

Had Ms F. actually slapped, punched, kicked, or otherwise injured and demeaned special and other students? The issue was ultimately a question of who was telling the truth. Ms F. said that the persons who testified against her were liars and that she was the object of a local witch-hunt and character assassination. There were two possibilities, said the chairman. Either there was a conspiracy by dishonest children who were totally fabricating the accusations or the inquiry by the school board had led to more and more facts coming to light.

Most of the school board's case depended on the testimony of the children, unsupported by testimony from adults. The chairman carefully

... made inquiry of all of the younger witnesses in order to ascertain if they truly understood the religious and moral implications of an undertaking to tell the truth and as well the great evil and public hurt that could flow from bearing false witness.

Some witnesses for reasons of religious interpretation and understanding chose to be affirmed, in one or two cases where there appeared to be no religious conviction calculated to render an oath serious and binding I accepted the witnesses' undertaking to tell the truth. We were conscious, as a Board, of a community which is overwhelmingly German Lutheran and embracing traditional values and beliefs. The testimony was offered with considerable solemnity. After careful scrutinizing examination of the evidence, including explanations and denials of [Ms F.] we find the following to be the facts.

The chairman listed a long series of incidents in which Ms F. had slapped or otherwise struck children, listing the testimony child by child. Testimony by adults concerning injuries to the children were included. Ms F. explained that this was all a conspiracy and that the witnesses were all liars. The chairman found this explanation 'pathetic and quite unbelievable.'

These incidents, he said, fitted the Criminal Code definition of common assault or assault causing bodily harm:

Speaking for myself and my colleagues we were not impressed with the need in the cases reviewed for any corporal punishment, my personal view is that the force applied was in no case justified or warranted.

The chairman described Ms F.'s personality:

This Board has come to the conclusion that [Ms F.] is an unusually strong personality, a willful person, tending to be a dominating personality – anything but submissive. She is no doubt inflexible, rigid and at times far too categorical. As [Dr X.], the psychologist, has noted she can be very stern and she can be bubbly – subject to wide and sudden swings of ups and downs. Her threshold of tolerance and control is severely limited.

The chairman then went on to discuss the acceptability of physical punishment in Canadian schools and to cite the testimony of one of the expert witnesses concerning shifting standards about how pupils should be controlled. This section of the report seems to us to be sufficiently important to be quoted at some length:

Because Canada places a particularly high value upon quality of life, because the thrust of Canadian law is so particularly oriented in the direction of protecting people – protection against many of the harsh vicissitudes of life and particularly against violence in any shape or form, because our laws are designed to hold in reverence human personality – the very young, the very old, the wise and the mentally disadvantaged, we as a Board of Reference would wish to draw attention to some of the testimony that was given by [Dr Y., named professor of education at named university].

Realizing always that our very costly education industry in Ontario is designed to serve the young, the youth and the future, let me read certain extracts of her testimony of February 3rd, last. The question was put to her by [name of counsel]:

'You heard me ask [Dr X., the psychologist] questions, Doctor, about the acceptability of physical punishment as a form of discipline in the school system. I'm wondering if you could comment on that, Doctor.'

Answer by [Dr Y.]: 'I find it very hard to think of a time when a teacher would be justified in using physical means to obtain compliance from a youngster.'

And then I intervened. I said, 'That used to be the rule you know in [old] school days. Do you think we're long removed from that?' And she gave an interesting reply. And then I went on to say, 'So what you're really saying is that the thrust of contemporary policy is against physical inflicting of pain, is that it?'

Answer: 'Against physical means for obtaining compliance. I think we in our society now, we think much more of discussion, persuasion. Ours is a selling society.'

And then I referred to the fact that some smart boys were smirking behind [Ms F.'s] back, but her answer:

'But you see, children are sent to school in our society to be taught, and we're teaching a number of things. We're teaching reading, writing, we're teaching behaviour and there are not very many people in our society that would think the best way to teach a child to behave is to use physical means doing it. We would want the child to follow, when they themselves run into difficulties, and the model we would expect them to follow is surely one of persuasion, one of trying to convince people to follow the point of view, or to accept the point of view, so the teacher is always a teacher in my opinion. And is always trying to help children understand what is expected in our society. What are behaviours that are acceptable.'

And then I put to her the remark, 'The teacher's the symbol? Is that what you're saying?' Her answer:

'The teacher's the symbol, but the teacher's a mod ... no, no. The teacher is the model.'

And I said, 'The model? The model of correct behaviour? Is that right?' And her reply:

'Yes. Acceptable behaviour, suitable behaviour, appropriate behaviour.'

The board of reference, therefore, unanimously recommended that Ms F.'s dismissal by the county board of education be upheld.

The chairman then said that his colleagues on the board of reference had some words to add. These words also bear quoting. The first to speak was the teacher's nominee. She said:

The expert witness referred to earlier in the report, Dr —, made a statement which concerns me greatly. Namely, that in faculties of education, student teachers are being taught not to touch students in any manner. The reason for this is the current social climate in which a teacher or any person who touches another may have that touch misinterpreted, and thus lay herself open for attack or criticism.

In my opinion, touch is the primary sense. It is the first means of communication between an adult and a baby. The adult touching and holding the baby, and the baby grasping a finger. And often the holding of hands at a deathbed is the last means of communication between two persons. But touch is also the prime communication during our entire lives. One gives and receives encouragement, comfort, and love, as well as punishment, through touching in various forms.

To deny teachers and students the opportunity for communication through touching for fear of misinterpretation is deplorable to me, and I would challenge this community to encourage both their teachers, and their children in the use of touching in the positive sense.

The nominee of the school board commented on the effects of the whole affair on the community. He said:

This event constitutes a tragedy in the most basic sense of the word. In this case there are no winners, there are only losers. [Ms F.] has lost her employment security, and in a very real sense her personal means of livelihood. The Board of Education, the parents, the children, and the community have lost a well qualified teacher. And from the evidence which has been presented, a talented and capable teacher. What has occurred is truly tragic. Therefore we should make every effort to ensure that it never is repeated.

While this event may assure us that our democratic system works, it also serves to remind us of the fragility of human nature. Teachers are no less susceptible, nor are they immune to this fragility. In recognition of the basic humanness of teachers, it would be hoped that the community through its elected Board and ultimately through the Board's administration, will examine the support system which is provided for its teachers.

As with [name of child] who ran in a desperate search for help for his very best friend, it is evident that some teachers may also be engaged in a similar desperate search. Surely the help that is available must extend well beyond that which might be deemed pedological [sic] or instructional.

As in the case of the children it is designed to serve, the system's interest must also extend to the psychological and emotional well-being of its teachers, for the health of the system depends on the health of its individual members, whether they be child or teacher.

Extended to this community, it would appear that all who have been involved in this unfortunate event have suffered inestimable hurt. The allegations, the denials, the accusations have all exacted their price. All who have been involved, have experienced their own personal agony. With this soul-wrenching experience, each of us must, if need be, be reminded of John Donne's epic in-sight, 'ask not for whom the bell tolls. It tolls for you and me.'

Because of what has happened here during the past two weeks, mankind has surely been diminished. Let us therefore, each in our own personal way, strive to be the first to embrace our fellow man and by doing so, take the first step toward forgiveness. Let each of us strive to meet the challenge posed to us almost 2000 years ago, that we love one another as He loved us.

This was the end of the comments by the member of the board of reference nominated to represent the school board.

Case 14: The Teacher Who Laid on the Lath

In these cases, we can discern a shift of educational opinion away from ideas that school discipline must be physically punitive to a gentler approach. Violent use of physical force or corporal punishment ceases to be judged acceptable as discipline and becomes judged unacceptable as assault. The standards of the community may still regard rough treatment as acceptable, however, while the teaching profession does not. Mr Earl Hjelter of the Alberta Teachers' Association (A.T.A.) told a story about a community and a teacher whose standards were *lower* than those set by the A.T.A.[11]

A certain teacher in a junior high school in a certain community disciplined his grade 7 boys by means of a lath of wood 76 centimetres long. He would call the boy who had misbehaved up in front of the class and order him to do push-ups. As the boy rose with each push-up, the teacher would strike the boy with the lath of wood.

Most of the boys and their parents seem to have accepted this 'discipline.' One set of parents, however, finding their son bruised by this treatment, charged the teacher with assault and took him to court. The court found the teacher not guilty of assault. The community and the teacher thought that since the court had not found the teacher guilty of assault, the offence against the boy was not serious.

The parents complained about the teacher's behaviour to the A.T.A. The A.T.A. investigated, called the teacher in front of the discipline committee, and punished him for treating the boys in this way. He was clearly told that he had offended against clauses 4 and 18 of the *Code of Professional Conduct.* Article 4 reads: 'The teacher treats pupils with dignity and respect and is considerate of their circumstances.' Article 18 reads: 'The teacher acts in a manner which maintains the honour and dignity of the profession.' The teacher's defence was that he had been doing this for several years and that no one had complained. Indeed, some persons in the local community approved of his methods.

In this case, the A.T.A. was setting a professional standard that was apparently higher than (or at least different from) the standard tolerated or accepted by the community. The executive secretary of the A.T.A. spent several days in the school district explaining to the teachers the decision of the discipline committee.

Use of Obscene or Vulgar Language

Using obscene or vulgar language does not appear, in cases heard by boards of reference during 1972–87, to constitute a serious offence by itself, whether in school or out of school. In school, however, it may be *evidence* of insubordination when directed at superiors or colleagues or of cruelty when directed towards students. Note the following case from New Brunswick.

Case 15: A Principal Who Labelled an 'S.O.B.' and a Teacher Who Protested[12]

In the presence of other teachers, the principal of the school labelled the grievor's brother a 'son of a bitch.' The brother, of course, was not present. The grievor objected to this comment and later repeated the phrase to her brother when she questioned him about the incident. The employer[13] considered that this discussion of a school incident outside the school premises was a breach of professional ethics and placed a letter of reprimand in the grievor's file. The grievor sought the removal of the letter from her file pursuant to the collective agreement.

The board of adjudication allowed the grievance. It ruled that the 'griever's conduct was reasonable in the circumstances and did not amount to a breach of the vague and undetermined set of behavioural standards under the expression "professional ethics."' The board ordered that the letter be removed from the grievor's file.

Dishonest Behaviour

In the introduction to this chapter, we argued that dishonesty is a fundamental offence against the teacher/student relationship. Evidence that a
teacher has a dishonest character must therefore be taken seriously. The
following cases show various forms of dishonesty and awareness of this
principle. Two of the cases show when dishonesty is not present and help
to define the nature of the accusation of dishonesty.

Case 16: The Teacher Who Possessed Stolen Goods

On 30 August 1982 Mrs F. was indicted in British Columbia Provincial
Court for having in her possession a radio that she knew to have been stolen. The police had found several stolen goods hidden in her trailer, but
she denied knowledge of them. Her seventeen-year-old son was involved
in the thefts. After expressing concern about Mrs F. being a teacher who
'has a public trust reposed in her dealings with children,' the court gave
her a conditional discharge with probation for a year. After suspending
her for a time, the school board reinstated her and then took no further
action. (The school board had learned, from a case elsewhere in the
province, that in a conditional discharge the accused, though being
found to have committed the offence, was deemed not to have been *convicted* of it.)

On 16 February 1983, Mrs F. informed the district superintendent of
schools that she was again going to be charged with possessing stolen
goods (stolen by the roomers in her apartment, one being her son). In
March of 1983 the school board suspended and then dismissed her for
misconduct, on the following specific grounds: '1. She did not take sufficient action in relation to suspicions concerning property not owned
by her, but in her home. 2. Possession of property in her home reported to have been stolen. 3. Condoning unlawful conduct. 4. Unwill-
ing and/or unable to accept the standard of conduct expected of
teachers.'

The board of reference (decision rendered 13 June 1983) heard her
appeal on 11–12 April 1983 and rejected it. Mrs F. had misconducted herself with respect to items (1), (3), and (4) of the school board's reasons
for dismissal. The board of reference described her conduct as 'a failure
of her duty to her employer, to her broader constituency, the community
and to her profession.' It was likely to detract from the esteem for education in the community. The dismissal was justified because she had done

similàr acts before and there was no assurance that she would not do it again '*in this community.*'

After her dismissal, the question was raised in the ministry about cancelling her teaching certificate. This question was dropped after the ministry learned in November 1983 that the Crown had stayed proceedings against Mrs F. and that she had left the community; the ministry then recalled that the board of reference had concluded only that she could not continue to teach in that community.

Case 17: The Principal Who Fiddled the Books

Mr Q., principal of a certain school in British Columbia, was suspended on 15 September 1983 and subsequently dismissed for misconduct, consisting of falsifying school records and thereby enlarging the apparent enrolment at his school so that the school received money to which it was not entitled.

The board of reference (decision dated 19 December 1983) agreed that misconduct had occurred and discussed whether dismissal was the appropriate penalty or whether it should be suspension followed by reinstatement as a teacher but not as a principal. The board noted that Mr Q. was currently 'having severe mental illness.' There was, however, no justification for his 'planned deliberate fraudulent conduct' that was 'inherently destructive' of the school system. Dismissal was the only appropriate course for the school board to take.

This affair reached the newspapers. The ministry discussed whether or not to make the board of reference decision public. The school board had no objection. The ministerial files contain an opinion that the board of reference decision is a report to the minister, not a public document, unless the case is appealed to the B.C. Supreme Court.

Case 18: The Principal Who Forged a Letter[14]

Mr P., a school principal in New Brunswick, altered a teacher's letter of resignation that contained remarks that reflected adversely upon Mr P.'s ability to administer the school and its staff. The school board dismissed Mr P. Mr P. appealed to a board of adjudication, where he argued 'that he had been dismissed without due cause and that the penalty was too severe in light of the circumstances.'

The board dismissed the grievance. According to the board, the forging of a teacher's letter of resignation crucially affected Mr P.'s responsibility not only to his employer but to the students and teachers under his authority. Because he occupied a position of trust, his wrongdoing was fatal. His employer thus dismissed him for just cause. For the board to reinstate Mr P. would be to impose upon the employer a principal whom the employer would no longer trust. The position of a principal requires the utmost integrity and honesty. Having lost their trust in Mr P., the school board, staff, teachers, and the community should not be expected to accept him back as principal.

Case 19: The Teacher Whose Principal Disbelieved Him

In this case from Alberta, the teacher, Mr Y., was accused of assaulting a student (though not one of his own students). When he was asked by the principal to explain what had happened, Mr Y. denied that he had touched the student. The principal did not believe Mr Y. and judged that he was lying. Subsequently, the school board terminated Mr Y.'s contract on the ground that Mr Y., having physically assaulted a student, had failed to provide a forthright, truthful, and accurate account of the incident.

At the board of reference hearing, the judge discussed the problems of credibility and differences in testimony. He concluded that though Mr Y. had actually struck the student, Mr Y. sincerely believed that he had not done so, and that he was not lying to the principal when he said that he had not struck the student. Mr Y. did not intentionally give an inaccurate or false version of the facts to the principal.

Mr Y. had also undergone a provincial court trial on criminal charges of assault. He had pleaded not guilty. The court found him guilty but gave him an absolute discharge pursuant to section 662.1(1) of the Criminal Code.[15] The judge at the board of reference said that this meant that the trial judge must not have felt the charge to be a serious one.

The board of reference also held that Mr Y. had not breached the school board's policy statement on corporal punishment and that the assault was not, in fact, of a serious or substantive nature.

Since the reasons given by the school board were thus false and since the assault was not of a serious nature, it was not reasonable to uphold the termination.

Mr Y., however, had left the employment of the school board and found new employment in another part of the country. The judge awarded him nine months' pay for damages and also awarded him the costs of moving to the other location.

Case 20: The Teacher Who Stole Chicken Parts

This case from Alberta is interesting for two reasons. First, it shows that stealing is not necessarily evidence of a dishonest character. Second, it helps to define the nature of a public outcry.

The issue before the board of reference was whether or not the school board ought to have terminated (as it had) the contract of employment of the teacher. The teacher, Ms P., was charged in provincial court with stealing a package of chicken parts from a Co-op store. She pleaded guilty. The judge who heard the case gave her an absolute discharge. The termination notice gave as a reason that there had been a theft charge with a guilty plea. It had not mentioned the absolute discharge, though the fact of this discharge was known to the school board.

This case is particularly interesting because the board of reference, in considering the evidence upon which the school board based its reasons for dismissal, assessed whether or not there was really evidence of indignation in the community. Since the details are important, we quote directly from the judgment by the board of reference. The grammatical unevenness in the excerpts is on account of the judgment having been delivered orally; the report of the board of reference is the court reporter's transcript of the judge's decision.

The school superintendent had testified that the functions of a teacher are twofold. The first is to perform the program that is assigned. There was no question that Ms P. could do this:

The question arises in function number 2, and that is a teacher is to be a role model in society and to maintain certain standards in the community and that the image must be there as it is, as a favourable image as that image is being viewed by the citizens in the area. It is [the school superintendent's] conclusion that if a teacher is involved in charges that a certain ambivalence is created whereby children make judgment and they should not be subjected to this ...

[The superintendent] indicated that the sole basis of the discharge was the charge and the conviction that followed. He had heard about the discharge and the upsetting incident was, through rumours he had heard that children were, in [Ms P.'s] classroom causing some disruption in taunting her with what I would interpret to be 'chicken sounds.' This was checked out with the principal and it was on this basis that he had heard from the principal that there really wasn't any great problem. However, there was an indication of criminal conduct.

[The superintendent] has indicated in his view that there is a difference in areas of criminal conduct. For example, if a person is charged with impaired driving and found guilty that this might be in fact a 'grey area' and not to be considered the same as theft and looked at differently because parties in our society, in his view, have somewhat a tolerance to this type of conduct. Therefore, if a person was within the School Board charged with impaired driving or convicted, this would not necessarily mean that there would be a dismissal for that reason alone.

It is interesting to note from the evidence of the school principal, [name], that there are teachers on the staff who have been convicted of impaired driving, that no action was taken ...

[The superintendent] states that it is because of public indignation that Ms P. could not be assigned to another school, and he concludes that her image in the community, and because of her conviction, resulted in her not being effective. Thus, the question that this Board must determine is whether or not the Board acted reasonably in accordance with the provisions of the Act as required, and determine whether or not that role model that he speaks of has been altered in such a degree where she is in fact not effective.

The basis on which [the superintendent] concluded that there is public indignation, from the evidence that I have heard, is as follows: that a personal friend attracted him to the situation as to Ms P.'s problem, the person being a local [occupation and name], who had no children at the school, complained. He had heard something from [another person], that there were some other complaints but he does not recall the name and doesn't give this Board any assistance as to the number. No students, according to [the superintendent], expressed concern.

The Trustee, Ms X., who is the chairman of the Board and has been on the Board from approximately eight years, indicates that she too received some complaints and people called her, [three names given], who were employees of Ms X., and I do not infer anything adverse as to those two latter people, other than they have easy access to her. Those are the two people that complained, and out of the 250 junior high school students, there were no complaints.

She has testified that the Board dealt with this complaint and that the decision was based on the fact that there was a criminal conviction and the Board reacted because in general, she states, that people addressed her on the basis of, 'what are you going to do about it?' Her concern in light of that was that someone teaching who committed a criminal offence results in unhappiness and that this person shouldn't have access to the classroom and influencing children because of the fact that a crime was committed. She didn't expect purity, but she didn't feel that this kind of a person would be a good influence on children and that the incident caused disappointment and indignation and thus a decision was made to terminate.

The question then is: was there such a public indignation within that commu-

nity whereby this person could not fulfill the role required of her, that model role
in society whereby the Board acted reasonably in the termination? I am satisfied
that they did not act reasonably in this situation. The amount of clamour from
within the neighbourhood in a town of 4,000, with a junior high school population of 250 without any complaints being heard from the students to either the
superintendent or these trustees, and only a limited amount of people in my view
does not indicate a public indignation. It is an expression of concern.

The judge then went on to say that in view of the absolute discharge
given to Ms P., the school board should have looked beyond the mere
fact of a criminal conviction to the wider circumstances. He reviewed
these circumstances, which were personal to Ms P., and said that these
did not warrant termination. Her principal and vice-principal had noted
no complaints about her behaviour and no impediments to her effectiveness as a teacher. She was still a role model in the eyes of the children. He
added:

I am somewhat impressed by the fact that [Ms P.] when initially being harassed
and while in a drama class, which is somewhat unstructured, and having heard
remarks which she initially ignored, had the strength of character to tell the class
that she did something foolish, something stupid. In making this admission the
matter then seemed to rest in that since then there has been no harassment. I
emphasize this, because if the decision was made on public indignation, or on the
basis of the conviction alone whereby the Board reached the decision that this
teacher could not any longer fulfill that secondary role so as to be effective, I am
satisfied that it was a wrong conclusion and that they did not act reasonably under
these circumstances ...

The judge had previously noted that Ms P. had not been present at the
meeting of the school board when it decided to terminate her contract.
In his final remarks, he mentioned this fact again:

Out of adversity of this nature sometimes the community can react positively. I
have seen evidence that after initial taunting it probably did that. The citizens of
[name of community] are perhaps to be commended if that is the way they treat
their citizens who have taught with them for a good number of years, to error [sic]
is human, to forgive is divine. I feel that no great condemnation can come upon
the decision makers in your board as perhaps if the hearing would have been conducted with [Ms P.] being present today's dissertation from this board might not
have been necessary.

Note that the judge distinguished expressions of concern by members of the community from public indignation by the community. Note also that he enquired whether or not the incident interfered with the ability of the teacher to perform her functions as a teacher. Note finally that (in a passage that we have not quoted) he distinguished this case as involving an absolute discharge by the court rather than a conditional discharge.

Discussion

What do these cases teach us? Let us review them briefly and discover if the players have been following the two 'value-centres' discussed in the introduction to this chapter.

Under 'The Abuse or Misuse of Alcohol and Other Drugs,' we discovered:

i)   a teacher whose addiction to alcohol led to frequent absences from work and finally to secret drinking on school premises; and
ii) a teacher whose alcoholism led to absences and finally to drunkenness in the classroom.

In both cases, the tribunal considered that alcoholism was a disease and should be treated as such. Rather than punitively dismissing the teacher, the school board should give her[16] a chance to cure her alcoholism. Of course, if the teacher persisted in her alcoholism, she would then be unable to do her job and would then have to be dismissed.

The value of rational self-control appears very obliquely in the board of reference decisions. It is not mentioned explicitly, but the notion of alcoholism as a disease is mentioned. The implication, then, is that the sufferer is not wholly responsible for the illness and the absences and actions that it causes. The sufferer is required, however, to take treatment to remedy this illness or lose her job.

Under 'Insubordination or Contrary-Minded Behaviour,' we encountered:

i)   a teacher with rough manners who argued with the principal in a rough manner on several occasions;
ii) a teacher who disagreed with the principal on several important matters and who, after trying to get a hearing from the principal's superiors, revealed his concerns in public;

iii) a teacher who had a disagreement with the principal, who was concerned with some opinions expressed by the teacher to students
regarding exemptions from the school's religious requirements;
iv) a teacher who had a disagreement with the principal over teaching
methods and whose dispute divided the community;
v) a teacher who supported students who boycotted classes in order to
demand a French-language high school of their own; and
vi) a teacher who promoted a boycott by pupils and parents in protest for
her suspension for allegedly unsatisfactory performance.

The value expressed in these cases is clearly obedience to authority.
The decisions of the boards of reference imply that the teacher must act
in such a way that the principal and other superordinates can rely upon
the loyalty of the teacher and can trust the teacher to follow orders. The
criticism of superordinate authorities by subordinates must proceed
through proper channels and not be made public in such a way that the
authorities are undermined.

Under 'Behaviour Showing Signs of Cruelty,' we discovered:

i) a teacher who habitually beat his children;
ii) a teacher who in physical education classes had appeared to be man-
handling and even sexually assaulting students;
iii) a teacher who lost his temper with a 'difficult' student;
iv) a teacher who was accused of verbally and physically abusing his students in class (as part of 'discipline');
v) a teacher who slapped students with 'loving strokes'; and
vi) a teacher who used a lath to discipline boys in his class.

The boards of reference declared that cruelty and the use of force was
unreasonable and that if the teacher had done such, the teacher should
be accordingly penalized. Standards change. What might have been
acceptable in former times was no longer acceptable. The cases turned
more on matters of definition and proof: had the teacher done what was
alleged to have been done? The value here is a revulsion against cruelty
and a consequent opposition to corporal punishment.

The one case under 'Use of Obscene or Vulgar Language' concerned a
principal who, when he insulted one of his teacher's relations at a teachers' meeting and heard that the teacher had told her relative, wrote a letter reprimanding the teacher for a breach of professional conduct. The
teacher grieved this reprimand and her grievance was upheld. Vulgar lan-

guage was not the issue here. *Abusive* language (by the teacher to the principal) was a concern in one case of insubordination. It was there viewed as evidence of the insubordination.

Under 'Dishonest Behaviour,' we encountered:

i)   a teacher who knew that her son was using her house to hide stolen goods and who was consequently convicted of 'possessing stolen goods';
ii) a principal who falsified his school's enrolment figures;
iii) a principal who fraudulently altered a teacher's letter of resignation because it adversely criticized the principal's abilities;
iv) a teacher whose principal accused him of dishonesty because the principal disbelieved the teacher's account of an incident; and
v)   a teacher who, in a moment of aberration, stole a package of chicken parts from a Co-op store.

Dishonesty and untruthfulness are clearly at issue in these cases. Where the dishonesty goes to the teacher's or principal's responsibility to the school board, the offender is dismissed.

Dishonesty is both serious in itself and serious for its effect on the school board. Dishonesty makes the school board unable to trust its employee. When such dishonesty becomes public knowledge, it may also render the community unable to trust a school board that keeps such a person on its payroll.

In general, therefore, the concern or value that is apparent in these cases seems to be primarily the character of the teacher as a reliable, trustworthy, obedient servant of the school board. If the teacher's conduct, whether inside or outside school, contravenes these requirements, the school board is entitled to dismiss the teacher. This, of course, is the old master-and-servant law in operation.

The second value that is apparent is a growing antipathy to cruel behaviour, whether physical or mental. If a public school teacher's behaviour, in the classroom or outside it, shows a disposition to be cruel to the children in his or her care, or raises the possibility of such a disposition, the school board is allowed, and almost obliged, to dismiss the teacher.

Both of these values seem reasonable grounds for school boards to dismiss teachers. If the teacher cannot do the job that he or she has been hired for – and dishonesty, for instance, certainly interferes with the job – then the school board must dismiss the teacher. If the teacher is treating the pupils cruelly, the teacher is not doing his/her job properly and should be terminated.

Where is the value that seemed at first to underlie all of these – that of the 'gentleman' or 'lady,' who is rational, self-controlled, courteous, considerate, and thoughtful? We cannot say that it is *not* present. Its presence, however, is in the background and not in the foreground.

Let us now go on to consider the second main class of misconducts, namely those concerned with sex. What *values* will the cases there reveal to us?

4

Sexual Misconducts

Introduction

Western educational theory, from Plato through the Christian era to today, has been dominated by the idea that the animal nature of human beings should be controlled in the interests of society and of spiritual or religious development. This animal nature has been described as unruly, selfish, evil, and corrupt. Consequently, human beings must be dominated, disciplined, and taught proper behaviour, while some of their grosser animal instincts must simply be suppressed or cut off. Young human beings must be taught that they cannot immediately gratify their animal impulses and must learn instead to do many things *now* for remote and distant rewards.

In the demand for training, Western educational theory is not unique. This demand, for instance, also characterizes the educational philosophy of Confucius, which is foundational to the traditional familial and formal educational practices in China. Confucianism, however, does not regard the animal nature as evil or corrupt: nature merely needs proper training.

The traditional Western theory has been challenged in the twentieth-century Western world by notions that impulse-gratification is not wrong, that repression and suppression of instinct and feeling are wrong, even pathological, and that egoistic indulgence is preferable. This alternative view has been encouraged by certain types of 'self-development' literature, by a popularized kind of psychoanalysis that advocates letting impulses free, and (no means least) by commercial advertising, whose message is, 'Indulge yourself – buy what we are selling.' We thus rush from one extreme to the other, instead of discovering a more balanced view that would do justice to the truth to be found in both views.

Of the impulses the traditional view deems most important to control, the sexual impulses are either paramount or next to paramount. Indeed, with some thinkers, the body is evil and dirty, sex is evil and dirty, and sex is permissible only within marriage for the purpose of the reproduction of the species. This extreme view itself testifies to an important fact about the sexual urge: that urge is both powerful and easily distorted or redirected. Given this long educational tradition and the fact that the sexual urge is both powerful and easily fixated on different objects, it is not surprising that teachers should sometimes be guilty of sexual misconducts. The teacher finds in the classroom a group of growing children and adolescents whose own sexual natures are stirring and forming and are in need of direction. If the students like their teacher and their teacher likes them (a relationship that favours successful teaching and learning), this mutual liking *can* become distorted and turn into sexual attractions. These sexual attractions can then potentially complicate the lives of both teachers and students and, if allowed to run their course, fundamentally distort the teacher-student relationship.

Part of the lessons the public schools have to teach concerns social and gender roles. Such roles are learned by children from their environment but particularly from family, friends, teachers, and television. The schools take up one-quarter of the growing child's and adolescent's life. The schools, therefore, must both deliberately instruct children in sexual and gender concerns and provide examples of relevant behaviours and attitudes. Refusing to discuss sex and parenthood sends a message concerning these issues. Sex and gender thus impinge on both the 'inherent necessities' and the 'adventitious content' of teaching.[1]

Teaching is a distinct kind of social action in which information, skills, attitudes, and values are communicated to, or induced in, a learner by a teacher. No matter what is communicated or taught, certain general principles must be followed if the teaching is to be successful. We may call these the 'inherent necessities' of teaching. For example, the teacher must be respected by the student if the teacher's messages are to be positively accepted and learned. However, these messages themselves are something other than the inherent necessities. They may be called the 'adventitious content.' The material to be taught has its own character that is different from the generic character of teaching as a kind of social action.

We should further distinguish this 'adventitious' material into two groups. The first group consists of subjects (e.g., geography) or skills (e.g., carpentry). The second group consists of moral or social habits, such as 'effective living' or 'family values.' In the first group, the off-the-job conduct of the teacher is appreciably *less* relevant[2] to the knowledge or skill the teacher is imparting. In the second group, this off-the-job conduct is *most* relevant. The teacher who has to teach such values as appropriate attitudes to authority, the duties and rights of citizenship, appropriate attitudes concerning gender, or ideals about family life and organization might well be expected to illustrate these attitudes and ideals in his or her off-the-job conduct. Such an expectation depends on the principle that inconsistency or contradiction between two messages reduces the plausibility of both, while consistency among messages increases their individual plausibilities.[3]

Only when the teacher's pupils become sexual objects or sexual partners does sexual activity *necessarily* interfere with the 'inherent necessities' of teaching.[4] This is because the teacher is in a position of authority over the pupil and could use that authority to impose sexual activities upon or to induce sexual favours from the pupil. 'Come sleep with me and I'll give you a good grade on the exam.' Or, if the pupil is 'street-smart' and the teacher's lusts are evident, the pupil may try to seduce the teacher and exchange sexual favours in return for preferential treatment. 'If you give me a good grade on my exam, I'll sleep with you.' In both these situations, our confidence in the integrity of the teaching becomes shaken.[5]

Beyond paedophilia and teacher/student liaisons, however, allegations of sexual misconduct reveal more about community values than about failures in teaching as such. If we classify the various occasions sexual misconduct by teachers has been alleged, we find the following major classes:

1. paedophilia, or sexual advances towards small children; and sexual abuse of small children;
2. seduction of, sexual advances towards, and even dating students;
   In this second class, the student has more initiative than in the first class and is usually older. The degree of consent and volition by the two persons involved is always relevant to this relationship.
3. sexual exhibition and lewdness;
4. heterosexual relationships outside marriage, including adultery;
   This blends by degree into the next class.
5. non-marital cohabitation, 'common-law' marriage, and heterosexual 'live-in' relationships;
   This may include out-of-wedlock pregnancies. In extreme cases, merely dating has been construed as misconduct.

6. homosexual (gay or lesbian) relationships, both public and private;
7. transvestism and transsexuality;
8. other: the residual class.

Classes 1 and 2 directly affect and indeed poison the teaching relationship. The remaining classes may or may not also involve students: sometimes they do; often they do not. The classes are not mutually exclusive. One could, indeed, imagine an affair which encompassed all seven categories. A further complication ensues when the sexual activity is also regarded as a criminal act, as for example in cases involving charges of 'gross indecency.'

These various misconducts therefore impinge upon teaching in different ways. Some directly affect the inherent necessities. Others have more to do with the kind of gender roles which students are expected to learn. Some merely outrage community standards. Let us follow each misconduct in turn.

We shall take each misconduct and describe it generally, speculating briefly on its character and the reasons for being concerned with it. We shall then outline one or more board of reference cases in which this misconduct was an issue.

Paedophilia, Proven or Alleged

By 'paedophilia,' we mean sexual advances towards small children with or without their consent. A key element is the child's ignorance of the implications of what is being done to him or her, regardless of whether or not the child likes it. The principle involved is the idea that small children should not be treated as sexual objects or in any way sexually used. The element of sexual abuse is clearly present when the child resists the teacher's advances but the teacher nonetheless persists. There may be a fine line between paedophiliac advances and behaviour intended to demonstrate affection and approval.

The child's consent cannot be used to justify the action. The child does not have the knowledge to give informed consent. In any event, whether the child thinks that he or she is consenting, there is a betrayal of the trust which ought to exist between the child and her or his caregiver. The teacher (or, for that matter, another adult or an older child) is in a position of control and dominance over the child. To use the child for sexual purposes is a gross abuse of that position. In our view, paedophilia is the most serious of these sexual misconducts. Board of reference cases con-

cerning paedophilia, however, have been few. They emerge where there
is doubt concerning either the actual occurrence of the alleged behaviour or the acceptability of the behaviour. The two cases cited here, both
from British Columbia, illustrate the issues which have concerned boards
of reference.

Case 21: The Teacher Who Touched Little Girls

On 25 January 1982 the principal of the elementary school reported that
mothers of two grade 4 girls had recently complained to him about Mr K.,
a grade 4 teacher, touching their children in an indecent way while marking their exams (the girls standing beside him at his desk while he did
this marking). Mr K. admitted to the principal that he had touched the
girls in an affectionate way but denied the indecencies. Other girls also,
upon investigation, admitted being touched by Mr K.

The school board suspended Mr K. on 2 March 1982 and, after interviewing him on 8 March, dismissed him on 9 March. Mr K. appealed, and
a board of reference was held during May and June. Twenty-seven witnesses in all, including the children, were heard.

The board of reference (decision rendered in June 1982) dismissed the
appeal. After hearing all of the girls involved and carefully considering
their testimony, the board concluded that the events alleged had
occurred and that Mr K. had a habit of touching the girls in a questionable manner which was *not* experienced by the girls as friendly encouragement for their good work (which was what Mr K. described himself as
giving them). There was no conspiracy on the part of the children and
their parents to discredit Mr K. as a teacher. The board described Mr K.'s
behaviour as 'gross misconduct.'

Mr K. appealed the decision of the board of reference to the B.C.
Supreme Court, but the court apparently[6] declined to hear the appeal
because criminal charges of indecent assault were being laid against Mr
K. arising from these allegations.

During 21–5 November 1982, Mr K. was tried in county court on the
criminal charges and was *acquitted*. According to newspaper reports, the
judge in his charge to the jury had discussed the nature of 'reconstructed
evidence,' in effect questioning the credibility of the girls as witnesses,
and this discussion may have influenced the jury.

The parents whose children were involved, and a number of other persons as well, were upset by the county court's acquittal and wondered why
the board of reference's and the county court's decisions were so

opposed. The county court's decision was *not* used as the basis for appealing the board of reference's decision, which (we infer) stood unchallenged. We should note, however, that board of reference decisions are based on the *balance of probabilities* according to the board's estimate of the evidence before it. A criminal act, by contrast, must be proven *beyond reasonable doubt*. Consequently, evidence that would be insufficient to allow a conviction in a criminal trial might easily be sufficient to warrant a board of reference deciding against a teacher.

This case also illustrates the 'triple jeopardy' facing any teacher who is convicted of a crime: (a) the teacher will suffer the penalty (fine or imprisonment and public obloquy) for having committed the crime; (b) the teacher will be dismissed by the school board (i.e., lose his or her job); and (c) the teacher may also lose his or her professional standing if the ministry cancels or suspends the teacher's certificate (i.e., the teacher loses his or her occupation). All of these threatened Mr K. In the end, however, the court acquitted him of the criminal charge, and the ministry consequently refrained from cancelling his certificate. Not only had Mr K. lost his job, his wife had left him, his reputation was thoroughly blemished, and he had a mental collapse requiring psychiatric help.

Case 22: The Teacher Who Was Too Affectionate

In this case, the students involved were somewhat older than those in case 21. On 24 June 1983, Mr M. was dismissed by the school board 'for his misconduct with respect to improper touching of female pupils.' For example, he was accustomed to putting his arm around them in order to show his appreciation of their work in school.

The board of reference (decision dated 12 November 1983) noted that this case raised serious problems of credibility. The board of reference also heard the pupils involved and observed them under cross-examination, whereas the school board had not. The board of reference concluded that Mr M.'s behaviour, including his style of teaching, was 'overly demonstrative' and 'caused some measure of discomfort and concern on the part of his students.' This was inappropriate. The testimony, however, did not support the full extent of the accusation. The board of reference, therefore, varied the decision of the school board from dismissal to a period of suspension without pay.

The major issue before the board was, as the board said, the credibility of the various witnesses. (Credibility was also an issue in case 21 above.) The second issue in the case was categorizing Mr M.'s behaviour:

was it simply an 'affectionate' manner of teaching or was it something more?

As people have become more aware of the possibilities of sexual overtones in touching children, especially small children, and of fondness becoming fondling, a countervailing fear of touching has resulted in response. In an Ontario case (see chapter 3, case 13) concerning a teacher who was accused of slapping her students (with no sexual overtones involved), one board of reference member commented on the growth of a taboo on touching. Her remarks seem worth repeating here:

The expert witness referred to earlier in the report, Dr —, made a statement which concerns me greatly. Namely, that in faculties of education, student teachers are being taught not to touch students in any manner. The reason for this is the current social climate in which a teacher or any person who touches another may have that touch misinterpreted, and thus lay herself open for attack or criticism.

In my opinion, touch is the primary sense. It is the first means of communication between an adult and a baby. The adult touching and holding the baby, and the baby grasping a finger. And often the holding of hands at a deathbed is the last means of communication between two persons. But touch is also the prime communication during our entire lives. One gives and receives encouragement, comfort, and love, as well as punishment, through touching in various forms.

To deny teachers and students the opportunity for communication through touching for fear of misinterpretation is deplorable to me, and I would challenge this community to encourage both their teachers, and their children in the use of touching in the positive sense.

This, of course, makes the trustworthiness of public school teachers even more important.

Sexual Liaisons with Students[7]

Sexual liaisons with students, in which the student is a consenting partner to the relationship, imply that the student is older than in the preceding class of cases. Because the teacher is responsible to persons other than the student, sexual relations between teacher and student will necessarily interfere with the teaching. When such liaisons involve consent by a student who is fully informed of the implications of the liaison, this offence is less heinous than paedophilia. When the teacher imposes sexual demands on the student as the price for the student's success in courses, however, the offence is as serious as paedophilia. We encountered no such cases in the board of reference decisions which we have been able to research.

Case 23: The Teacher Who Continued an Affair with His Student

This case is an Alberta case. In Alberta, the board of reference consists of a single judge sitting as the board. Case 23 stipulates the basic principle concerning sexual liaisons between teachers and students. If the student is in the teacher's own class, the teacher must have no sexual liaison whatsoever with the student.

A forty-three-year-old male schoolteacher, separated from his wife and depressed in mind, engaged in 'consentual[8] sexual intercourse' with a seventeen-year-old female student in one of his classes. The student was living with the teacher at the time of the board of reference hearing, some time after he had been dismissed. The teacher had admitted his activities to the school authorities, and his contract of employment had been duly terminated by the school board. He appealed to the board of reference essentially on the grounds that the school board had no reasonable basis for dismissing him, and he asked, not for reinstatement, but for monetary compensation in lieu of notice. The immediate issue before the board of reference was, therefore, whether the compensation was justified. The judge gave his decision on 8 May 1988.

The judge observed that the teacher had committed a breach of trust, and had admitted this:

He shows no remorse in that he is still living with the student. This is not a case of a teacher having sexual intercourse with a student in some other school or even some other class but it involved a student in his own class over whom he would have some measure of control and whose examination papers he would be required to grade.

A psychiatrist gave evidence that the teacher would be unlikely to repeat his unacceptable behavior. However, the teacher is now living with the girl and he was separated from his wife at the time of the sexual intercourse with the girl. Furthermore, he has not asked for reinstatement and he won't be given the chance to repeat.

The judge concluded:

I agree with the decision of the school board in this inquiry. It would be wrong of them to send a message to teachers that they can expect anything less than instant dismissal if they engage in sexual activities with their students. Parents have the right to expect that they can continue to send their children to school without fear that they will be treated in such a manner. The appeal is dismissed. The decision of the school board is upheld.

This case is straightforward. What makes it interesting is that the judge quoted from three British Columbia cases and from one case from the State of Washington. These quotations concerned the function of teachers as role models, the importance of maintaining public confidence in the school system, and the heinousness of sexual relations between a teacher and his student.[9]

Case 24: The Teacher Who Wrote Romantic Letters

This is a British Columbia case. The student was in the teacher's school but not in the teacher's own classes. Since the teacher was married, it also falls under class (4), extramarital heterosexual relationships. Note that the board of reference was less severe on the teacher than was the school board.

The teacher was dismissed on 2 June 1983 by the school board for having had sexual relations with a seventeen-to-eighteen-year-old girl who was a student in his school but not in any of his classes. He had written romantic letters to her, and her parents found the letters. The affair thus became known to her parents, the teacher's wife, and the school board.

At the hearing before the school board, the discussion turned on the role of teacher and student and on the exercise of authority by a teacher. The school board decided, though not unanimously, to dismiss the teacher.

The board of reference (decision dated 6 October 1983) varied the school board's decision. The board of reference observed that though the girl was a student, she was not a student of the teacher. The teacher was remorseful and said that the relationship was over. There had been no attempt by either the teacher or the student to use the other for his or her own advantage. The board of reference held that the teacher's behaviour was misconduct but that the appropriate penalty was suspension without pay and transfer to another school.

Case 25: The Teacher Who Dated a Fourteen-Year-Old Girl

This is a case from British Columbia that has been noticed several times in B.C. board of reference decisions and in decisions of the B.C.

Supreme Court, though the details of the case are usually not given. It was one of the earliest B.C. board of reference cases. It illustrates well the concern of the school board both for the moral welfare of the students under the school board's care and for the reaction of the community. The school district in the story may be identified as a large rural one.

Note that the teacher had met the student while she was at a school where he taught but that the affair proceeded when she was, though still a student in the school district, at a school other than the teacher's. Note as well that her parents approved of the relationship between her and the teacher.

In June 1972, Mr T. was appointed to a teaching position in one of the elementary schools of the School District of Y—. During the summer of 1973, he participated in a youth group program at a certain lake and there developed an attachment to Miss F., a fourteen-year-old whose parents lived in the vicinity. Miss F. had been, during the 1972–3 school year, a pupil in the school where Mr T. taught. Mr T. at this time was having marital difficulties that he would later deny to be caused by his attachment to Miss F.

In September 1973, Miss F. moved to the town of Z—, to attend school and to live in the dormitory maintained by the school board for out-of-town students. There, Mr T. saw her frequently during weekdays and, on Friday evenings, would pick her up in his car and take her home to her parents for the weekend.

The result was that some persons in the community began to gossip about Miss F. and Mr T. ('a married man'), and this gossip reached the ears of the district superintendent of schools. The district superintendent met with Mr T. on 17 September. At that meeting, the superintendent thought that he had received an undertaking from Mr T. that Mr T. would not see Miss F. on weekdays in Z—, and would restrict his social intercourse with her to 'weekends under the aegis of the girl's parents' (as the superintendent phrased it in his letter of 23 October). Mr T. (as he explained later) thought that he had agreed only not to be seen with her in public on weekdays.

The relationship continued and apparently so did the gossip. The superintendent wrote to Mr T. on 23 October, chiding Mr T. for not living up to the agreement and noting, 'Your public behaviour occasions much derogatory talk in the community, from your colleagues, school board members, and members of the general public.' Since Mr T. did not seem to appreciate the seriousness of his acts (the superintendent wrote), he, the superintendent, must consider further action.

The further action came on 30 October 1973. The school board wrote to Mr T. and suspended him, on the following grounds:

That you did and do consort with a fourteen-year-old girl pupil in this School District; and that the young lady is resident in the Dormitory and was last year a pupil in the school in which you taught; and that you declare that there is a very affectionate relationship between yourself and the young lady, which you describe as 'being in love' and which you demonstrate by way of holding hands, cuddling, and kissing; and that this relationship did develop during the summer of 1973 at a youth group program at —, in the attendance area of your school of the 1972–73 school year; and that you are twenty-five years of age, a teacher in an elementary school in this School District, and a married man.

On 5 November, the school board met with Mr T. to hear his side of the affair. There Mr T. stated that he was quite aware of the unpleasant remarks being made by 'disturbed people' in the community and he was quite prepared, both before and after his divorce, to limit his appearances with Miss F. in Z—. This relationship did not reduce his effectiveness as a teacher.

The board discussed his relationship with Miss F. At one point, he said that Miss F. knew what she was doing; she was, he said, a very mature girl. Trustee A. retorted, 'Some of us are a little more equipped at looking ahead than a 14 year old girl.' Did Mr T. and Miss F. really know their own minds? Trustee B. asked if they would accept separation for one year; then they would know better how they felt about the relationship. Mr T. would not accept a year's separation.

The district superintendent found the problem to be in the fact that Mr T. was teaching pupils only one or two years younger than Miss F. 'It is suggested that because you are a teacher, there are certain restrictions [and] disciplines upon you that make this not quite the right thing for you to do.'

Trustee B. had not heard any gossip about Mr T.'s affair. She was, however, concerned that the school board was 'totally responsible' for the students in the dormitory. Trustee C. added, 'Any time a married man is taking a girl out from the Dorm we would be looking in to it.'

Some trustees thought that it was wrong for Mr T., as teacher and an older man, to be encouraging the strong attachment that Miss F. had formed for him. One trustee remarked that it was quite common for fourteen- or fifteen-year-old girls to form such an attachment. Mr T. did not admit to doing anything wrong, and D., the chairman of the school board, commented on this. Trustee B. said to Mr T., 'This may cause Miss F. to leave school. What would you do?' Mr T. answered, 'Put her back in school.' Chairman D., who was a woman, observed, 'How can you put a mature woman back in school?' and added, 'I cannot imagine any man putting me where I did not want to go.'[10]

This meeting did not resolve to dismiss Mr T., but a later meeting of the board did, and on 8 November 1973 the school board officially dismissed him. The letter of dismissal dismissed him for misconduct and cited as grounds the same passage as in the letter of suspension. Mr T. duly appealed his dismissal, and the machinery for a board of reference hearing was set in motion.

Mr T.'s appeal was heard in Z— on 18 and 19 December 1973, and the board of reference gave its decision in writing on 25 January 1974. The majority of the board of reference dismissed Mr T.'s appeal and upheld the school board, while the minority allowed the appeal. Both majority and minority agreed that Mr T.'s ability to teach had not been questioned and that the school board was not alleging that his effectiveness as a teacher had been impaired by reason of his association with the girl. Neither majority nor minority were prepared to find that Mr T. had broken the code of ethics of the British Columbia Teachers' Federation. The members of the board of reference then parted company.

The majority held that

... [Mr T.'s] continuing association with the girl justified the school board in concluding that it would not be fulfilling its responsibilities to the community and particularly to parents of the School District's school children, if it did not take steps to terminate the association. However, the evidence is clear that although [Mr T.] was prepared to make certain concessions with regard to his relationship with the girl, such as limiting public appearances, he was not prepared to terminate the relationship.

In the opinion of the majority of the Board of Reference, [Mr T.'s] decision to continue the association with the girl was misconduct within the meaning of the Public Schools Act in that the continued association would likely bring the school board into disrepute in the community and amounted to a refusal to obey a lawful direction by the school board.

These words by the majority echoed an argument by counsel for the school board that

... it is misconduct if a teacher's conduct was likely to bring his employer into disrepute or if he does anything incompatible with the due or faithful discharge of his duty or if he refuses to obey a lawful direction of his employer.

This argument is, in fact – though the board of reference did not say so – a fairly standard notion of misconduct in the law of master and servant or of employee discipline.

The minority of the board of reference disagreed with the majority's view that Mr T.'s conduct amounted to a refusal to obey a lawful order of the school board. Mr T. had been dismissed, not for such a refusal, but only for misconduct as defined in the school board's motion. The minority considered that, following the intent of the Public School Act, misconduct governs only the carrying out by the teacher of the duties assigned under the Public School Act and its regulations and that the Public School Act does not govern the social life of teachers. Since there was no evidence that Mr T.'s teaching had been adversely affected and though Mr T.'s actions 'were unwise and are not condoned,' the minority approved Mr T.'s appeal.

Mr T. apparently appealed the decision of the board of reference to the B.C. Supreme Court, but we have no data on what happened to this appeal. In any event, sometime after his dismissal, Mr T. obtained his divorce and duly married Miss F. He and she left the school district, and Mr T. continued to teach in other school districts. It would appear that he was successful as a teacher and eventually also attained a position in school administration.

The case seems, at first, straightforward. A young but married teacher starts dating a student who had, the previous year, been a pupil in his school. The pupil is just below the legal age of consent and is a resident in a student dormitory managed by the school board. The relationship, however, is with the knowledge and consent of the girl's parents. The girl, by those who know her, is considered to be mature for her age. The teacher's marriage is apparently already experiencing difficulties. Persons in the community, perhaps including colleagues of the teacher, notice the developing relationship and start to gossip, sometimes rather adversely. The relationship comes to the attention of the district superintendent of schools, who investigates and tries to secure from the teacher an undertaking to stop the relationship, at least in public. The teacher agrees to be discreet but will not stop the relationship. The school board suspends the teacher and interviews him. They are not wholly certain what to do but agree that what the teacher is doing is somehow wrong and should cease. The teacher insists on maintaining the relationship.

Shortly thereafter, the school board dismisses him for misconduct, citing his conduct and the circumstances as the reasons therefor. The board of reference in a two-to-one split decision upholds the school board and allows the teacher's dismissal for misconduct; the minority opinion holds that there was no misconduct, although the teacher's behaviour was 'unwise.' The majority also held that the teacher had, in refusing to end the relationship, refused to obey a lawful order of the school board.

Just what had happened? What had upset the district superintendent and the school board? Were the reasons given by the school board and by board of reference soundly based on the facts? Was there perhaps an underlying principle not fully enunciated by the case? Also, were there differences between the way the school board understood the affair and the way the board of reference understood and rationalized it?

On the basis of the letter of the district superintendent and the transcript of the meeting of the school board, we infer four interlocking concerns:

(a) The first concern seems to have been that teachers should not date students, even students other than their own. The teacher-student relationship is not compatible with the dating relationship. Teachers are, in a sense, in a quasi-parental relationship or in a relationship of moral and pedagogic authority vis-à-vis students. That relationship cannot be maintained if students or teachers are allowed to think of the other as datable or as a possible sexual partner. The two kinds of relationships interfere with one another and the district superintendent and the school board were aware of this. Mr T. did not, however, *clearly* fall into this category. Miss F. had been, but then was not, a student in the school where Mr T. taught, and was not likely to be Mr T.'s student in the future.

(b) The second concern seems to have been the responsibility of the school board for the morals of the students in the dormitory managed by the school board, where the school board was clearly *in loco parentis*. Miss F., a fourteen-year-old girl, was dating not merely a man eleven years her senior but a married man at that. This was immoral and parents might object. Had Miss F.'s parents objected, the school board's case would have been clearer; but, in fact, not only did Miss F.'s parents not object, they also wrote a 'To Whom It May Concern' letter stating that Mr T. had been 'nothing short of a gentleman' and objected to the charges of immorality against their daughter. The fact that such charges were being made, however, might still give the school board grounds for concern about the damage ensuing to the image of the school board. Perhaps the morals of the students in the dormitory were not, in themselves, a concern of the school board, as much as the failure of the students to live up to the moral demands of the parents, of whom the school board must consider itself the agent. Perhaps the school board did not distinguish between these two aspects.

(c) The third concern seems, therefore, to have been the effect of the affair and of the gossip about the affair upon the public image of the school board. If what Mr T. and Miss F. were doing was in some sense wrong, then the school board's not taking action (if action were proper and legal in the circumstances) would be interpreted by some members of the community (how many? how widely?) as condoning the wrong. This may reduce (but by how much really?) the prestige and influence of the school board in the community and may by association besmirch the individual reputations of the members of the school board and the school district administration. It would therefore be important that the school board be seen to be responding positively to community standards and not condoning the wrong-doing of Mr T. and Miss F. In this situation, this would mean reprimanding the more legally responsible of the two, namely Mr T., both as adult and as teacher. Alternatively, the school board could have defied the tale-tellers in the community and stated that in their view Mr T. was doing nothing wrong. That would also be a clear message that the school board was acting responsibly. The values that the board would have been declaring, however, would then have been different from those they did, in fact, declare.

(d) The fact that Mr T. was married was referred to more than once and was expressly included as part of the grounds in the letters suspending and dismissing him. Would the affair and the gossip have been different if he had been a bachelor? Without further evidence, we cannot say. We can imagine, however, the scandalous overtones his being married must have given to the gossips. 'Oh dear, not only is the teacher going out with a student, but he's also committing adultery!' Or, 'Have you heard the news? A teacher is committing adultery, and with a student, too!' The fact that Miss F., according to her parents' letter, was being accused of 'immorality' suggests that accusations of adultery were being passed on by gossip. In effect, the school board, by dismissing Mr T., and the board of reference, by upholding the school board, were saying, 'Thou shalt not commit adultery.'[11]

The school board had the power to dismiss Mr T. for misconduct, for neglect of duty, or for refusal to obey a lawful order of the board. Considering that what he had done was wrong and that he was not going to change, they dismissed him for misconduct. This action upheld their own

sense of what was right and also upheld the reputation of the school
board in the community as a responsible defender of certain moral
values.

The school board's decision had to then be defended before the
board of reference. The dismissal was for 'misconduct,' the term in the
statute which captures the element of moral judgment. ('Refusal to
obey a lawful order of the board' does not have the same moral connota-
tion.) 'Misconduct,' however, is not defined in the statute. The board of
reference, therefore, was faced with the *legal* problem of construing the
intent of the statute in order to decide what the statute meant by 'misconduct'; or of taking the meaning of the term 'misconduct' either from
prior legal meanings of the word or from the meanings in common
speech. The minority decision considered the intent of the Public
School Act and held that 'misconduct' governed the carrying-out by the
teacher of those duties which were assigned by the Act and its regulations. The Act, so wrote the minority, does not govern the social lives of
teachers. Since Mr T.'s teaching had not been affected, there had been
no misconduct.

The majority followed, but less explicitly, the second line of argument.
They noted the idea of 'misconduct' proposed by counsel for the school
board, including the comment that 'it is misconduct if a teacher's conduct was likely to bring his employer into disrepute ...' This, as we have
noted, is a standard conception of misconduct in the law of employee discipline. The majority put Mr T.'s behaviour into this category and found
it to be misconduct. They came to the logical conclusion that if an
employee's outside behaviour could bring the employer's reputation
down, the employer was lawfully entitled to order the employee to desist.
The school board was quite properly concerned with what parents might
think and so quite properly asked Mr T. to terminate the relationship. Mr
T. refused, thereby not only continuing his misconduct but also refusing
to obey a lawful order of his employer. The school board was therefore
legally entitled to dismiss him.

Here we discover a narrower construction of 'misconduct' by the
minority and a broader construction by the majority. In both instances,
however, the legal judgment abbreviated the complexities of the actual
situation. The conflict of moralities implicit in the affair is not addressed,
and the issue is reduced, in essence, to whether or not an employer has
the right to dismiss an employee whose behaviour in some way threatens
the reputation or public image of the employer. The majority clearly considered that the employee's behaviour did threaten the employer's repu-

tation in the community. The minority also, one could infer, thought the same even though the minority did not construe Mr T.'s acts as misconduct.

Since maintaining the good reputation of the school board is thus construed to be a necessary element in the work of the school board, *any* controversy over an employee of the school board can threaten the reputation of the school board. Hence, any widespread rumours in the community about a teacher (provided that they be reasonably grounded in fact) can provide the school board with an issue of misconduct. The community, therefore, is able to use the threat of dismissal by the school board as a means to hold teachers to whatever standards of behaviour the influential or vociferous section of the community believes teachers should follow.

In this affair, was Mr T. wrong? Imprudent, surely, but, arguably, not necessarily morally wrong. Mr T.'s marriage (if we accept his statements) was already breaking up, and Miss F. was not the cause of the breakdown (although her existence may have accelerated it). He behaved, as her parents testified, 'like a gentleman.' He did not commit adultery in the strict sense, although he came close to the line. He declared himself to be in love with Miss F. and intended after his divorce to marry her (as he in fact did). Miss F. was not a student in his school during the affair, and he was in no position of authority over her. Given these facts, he could only insist on maintaining the relationship in the face of the school board's disapproval. To have broken off the relationship would have been to *make* the relationship immoral, to besmirch Miss F.'s reputation (by retroactively approving the gossips) and to betray their feelings. He had to risk dismissal, if he had the courage of his declared convictions.

On the other hand, was the school board wrong? Judging from the transcript of the meeting between the school board and Mr T., the school board was concerned that something was wrong but unable to state clearly just what was wrong and why it was wrong. The school board was acting from a sense of responsibility to the community, the schools, and the education system. They tried to demonstrate that the board was worthy of its trust in representing the community within the education system that had so much responsibility for the well-being of the children of the community. The fact remains, however, that in firing Mr T., the school board took the politically expedient way out. They bowed to public opinion (of part of the community) and rid themselves of an irritant in their midst.

There are two principles which can be discerned in their decision. The first principle is that teachers, being entrusted with the care of children and having a position of authority over children, must not do anything or appear to do anything which might compromise that responsibility or exploit the dependent position of the children. The second principle is that teachers, again because of their position, must be moral exemplars off the job as well as on the job and so must at least uphold the moral values of the community in which they teach. On the basis of these two principles, Mr T. was in a distinctly ambiguous position. 'Putting a fence about the law,' the school board, in effect, decided that such ambiguities should be avoided and to be, as it were, on the safe side, they dismissed Mr T.

This case is a good example of the school board responding to the expression of moral values in the community (by some segment of the community) and punishing the teacher for not complying with such moral values. The case also shows how response to community values is entangled with notions about the responsibilities of the teacher towards children, the schools, and the school board. The case demonstrates how, as the dispute moves from the school board to the board of reference, it becomes abstracted from its context in the community and 'molded' to fit the thought-forms of the legal tradition.

Case 26: The Teacher Who Developed a Relationship

This case from British Columbia forms a neat complement to case 25. The setting is urban rather than rural, and the case is ten years after case 25.

His marriage having fallen apart, Mr L. developed a relationship with N. O., who *had been* a student at the school at which he taught. This was in 1982. Her parents learned of this and wanted N.O. to finish grade 12 without undue influence from Mr L. Mr L. agreed and took a year's leave of absence outside the province. During that year, he corresponded with N.O. but did not see her. N.O. became eighteen in April 1983 and graduated in June. In June, Mr L. returned to the school district and in July, N.O. moved into his house. Mrs O., the young woman's mother, and B.O., N.O.'s brother, subsequently alleged to the school board that Mr L. had had a sexual involvement with N.O. and had smoked marijuana with other students in 1981, including B.O.

On 7 September 1983 the school board suspended Mr L. for misconduct. On 12 September, the school board heard Mr L. He denied most of the allegations but admitted seeing N.O. secretly in 1982 and smoking marijuana with her brother. Subsequently, the school board dismissed Mr L. for misconduct and he appealed.

The board of reference (decision rendered 31 May 1984) rejected the evidence given by B.O. but agreed that misconduct had occurred. The board wrote, '... a petting and caressing relationship by a teacher with a student in the school system as admitted amounts to misconduct and the smoking of marijuana with students in the school system amounts to serious misconduct.' Dismissal, however, was too harsh a penalty. The board of reference substituted suspension until 1 January 1985. The board also held that the teacher's capability was relevant to assessing the adequacy of the penalty, though not to whether or not the teacher was guilty of misconduct.

Cases 24 and 26 both occurred in the same school district and involved the same school board. Note in case 26 that the board of reference referred not to 'the school' or 'the school district' but to 'the school system.' This is broad and vague: does 'school system' mean the schools of the school district only or does it mean all the schools of the province? We imagine that the board of reference meant only the school district since that was the system over which the school board had jurisdiction, but, nonetheless, the board of reference did use the wider, vaguer term.

Sexual Exhibition or Lewdness (Alleged)

Sexual exhibition or lewdness is an issue for teachers simply because school boards and the communities which they presumably represent have certain ideals about proper sexual behaviour in public. Some of these ideals may be recognized in the Criminal Code under such headings as 'gross indecency' and 'indecent exposure.' When teachers are expected to be moral examplars and the morals in question define certain sexual behaviours as indecent, obscene, or lewd, the possibility emerges that teachers off the job may misconduct themselves, wittingly or unwittingly.

Case 27: The Teachers Who Published in Gallery[12]

This British Columbian case received national TV and newspaper publicity when it occurred and thereafter, as it wound its way to the B.C. Court of Appeal, and has been cited more than once in discussions examining the duties and rights of public school teachers in their lives outside school and classroom.[13] Indeed, the offending picture itself appeared on

CBC TV as part of the news report concerning the decision of the Court of Appeal (in 1987). There seems no point, therefore, in our trying to maintain the anonymity of the teachers involved.

Brief Outline of Events

Some time in mid-1984 John Shewan, with his wife's agreement, submitted three photographs showing her in a semi-nude pose, along with an entry form and essay, to *Gallery* magazine. He was responding to the magazine's 'Girl Next Door Amateur Erotic Photo Contest.' His purpose was personal – to encourage his wife's self-image by having her picture appear in a national magazine. Subsequently, in the February 1985 issue of *Gallery* (which appeared on the stands in January), a picture of Mrs Shewan appeared identified as 'Ilze S, 34, teacher, Clearbrook, B.C., Canada. Photography by her husband, John.' On about 23 January, a radio reporter who had heard of or seen the photograph telephoned the superintendent of schools for Abbotsford School District and enquired about the photograph. The superintendent duly investigated and held the requisite hearings. On 4 and 5 February respectively, Ilze and John Shewan were formally suspended without pay for six weeks. From 29 January to 7 February, the Shewans' behaviour and the school board's response were reported and commented on by several newspapers in the Lower Fraser Valley and Greater Vancouver areas. Some persons supported the school board. Others declared that the school board was making a great fuss about nothing.

The Shewans appealed their suspensions to a board of reference. Two out of three members of the board of reference decided that the behaviour of the Shewans fell within accepted standards of tolerance in Canadian society and did not constitute misconduct. They ordered that the school board's decision be set aside and that the Shewans should receive their full back pay. The third member of the board of reference held that the Shewans' behaviour was misconduct, but reduced the suspension from six weeks to ten days. The school board appealed to the B.C. Supreme Court. The judge held for the school board that the Shewans were guilty of misconduct, as defined in law, but set the suspension at one month. The Shewans next appealed to the B.C. Court of Appeal. This court dismissed their appeal and held that the behaviour in question constituted misconduct. The Court of Appeal upheld the one-month suspension.

In this outline, we can trace the following phases of the dispute:
(a) The offending behaviour is committed: the picture appears in *Gallery*.

(b) Some persons discover it. (c) News of the offending behaviour is communicated to the superintendent of the school district, who investigates. (d) The superintendent communicates his findings to the school board. (e) The school board comes to a decision to suspend the teachers. (f) The school board formally communicates its decision to the teachers as required by the School Act and holds the formal hearing which is required. Had the school board not held this formal hearing at which the teachers had an opportunity to defend themselves, its decision to suspend would have been overturned by the board of reference on the grounds that the school board had failed to follow principles of natural justice and fairness. (g) After the hearing, the school board suspends the teachers for six weeks. By suspending them for more than ten days, however, the school board enabled the teachers to take advantage of the relevant provisions in the School Act and apply for a board of reference. (h) The parties to the dispute prepare for the board of reference. (i) The hearing is conducted before the board of reference. (j) The board of reference communicates its decision to the school board and the teachers, and its decision is duly communicated by the school board and the teachers to the public. In British Columbia at this time, board of reference decisions were considered private arbitration judgments and were not made public unless one of the parties to the dispute chose to make them so. In this case, publication by one or both the parties was inevitable. (k) The school board appeals to the B.C. Supreme Court on the legal ground that the board of reference has applied the wrong law. (l) The Supreme Court judge finds for the school board. (m) The Shewans appeal to the B.C. Court of Appeal. (n) The Court of Appeal dismisses their appeal and upholds the decision of the Supreme Court. (o) The Shewans decide that there is no point to pursuing the matter any further. The court cases are open to the public and are duly reported in the news. Thus the whole process, from the discovery of the picture in *Gallery* magazine to the final Court of Appeal decision, has been conducted in the 'goldfish bowl' of public scrutiny.

The Community
The suspension was justified by the superintendent and the school board on the grounds that teachers are expected to be role models for their students and that this role includes upholding the values of the community outside the classroom as well as in it. In appearing all but nude in *Gallery* magazine, Mrs Shewan had offended community standards and certainly not provided a proper role model for her students. In sending the photo-

graph to *Gallery* magazine, Mr Shewan had caused the whole affair and was as responsible for it, if not more so, than his wife. The School Board was not only themselves offended by this, but they knew that some persons in the Abbotsford and Matsqui School District would also be offended. The school board therefore had to act and show their displeasure at the Shewans' behaviour in some decisive manner. They chose, as noted above, six weeks suspension without pay.

But what was the community, and what sort of standards were expected? Why would appearing nude in *Gallery* upset people in School District 34?

School District 34 consisted of the two municipalities of Matsqui and Abbotsford in the central part of the Lower Fraser Valley. The areas of each of the municipalities are approximately the same, but populations differ. As of 1990, Matsqui's population was approximately 62,000, while Abbotsford's was approximately 18,000 persons. Matsqui as the more western municipality is nearer Vancouver. The two municipalities form a single economic unit. The main economic activities are dairy farming, egg and poultry farming, berry farming, and vegetable farming. There is some light industry. Matsqui, especially, is also becoming a dormitory suburb for Vancouver. Fraser Valley College has campuses in Abbotsford as well as in the municipality of Chilliwack on the eastern side of Abbotsford. So far, Matsqui and Abbotsford are like many Canadian communities.[14]

The peculiarity of Abbotsford and Matsqui, however, is that (along with the municipality of Chilliwack) they contain a great many churches belonging to strict Protestant denominations whose members take their religion seriously. There are three bible colleges and several private schools founded on religious principles. Voting patterns show a certain conservative temper and a desire to emphasize family values, including values founded on Scripture. Abbotsford, Matsqui, and Chilliwack together are sometimes called British Columbia's 'bible belt' Protestant ministers have sometimes been elected to the B.C. legislature by the electors of this area. With such a cultural background, a great many people in these municipalities might reasonably be expected to object to schoolteachers appearing nude in magazines which are sold on newsstands where their children can get them.

The Suspension
The school board's decision to suspend the Shewans was taken pursuant to section 122(1)(a) of the then B.C. School Act, R.S.B.C. 1979, c. 375,

which allowed school boards to suspend teachers for misconduct, neglect of duty, or refusal to obey a lawful order of the school board. This suspension could take effect immediately or not, as the school board decided. However, the board was required to immediately notify the teacher of the suspension formally in writing, and the teacher then had to be given the chance within one week of the date of this formal notice to present his or her defence in a formal hearing by the school board. After this formal hearing (and not until, unless the teacher let the matter go by default), the school board could decide to extend the suspension beyond ten days or to dismiss the teacher. But if the board chose to extend the suspension or to dismiss the teacher, the teacher had the right to apply to the minister of education for a board of reference.

The district superintendent heard the Shewans before making his report to the school board. He did not agree with Mr Shewan's argument that what Mr and Mrs Shewan had done did not violate community standards, and he recommended to the school board that a period of suspension without pay was in order. This meeting between the superintendent and the Shewans took place on 24 January.

Shortly after this meeting, and before 30 January, the superintendent gave a television interview in which he said that he was shocked and sickened by the whole episode.

The school board heard Mrs Shewan on 30 January. Mrs Shewan agreed that appearing in *Gallery* was indiscreet but said she did not think it was against community standards. The board confirmed its suspension of Mrs Shewan and decided also to suspend Mr Shewan. The grounds for the suspensions was 'misconduct' The board duly held a formal hearing for Mr Shewan on 2 February, and subsequently suspended him without pay for six weeks. Mr Shewan agreed that there had been an indiscretion, but he said that he thought *Gallery* magazine met community standards. The six weeks' suspension without pay meant that the Shewans would lose in pay approximately $7,000 together.

The Teachers
Both teachers had taught in School District 34 for about ten years (John Shewan since 1972 and Ilze Shewan since 1976). John Shewan taught at Abbotsford Junior Secondary School and Ilze Shewan at Clearbrook Junior Secondary School. Both were regarded as good teachers and both were active in community affairs. Neither therefore could be considered to be ignorant concerning the values held by people in Abbotsford and Matsqui.

The Offending Picture

The picture in *Gallery* magazine showed Mrs Shewan lying on her back, head towards the viewer, with her knees drawn up. She was wearing only a suspender belt, stockings, and high heeled shoes. The pose in fact was similar to those that used to appear in 'pin-up' calendars of an old-fashioned sort, and was only modestly revealing compared with other pictures in *Gallery*. Unfortunately it bore the following caption: 'Ilze S., 34, teacher, Clearbrook, B.C., Canada. Photography by her husband, John.' There was no doubt.

The school board suspended the Shewans. The Shewans applied for a board of reference. The minister of education set up the board of reference. The board of reference met in Vancouver from 9 April to 18 June 1985.

The Board of Reference

The issue before the board of reference was whether the Shewans' behaviour constituted misconduct, as the school board asserted, or whether it was merely, as one member of the board of reference would say, 'an appalling lack of judgement'?

Expert witnesses were called by both sides to testify before the board. Among those called by the Abbotsford School Board was Dr Dante Lupini, superintendent of schools in Vancouver. His opinion was that the Shewans' behaviour was 'misconduct, namely conduct unbecoming a professional teacher.' He stated that a teacher is regarded by both students and parents as a role model, and should be entitled to respect from them. The appearance of the picture of Mrs Shewan in *Gallery* reduced the professional relationship to an unacceptably 'familiar or personal level.' It would create a loss of respect for her as a teacher. The Shewans, he opined, ought to have known this. Furthermore, publication of Mrs Shewan's picture 'could create unnecessary debate and unnecessary criticism' in the school district, and the Shewans ought to have known this as well. The two other expert witnesses for the school board gave similar opinions.

Among the expert witnesses called on behalf of the Shewans was Dr Michael Manley-Casimir, a professor in the Faculty of Education at Simon Fraser University. His opinion was that the Shewans' behaviour was a foolish indiscretion; however, it did not amount to misconduct. He stated:

[F]or example, a teacher who engages in an affair with a student in his/her charge, to my mind, clearly commits misconduct. This is so because the effect of the affair is to breach the fiduciary relationship, to subvert the integrity of the professional relationship between teacher and student, and may substantially and materially impair the teacher's ability to perform his or her professional duties or responsibilities in the classroom.[15]

In his view, the Shewans' actions in causing the publication and distribution of Mrs Shewan's picture in *Gallery* had not demonstrably adversely affected the relationship between themselves as teachers and their students.

After hearing the school board, the Shewans, various persons from Abbotsford and Matsqui, and the various expert witnesses, the board of reference held in a two-to-one decision that misconduct had not occurred. Hence the suspension by the school board was invalid, and the Shewans should be reinstated with pay.

The chairman of the board of reference, Marvin Storrow, Q.C., who wrote the board's minority decision, held that the Shewans had committed misconduct. He considered that the Shewans ought to have been aware that Ilze's photograph, if accepted by *Gallery*, would come to the attention of their employers and the general public and would cause controversy. He went on to say:

A person who is known in a community in whole or in part because of his occupation must be wary of his activities outside his occupation. One becomes identified with his or her occupational calling and must be very cautious about extracurricular activities for fear of bringing disrespect or dishonour upon the occupation that he or she represents. This is even more important when one is considering those professions which depend upon the confidence that others have for it or the impression that others have of it in order for it to achieve its legitimate ends. The medical profession, the legal profession, and the teaching profession are all examples of this.[16]

He had difficulties with the argument that if the actions of the teachers outside their office of teacher did not affect their relationship with their pupils, then those actions did not amount to 'misconduct.' If this criterion were applied, there would have to be a period of observation of the particular teacher for some time after the supposed misconduct in order to find out whether or not it had adversely affected the teacher's relationship with his or her pupils.

He examined the definition of 'misconduct' in legal dictionaries and

in Batt's *Law of Master and Servant*. He quoted Batt's as follows: 'Misconduct comprises a positive act and not mere neglect or failures. *It is conduct
inconsistent with the due and faithful discharge of the duties of service.*'[17]

He went on to argue that the Shewans' behaviour in submitting the
photograph knowing that it might be published and distributed to the
public, including the Abbotsford public, was 'misconduct' because a size-
able portion of the community regarded such a public display as intolerable, and this portion would therefore lose confidence in the integrity of
the Shewans as teachers, in particular, and of teachers and the school system, in general. He went on to say:

A school teacher, particularly one teaching pre-university students, works in a very
sensitive area while working in a classroom. Whilst there he or she shapes attitudes of young people towards the community in which they live. In this the community has a vital concern and a role to play. The community, through its school
boards, must preserve the integrity of its schools. It cannot be doubted that school
authorities have the right and the duty to screen and discipline teachers and
other employees as to their fitness to maintain the integrity of the school system
as part of a properly ordered society.[18]

This requires that teachers must behave in a manner which justifies and
upholds the 'high esteem' and trust which they are given.

On the other hand, Gordon Eddy and Phillip Rankin, the other two
members of the board of reference, considered that the Shewans' behaviour was not misconduct. In their view, the context of the word 'misconduct' in section 122 of the School Act showed that in that statute
misconduct is 'related to the employer/employee relationship.' They
cited Brown and Beatty's *Canadian Labour Arbitration*,[19] to the effect that
'unless a substantial and legitimate business reason exists, the employer
has no authority, control, interest or jurisdiction over an employee's
behaviour outside the hours of his employment.' They all agreed, however, that 'off the job conduct may be misconduct in the right circumstances.' Had the photograph shown the Shewans in lewd acts, that might
well have been misconduct.

But, in the end, the majority of the board simply held that the behaviour of the Shewans could not properly be considered misconduct:

We are not convinced that an employer can demand more of a teacher than they
exhibit enough decorum and formality to do their job. Teachers are not on duty 24

hours a day. Surely their main function is to teach, not to be emulated. When teachers are off the job, they ought to be allowed far greater latitude in their lifestyle.[20]

They agreed that some persons in Abbotsford had clearly been offended by the picture in *Gallery* magazine. But this, they thought, was not the proper standard. The standard to be applied was not whether 'the Shewans' conduct fell below some of the community's standards but whether it was within the accepted standards of tolerance in contemporary Canadian society.' In their judgment, the Shewans' behaviour was within these accepted standards. They said, 'British Columbia teachers do not have to have different standards of behaviour depending on what community they teach in.'

Decision of the B.C. Supreme Court
The dispute appeared before Mr Justice Bouck of the B.C. Supreme Court on 19 December 1985. On 30 January 1986 the judge handed down his decision. He found that the board of reference had erred in law in making its determination, that the Shewans' behaviour was misconduct, and that a penalty of one month's suspension without pay was appropriate. In the words of the judge's summary:

(1) The Board of Reference fell into error when:
   (a) It applied the obscenity test of the standard of tolerance of contemporary Canadian society when it should have applied the test of the moral standard of the community, namely, the community in the Abbotsford area;
   (b) It admitted expert opinion on misconduct and allowed itself to be improperly influenced by the experts called on behalf of the respondents. The proper way to test whether the conduct complained of amounted to misconduct was to hear objective evidence about the activities of other teachers in the community and to compare similar situations where teachers or other public sector employees were disciplined for wrongful behaviour;
   (c) It decided the word 'misconduct' as set out in s. 122 of the School Act has little application to behaviour of teachers outside of their normal school duties.
(2) Teachers are among the leaders in the community. They are supposed to set an example for their students to follow. This includes their behaviour both on and off the job.
(3) A fair inference to be drawn from the testimony heard by the Board of Reference is to the effect that other teachers in the Abbotsford area do not send

their nude or semi-nude pictures to men's magazines for publication. Consequently, the conduct of the respondents was abnormal.

(4) A teacher owes a duty of good behaviour to the school board as his or her employer, to the local community and to the teaching profession. Looking at the facts of these cases and the abnormal behaviour of the respondents as described by the evidence, one can only conclude that in this instance their behaviour amounted to misconduct.

(5) The penalty of six weeks' suspension was excessive given the past favourable history of the respondents and looking at cases where penalties have been imposed upon teachers for improper conduct. A more reasonable penalty in keeping with these awards is one month's suspension.[21]

Mr Justice Bouck began by reviewing the history of the dispute. He gave a capsule summary of the testimony given before the board of reference. Then he defined the issues before the court: (1) What was the character of the appeal jurisdiction which section 129 of the School Act gave the Supreme Court? (2) Assuming the Supreme Court had the jurisdiction of the Court of Appeal (and Mr Justice Bouck duly decided that it did), did the board of reference err in law or in fact when the majority thereof found that there had been no misconduct? (3) If misconduct had occurred, what penalty was appropriate?

Misconduct was not defined in the School Act. The judge cited definitions from the *Canadian Law Dictionary*, the *Shorter Oxford English Dictionary*, and *Black's Law Dictionary*, 5th ed. (1979):[22]

From the *Canadian Law Dictionary*:

Any transgression of some established and definite rule of action, a dereliction from duty, unlawful behaviour, willful in character, *improper or wrong behaviour*. [Bouck J.'s emphasis]

In the law of master and servant there is no fixed rule of law defining the degree of misconduct which will justify dismissal. The particular act justifying dismissal must depend upon the character of the act itself, upon the duties of the workmen and upon the possible consequences of the act. The conduct complained of must be inconsistent with the fulfillment of the express or implied conditions of service.[23]

From the *Shorter Oxford English Dictionary*:

1. Bad management; mismanagement. Often quasi- *spec.*, malfeasance.
2. Improper conduct. Often *spec.* in the sense of adultery.

From *Black's Law Dictionary*:

A transgression of some established and definite rule of action, a forbidden act, a dereliction from duty, unlawful behavior, willful in character, improper or wrong behavior; its synonyms are misdemeanor, misbehavior, delinquency, impropriety, mismanagement, offence, but not negligence or carelessness.[24]

The board of reference had erred, the judge said, in applying the test for obscenity, which was whether or not the offending behaviour was within the standards of what contemporary Canadian society would tolerate. The proper test was

... the 'moral standards of the community' where the respondents taught and lived and not the Canadian standards of tolerance test applied to obscenity cases. I say this partly because the moral conduct of a teacher amounting to misconduct may have nothing to do with obscenity as defined under the Criminal Code. Lying by a teacher is an example. A lie amounts to a breach of morality and may be misconduct but it is not obscene. Hence, using the 'tolerance' test which was designed for obscenity cases is a poor way of testing 'moral conduct.'[25]

The judge then considered whether the board of reference had heard evidence which could support the conclusion that the behaviour of the teachers had not offended the moral standards of the community and was therefore not misconduct. He considered the opinion evidence heard by the board. He cited authority to show that legal opinion concerning what is or is not misconduct is irrelevant. It is irrelevant because the decision that behaviour is or is not misconduct is a matter of law to be decided by the court. Then he considered the expert evidence. He concluded that case authority showed that expert opinion concerning a teacher's misconduct has little probative value and is largely irrelevant when the facts concerning the disputed conduct are before the court. The test for misconduct depended on objective testimony concerning the moral standards of the community.

The test requires that the judge apply not his own personal scale of values, but rather the community standard. How, then, may this community standard be assessed?

One test was whether or not the behaviour of the teachers was abnormal:

In this instance, the Board of Reference had the right to hear evidence about what a teacher does from day to day and his or her position in the community at large. In this way it could assess the conduct of the average teacher. Then it could examine the alleged act of misconduct. From this evidence it was in a position to decide if there was misconduct because it could compare the conduct of the average teacher as shown by the evidence with the evidence presented to show an act of misconduct on the part of the teacher who was charged. It might not be misconduct for a person in some other trade or calling but the same act committed by a teacher might indeed amount to misconduct. All of that was for the Board of Reference to decide and not for a witness. While it was an issue of fact as to whether there was misconduct, the question the board had to answer in the end was whether those facts amounted to misconduct in law.

Did the respondents meet the moral standard of the community by the publication of the nude picture in Gallery Magazine and, if not, did that have any effect on their ability to teach. One way of determining the point is to look at the conduct of other teachers. If a good number of teachers in or about Abbotsford are publishing their nude photographs in a magazine such as the one in question, then the conduct of the respondents may be within community standards. If no other teachers are doing this, then it may be misconduct. Evidence of this nature was not heard by the Board of Reference but I believe I am entitled to draw an inference from the proven facts as to whether a substantial number of teachers in the Abbotsford area do indeed publish their nude pictures in men's magazines. It seems clear they do not.[26]

Having said this, the judge shifted ground and brought in another test. Referring to the test of abnormality, he said:

This is not a conclusive test because the key ingredient is whether the act of misconduct affects the teacher in his or her educational capacity. If it does not, then it is not an offence under the School Act.[27]

He then reviewed a number of cases involving persons in positions of public responsibility whose behaviours off the job could affect the ways in which the public regarded these persons' employers. The jobs were those of a fireman, a nurse, a bus driver, an airline company employee, and four teachers. The cases all emphasized the duty of the employee to maintain the reputation of the employer and public trust in the institution. He concluded:

What do these decisions tell us? They say a teacher is an important member of the community who leads by example. He or she not only owes a duty of good behaviour to the school board as the employer but also to the local community at large and to the teaching profession. An appropriate standard of moral conduct or behaviour must be maintained both inside and outside the classroom. The nature of that standard will, of course, vary from case to case. Moral standards are those of the community where the teacher is employed and lives not those of some other city or municipality. In most instances there will be little difference, but what may be acceptable in an urban setting may occasionally be misconduct in a rural community and vice versa. For example, a small religious community might find it unacceptable for a female teacher to live with a man out of wedlock or a male teacher to live with a woman who is not his wife. On the other hand, these kinds of relationships may be tolerated in an urban setting where the two people are lost in the anonymity of the crowd because they live far away from the school or because the values of the city are different from the values of the country.

Initially, I should not find whether there is misconduct in these kinds of situations simply by looking at the act complained of and then expressing my personal opinion whether it offends the School Act. Instead, I must see what other objective non-opinion evidence exists to help categorize the nature of the conduct. But at the end of the day, I am required to state my opinion. The difference is that my opinion is based upon outside evidence and not just a personal reaction to the allegations of misconduct.

There was an act of misconduct in this case since the incident amounts to abnormal behaviour which reflects unfavourably on the respondents. They are supposed to be examples to the students. Their actions lower the esteem in which they were held by the community including the students, because they set a standard that the community found unsuitable. All of this amounts to misconduct. The appeal is therefore allowed and I now turn to the issue of penalty.[28]

Mr Justice Bouck then reviewed a number of board of reference cases, expressed a certain sympathy for the dilemma of the school board in assessing suitable penalties, remarked that penalties should be consistent from case to case, noted that the ordinary behaviour of the teachers was good and that putting the photograph in *Gallery* was an abnormal incident, and assessed the proper penalty as being one month's suspension without pay. 'This will mean,' he said, 'a total past loss of income after taxes between both of them, of about $4,600.'[29]

Decision of the B.C. Court of Appeal
The Shewans appealed the decision of Mr Justice Bouck. Their case was heard before the B.C. Court of Appeal on 9 December 1987; the court brought down its ruling on 21 December 1987.

The principal issue in the appeal, as the court viewed it, was 'what meaning to give to the word "misconduct" as used in s. 122(1) of the School Act, and what standard to apply in determining whether certain conduct constitutes misconduct within the meaning of the statute.'

Misconduct, which is 'bad,' 'wrong,' or 'improper' conduct, may include off-the-job conduct as well as conduct in the classroom. This is because

a teacher holds a position of trust, confidence and responsibility. If he or she acts in an improper way, on or off the job, there may be a loss of public confidence in the teacher and in the public school system, a loss of respect by students for the teacher involved, and other teachers generally, and there may be controversy within the school and within the community which disrupts the proper carrying on of the educational system.[30]

Therefore the minimum standard of morality that will be tolerated in a given community is not necessarily the minimum standard for a teacher:

Teachers must maintain the confidence and respect of their superiors, their peers, and in particular, the students, and those who send their children to our public schools. Teachers must not only be competent, but they are expected to lead by example. Any loss of confidence or respect will impair the system, and have an adverse effect upon those who participate in or rely upon it. That is why a teacher must maintain a standard of behaviour which most other citizens need not observe because they do not have such public responsibilities to fulfill.[31]

Did the action of the Shewans amount to misconduct? The photograph had appeared in a magazine which was designed to exploit sex

... and to be devoted to the display of the private parts of a female form. Clearly, it is not a magazine which one would make available to an adolescent. These two teachers testified that they would not recommend it to their students, who are at an impressionable age, and yet they endorsed it by permitting Mrs Shewan's photograph to be published in it. In doing so, they undermined any influence they might otherwise have possessed to discourage students from reading such material.

In fairness to Mrs Shewan, the pose which she assumed was modest in comparison with the others whose photographs appeared in the magazine. But it is to be inferred that she knew it was wrong to display herself in that way in that company, and that such conduct was well below the standard expected of teachers. That is borne out by the fact that when she saw the magazine she was 'alarmed' and 'concerned' that if the school board members saw it, her job would be in jeopardy. When the matter was publicized there was controversy in the school and in the community, with attendant disruption of the educational system.

Mr and Mrs Shewan conducted themselves in a manner contrary to a standard acceptable to teachers.[32]

The Court of Appeal next picked up a matter which Marvin Storrow had mentioned in his minority report but which Mr Justice Bouck had not mentioned in his decision:

The teaching profession has adopted a policy with respect to magazines which portray its subjects as sexual objects. The British Columbia Teachers' Federation condemns the public display of all pornographic material and defines pornography as exploiting those it portrays by depicting them as sexual objects. This publication would come within the concerns of the B.C. Teachers' Federation.[33]

On these several grounds, the court concluded:

We are of the opinion that the publication of such a photograph of a teacher in such a magazine was bound to have an adverse effect upon the educational system to which these two teachers owed a duty to act responsibly.[34]

The circumstances therefore justified a finding of misconduct.

The court upheld the penalty assigned by Mr Justice Bouck.

Comment
The case arose because the Shewans did something which, when brought to the attention of the superintendent and the school board, was found by those authorities to be reprehensible and inconsistent with their expectations concerning how public school teachers ought to behave. These expectations were shared by some other residents of the Abbotsford and Matsqui districts, though not by all. This sharing was revealed by a measure of public comment both in and outside the news media, and by some of the testimony before the board of reference. The school board decided to suspend the teachers without pay for six weeks. Since their power to do this, however, was given them by the School Act, they had to find some justification to defend their decision. The only rubric available was 'misconduct.' Thus the school board suspended the teachers for misconduct, and the teachers appealed, as they were entitled, to a

board of reference. The original sense of outrage which the superintendent and school board had was thereby drawn within the categories of
law.

Misconduct, therefore, but misconduct in what sense? The board of
reference was divided on the issue, and their decision was duly appealed
to the B.C. Supreme Court. The cases cited by Mr Justice Bouck indicate
that underlying his decision was the principle that an employee must not
damage the reputation of his or her employer. Hence the employee's
behaviour outside the workplace may constitute misconduct warranting
discipline by suspension or even dismissal without notice. Teachers are
expected to be role models for the children of the parents who send their
children to the school. A failure to meet this standard or to uphold the
moral standards of the community damages the reputation of the school
system in the community. This argument comes out clearly in Mr Justice
Bouck's decision and was enunciated again in the Court of Appeal decision which followed.

Granting that teachers must uphold community standards, how are
these standards to be determined? The majority of the board of reference
noted, 'Although evidence was lead [sic] on the community standards in
Abbotsford, neither party established to our satisfaction what those community standards were.' Mr Justice Bouck's suggested test is not really
very satisfactory. Determining whether a teacher's behaviour departs
from the behaviour usual among other teachers in the community is at
best a very oblique way of assessing the community's standards. In the
end, though the judge said that imposing his personal values was not
the right thing to do, he imposed his own personal assessment that the
Shewans' behaviour (evident in the photograph in *Gallery* magazine)
would tend to cast the educational system into disrepute. So the question
concerning how community standards are to be assessed remained unanswered.

The case does not distinguish between employee misconduct and professional misconduct. It applies the principles of master-and-servant law
concerning employee misconduct. However, the teachers' behaviour was
typified, especially by the expert witnesses for the school board at the
board of reference, as 'unprofessional.' Perhaps it was unnecessary in this
case to have distinguished the two sorts of misconduct. But once we make
the distinction, questions emerge.

While a school board, as an employer, is presumably competent to
decide whether or not an employee's 'off-the-job' conduct imperils the
reputation of the school in the community, is a school board really com-

petent to judge whether or not a teacher's conduct is unprofessional? Surely the judgment concerning unprofessional conduct is properly left to the professional association which has been given the jurisdiction to make such judgments.

Mr Justice Bouck remarked that a teacher has a duty to the school board which employs the teacher, to the local community, and to the teaching profession. There are three sets of obligations implied in this statement, namely, to the school, to the profession, *and to the community*. Might it be that the duties to the community, though involved in practice with the other two sets of duties, are nevertheless separately anchored in the status of the public school teacher as an agent of the community or of the state (in this case, the provincial government), which is in theory at least an agent of the larger society? A teacher, the cases say, is expected to be a role model, portraying the values of the community for the benefit of the students. It is a perilous obligation.

Case 28: The Teacher Who Appeared Nude

This is a case similar to case 27. It occurred in Quebec and has been reported as a board of arbitration case.[35]

The teacher, a man with an untarnished teaching record of eleven years, posed nude with his live-in girlfriend, who had been voted Miss Quebec Nude in a nudist camp. The photograph of the couple appeared in a newspaper with a circulation of twelve to eighteen thousand copies. This occurred during the summer holidays. The girlfriend had been a student at the school at which the teacher had taught one year before the photograph was taken.

Upon learning of this event, the school board suspended the teacher for one and a half months. (Note that this was the same penalty imposed by the Abbotsford School Board upon the Shewans.) The school board charged the teacher with negligence in the performance of his duties and professional obligations, incapacity, misconduct, and immorality. Further, the board alleged that the teacher had contravened Catholic precepts by exhibiting himself in the nude and had so failed to respect the religious principles of the institution where he worked.

The teacher grieved this suspension to a board of arbitration. The board of arbitration found that the one-and-a-half-month suspension was 'draconian' and out of proportion with the teacher's misconduct. The board, however, also reproached the teacher for his indiscretion and noted that the case would have been much more serious had the incident received greater publicity and had parents expressed concern.[36] The board of arbitration also held that the employer had failed to satisfy the board that nudism violated the principles of Catholicism.

The school board subsequently applied to the Quebec Superior Court for a judicial review of the decision of the board of arbitration, on the grounds that the board of arbitration had acted beyond its jurisdiction and had substituted its own morality for that of the Catholic school board. The Superior Court agreed with the arbitrators; that the onus was on the employer to show that the action against the teacher was reasonable and to prove that the teacher's behaviour contravened Catholic principles. The Superior Court upheld the decision of the board of arbitration.

The school board then appealed to the Quebec Court of Appeal, which dismissed the appeal without significant comment.

Extramarital and Non-marital Heterosexual Relationships

These two headings may conveniently be considered together.

Under 'Extramarital Heterosexual Relationships,' we mean affairs between a teacher and someone of the opposite sex when one or both of the offending persons are married to someone else; in short, when adultery is at least formally involved. Such acts are regarded as offensive when there is an ideal that married persons should have sexual relationships only with their own spouses and when teachers are expected to uphold this ideal.

When a public school teacher is working for a denominational school board and the religious denomination's beliefs forbid divorce and remarriage, if the teacher has a civil divorce and remarries, he or she may be regarded as failing to uphold the moral values of the denomination and may therefore be dismissed. The following questions emerge: Is the teacher a member of the denomination or not? Does the teacher change denominations (or merely leave one) as a result of the civil divorce and remarriage, or in order to allow him or her to divorce and remarry? How do such memberships and changes of membership affect the contract of employment between teacher and school board?

In such cases, however, the issues are not so much presumed adultery but the implications of membership or non-membership in the denomination and the right of a denominational school board to impose the denomination's expectations on the teachers employed by the board. Case 29 below illustrates some of these concerns.

By 'Non-Marital Heterosexual Relationships,' we mean all sexual relations between persons of opposite sex in which *neither* person is married.
Such relations may be ephemeral or they may be long-lasting, as in a so-
called 'common-law marriage.' This becomes a matter of concern when
the school board, or the community that it presumably represents, holds
that sexual intercourse outside marriage is wrong and that teachers
should be moral exemplars. Otherwise, if the teacher's sexual partner
is not a student in the teacher's school, we should find no justification
for regarding non-marital heterosexual relations by themselves as
misconduct.

Case 29: The Teacher Who Pursued an Incompatible Lifestyle

This is an Alberta case in which the teacher's lifestyle was expressly given
as a reason for termination. The Charter rights of denominational
schools and of the teachers who work in them were also discussed.
    The issues before the board of reference were summarized by the
judge as follows: 'Were the reasons for the termination of contract fundamentally lawful, and had the respondent school board acted reasonably?'
    The school board, which was a Roman Catholic separate school board,
gave the following reasons for terminating the contract of employment of
the teacher, Ms F.:

1. By pursuing a lifestyle which has resulted in having become pregnant for a second time outside of a marriage relationship, you have failed to conduct yourself
in a manner consistent with the philosophy of this Roman Catholic School District, its policies and guidelines and the Canon law, and you have failed to be a
positive role model to students and others in the community in contravention of
Board philosophy and policy.
2. Failure to comply with directives of the Board ... in that you have once again
become pregnant out of wedlock.

    Behind this notice of termination were the following facts. Ms F. was an
unmarried teacher and remained unmarried throughout the time period
of this case. When Ms F. was first hired by the school board, she was
already pregnant and did not disclose this fact to her employer until she
had taught for approximately three weeks. The school board investigated
and, though concerned with the effect on the students vis-à-vis her role as
a Catholic schoolteacher, granted her maternity leave and kept her on
staff for compassionate reasons. She was warned that any further premar-

ital sexual intercourse would be unacceptable and would result in her dismissal. Her baby was born in December of the year in which she was hired.

Her teaching being satisfactory, Ms F. was offered and accepted a permanent appointment to start on the 30th of August of the year following the year in which she was first hired. In mid-August of that year, however, she was again pregnant and she told her principal. Ms F. asked for maternity leave and for an extended leave of absence without pay. The school board decided to terminate the contract.

Ms F. was aware that extramarital sexual intercourse was contrary to Roman Catholic doctrine.

Legal counsel for Ms F. argued that the action of the school board was 'discrimination against catholic teachers in general and the appellant in particular.' The judge of the board of reference, however, held that

specifically, denominational schools have the right to discriminate on religious grounds in the terms of employment of their teachers. (See Caldwell et al. v. Stuart et al., (1985) 15, 1 D.L.R. (4th), 1, S.C.C. where it was held that a Roman Catholic school was entitled to dismiss teachers who, contrary to catholic doctrine, married divorced spouses.)

The judge concluded that 'any alleged discrimination by the respondent was on the permissible basis of catholic doctrine ... the appellant was [not] treated differently than would be any other catholic teacher, male or female.'

Section 29 of the Charter of Rights also nullified any benefit that the appellant sought to get from the equality provisions of section 15. Section 29 must be interpreted here, the judge ruled, 'so as to unfetter a catholic school board's pre-Charter right to exercise control on the moral character of its teaching staff.' The judge went on to say,

It is trite to say that a school teacher serves as a role model to his or her students. It must also be trite that any school board, public or Roman Catholic, has the responsibility to exercise certain control over the moral conduct of its teachers, especially as it might have an effect on a school's teachers ... The evidence established that the respondent adopted a philosophy which, among other things, required of its teachers, (a) to practice integrity and not deceit in discharging their duties; (b) to be a role model for the pupils within their charge, and, (c) to avoid scandalizing the students and jeopardizing the common good of the school.

These standards were reflected in the policy of the school board and in what the teachers were asked to be mindful of. Though high, these standards and policies were not unreasonable. Ms F. was aware of these policies and procedures when she accepted employment and she had undertaken to follow them:

Conduct amounting to sexual intercourse outside the marriage sacrament is clearly contrary to the respondent's policies and philosophy, and the appellant therefore breached the terms of her contract of employment ... She put the board in a very difficult position. Her action clearly scandalized the students; that is, it offended their moral sensibility.

The board, therefore, had sufficient legal cause to dismiss her.

The judge believed that, given Ms F.'s employment circumstances and the probable necessity for her to move from the school district, Ms F. should be granted an extra three months' salary.

Ms F. appealed the decision of the board of reference to the Alberta Court of Queen's Bench. The first issue concerned the right of separate, denominational schools to dismiss teachers for denominational causes. The court concluded, citing among others *Caldwell et al. v. Stuart et al.*,[37] that the right to establish separate schools included the right to maintain the denominational character of the school and therefore to impose rules requiring teachers to adhere to certain religious and moral standards. Section 29 of the Charter protects constitutional rights to establish separate schools and overrides not only individual rights granted by the Charter but also individual rights granted by provincial legislation. This limitation on individual rights, however, can only be permitted in cases in which a dismissal or termination is based on a *bona fide* denominational cause.

The court agreed that Ms F.'s pregnancy 'was not the cause for the termination of employment. The cause for terminating the contract was the lifestyle which the pregnancy evidenced.' It also found that Ms F. was not being specially discriminated against:

It is clear on the findings made by the Board of Reference that the rule which was breached by the Applicant was the prohibition of the Roman Catholic Church against participation in sexual intercourse outside the marriage sacrament. This rule applied equally to all Catholic teachers, both male and female. Although evidence of a breach of the rule was more readily available in the case of a female teacher who was pregnant, the rule did not result in any intentional or unintentional discrimination against the Applicant as a female teacher.

Homosexual (Gay or Lesbian) Relationships

Homosexuality is a special class within sexual misconduct only because school boards, communities, legislators, and religious and secular authorities have made it so. So long as the teacher's student is not involved, there is no reason inherent in the teaching relationship why homosexual relationships, whether gay or lesbian, should make a teacher unfit for teaching any more than heterosexual relationships do. Only if the values of the school board or the community which the school board presumably represents forbid sexual relationships between persons of the same sex, and if the teachers are expected to exemplify these values, can homosexuality as such be considered misconduct.

We have then to ask such questions as the following: What sorts of gender roles are preferred or even prescribed by the community and so are included as part of the moral standards teachers are expected to promulgate and exemplify? Does the community or the educational system select as desirable a few out of many logical possibilities, or does it provide a wide range of acceptable patterns for its youth to adopt? Does it accept different patterns and provide students with the principles for choosing between them? Does it confine the acceptable pattern to only one or two alternatives and castigate the others as evil, immoral, or mentally ill?

Homosexuality, whether male or female, has been regarded in the Western world for the last two thousand years, by and large, as officially undesirable. Actual attitudes have varied from open acceptance to persecution. This official attitude has been reflected in legislation aimed at reducing or eliminating at least the public expression of homosexuality.

The three cases which follow are complicated by the fact that two of them (cases 30 and 32) also involve criminal charges and convictions for 'gross indecency' (meaning, in these cases, homosexual acts in men's washrooms). All three cases involve male teachers, and it is quite unclear what would have been the outcome if the teacher's homosexuality had been circumspect and private even if known to the school boards concerned. We suspect that in the B.C. case (30) the teacher would still have been dismissed. In the Saskatchewan and Ontario cases, the teachers probably would not have been dismissed.

Case 30: The Teacher Who Did a Gross Indecency

In this case from British Columbia, Mr X., under his former name of Mr Y., was accused of gross indecency with a young man in a public washroom under section 157 of the Criminal Code. On 25 September 1978 he was found guilty and was given a conditional discharge. Mr Y. changed his name legally to Mr X. in June 1978.

On 4 January 1979 the school board learned[38] that Mr X. was, or had been, Mr Y., of whose offence the school board had learned in late December of 1978. On 6 February 1979 the school board suspended Mr X. for misconduct under section 130(1)(a) of the Public Schools Act, and on 20 February they dismissed him. As was the standard practice, the school board notified the Ministry of Education concerning this dismissal. On 28 February, the director of teacher services also informed Mr X. that the director would be recommending the cancellation of Mr X.'s teaching certificate (a proceeding separate from suspension and dismissal by a school board). Mr X. appealed and a board of reference was set up.

The board of reference (decision dated 28 August 1979) agreed with the school board's argument that a teacher is more than just a skilled technician in a classroom; a teacher is also a role model whose behaviour outside the classroom is relevant both to his teaching role vis-à-vis his pupils and to the maintenance of public confidence in the school system. Teacher discipline was compared to professional discipline, like disbarment. Mr X. lost his appeal.

The cancellation of Mr X.'s teaching certificate remained 'in the air' until 5 April 1984, when it was cancelled.

Case 31: The Case of the Gay Pest

This story comes from Saskatchewan. On 17 May 1979, Mr G., the teacher, was dismissed (effective 30 June 1979) by the school division for conduct during the months of January through April which 'constitutes and evidences professional misconduct, immorality, neglect of duty and mental instability.' This conduct involved (a) indecently assaulting Mr A. and Mr B. (the parent of a pupil in Mr G.'s classroom); (b) allowing a pupil to overhear a conversation between Mr G. and the pupil's mother defending Mr G.'s homosexual activities; (c) using this pupil to deliver personal notes to Mr A.; and (d) exhibiting mental instability by taking an overdose of alcohol and vallium and by sending a letter of resignation to the school board. The school board's letter of termination also stated, as item 2 in the letter, that Mr G.'s conduct 'and the awareness of the same by the parents, students, and other teachers' made it impossible for Mr G. to fulfil his duties and obligations as a teacher under the Education Act, S. S. 1978.

At the outset, the board of reference was faced with a question of law, concerning both the jurisdiction of the board of reference and the role of community standards. Counsel for the school division proposed to argue that Mr G. was a homosexual and therefore unsuitable to teach in the school division because the community standards considered homosexuality as immoral. 'Counsel cited several cases at law, and a recent article from the "Canadian Bar Review" to support his contention that the local community standards of immoral behaviour take precedence over national, or provincial standards of behaviour.' Counsel for the teacher took the view that the jurisdiction of the board of reference was restricted to the specific allegations contained in the written notice of termination of the contract. The board of reference agreed with counsel for the teacher.

Mr B. complained, apparently sometime in March, to a member of the local school board about Mr G.'s conduct. This complaint and some other affairs culminating in Mr G.'s (apparently) overdosing on or shortly after 13 March led the local school board in a letter dated 26 March 1979 to request that the school division seek Mr G.'s resignation. If the resignation was not forthcoming, the school division was to terminate his contract immediately. The school division did seek Mr G.'s resignation, found his conditional resignation unsatisfactory, and dismissed him for the reasons given.

The incidents in question transpired as follows. First, on 13 February 1979, Mr B. was approached by Mr G. in a bar and pool-room and was persuaded by a mutual acquaintance, Mr K., to take Mr G. home in his, Mr B.'s, truck. On the way home, Mr G. began making homosexual advances to Mr B. Mr G. talked about his affair with Mr A., who was Mr B.'s brother. This was Mr B.'s testimony. Mr G. claimed that Mr B. made the first advances, to which Mr G. responded favourably.

Second, there was the 'affair' with Mr A. On 2 or 3 February, Mr A. and Mr G. went to a neighbouring town to seek some female friends. They could not find them and so stayed overnight at a motel. In his testimony before the board of reference, Mr A. claimed that Mr G. made homosexual advances to him at the motel. Mr G. claimed that Mr A. made the first advances and that he, Mr G., responded favourably.

The third incident began on 13 March 1979 at the home of Mrs T., a widow who was a close friend of Mr A. and who also knew Mr G. At midnight on that day, Mr G. and Mr K. arrived in a truck which became stuck in the snow. Mr A., who was with Mrs T. at the time, helped free the truck, and the three men entered the house. Mrs T. then asked Mr G. about the incident in the motel. Mr G. began a lecture on the virtues of homosexuality, claiming a five-year relationship between himself and Mr A. (denied by Mr A.). Mr G. took some pills and acted as if he were deliberately overdosing. Mrs T. called a neighbour, Mr C., to take Mr G. home. This was done, and Mr G. was left in his car in front of his home. Mrs T. and Mr A. later had second thoughts. They went to Mr G.'s home to see if he was all right. They found Mr G. in his car and solicited the help of an 'ex-police' officer, who took Mr G. inside. This was Mrs T.'s testimony. Mr A. corroborated this testimony, claiming that Mr G. was talking loudly and threatening to kill himself.

Mr K. and Mr G. told a somewhat different story. Mr G. accused Mrs T. of spreading rumours about his, Mr G.'s, behaviour and of ridiculing Mr A. about his sexuality. Mr G. took some pills, 'to get a good sleep tonight.' Mr K. and Mr G. denied that Mr C. had driven them home. Mr K. and Mr G. denied that Mr G. had threatened suicide. Mr G. said that the first encounter he had with the police was at 6 a.m., when three policemen arrived at his home because of a report that Mr G. had taken an overdose of drugs. Mr G. was persuaded by the police to go to the hospital, where apparently he stayed two weeks for what he claimed was a bladder infection. Counsel for the school division called several witnesses

who generally stated, that because [Mr G.] was a homosexual, and his behaviour was known, that in their opinion, made him unsuitable to continue teaching at [name of locality] and in the [name] School Division. It was their opinion that such behaviour was immoral, within the standards of the community.

We can almost hear the members of the board of reference sighing (even though the hearing apparently took only two days, viz. 20–1 August 1979):

The nature of the case has caused untold difficulties for the Board of Reference, due to the legal questions of procedure to be answered, the large number of witnesses, what is expected to be nearly one thousand pages of evidence, and the conflicting nature of the evidence adduced during the investigation.

Concerning the jurisdictional issue, the board of reference concluded that its jurisdiction was confined to assessing the reasons given in the letter of termination. These reasons were the grounds alleged for the termination. The board could, therefore, not go to the general question whether 'admitted homosexual activity ... was immoral conduct within the standards of immorality in the community ...'

Concerning the burden of proof required by the school division, the board of reference held that it 'is more than just meeting a "balance of probabilities," and falls somewhere short of "proving beyond reasonable doubt," this being a case of termination.'

After this ruling, the majority and minority of the board of reference parted company. The majority held that the conflicting nature of the evidence was so great that the burden of proof required against the teacher had not been met. The evidence left many unanswered questions. The evidence appeared to be 'coloured.' Then the majority stated:

[Mr G.'s] admissions of being bi-sexual, with homo-sexual tendencies, and his homo-sexual relations, are no doubt a genuine concern of the [name] School Division and at least some of the area residents.

If [Mr G.] were to return to teaching at [place name] or for that matter at any school within the [name] School Division, his effectiveness as a teacher would be severely limited, to a point of causing impairment to his pupils' progress.

Mr G. had promised under oath to resign, so that the board of reference ordered reinstatement and urged him to resign forthwith.

The minority member, representing the board of education, held that the burden of proof *had* been satisfied by the school division. He said:

The conflict of evidence that was presented to this Board, as summarized in part by the Majority Award, is so dramatic, that it can lead only to the conclusion that one or more of the witnesses in their testimony to this Board have lied as to the events which they testify to.

He found the stories of Mr A. and Mr B. much more logically consistent and credible than Mr G.'s. Another witness, Ms D., also contradicted Mr G.'s testimony in key respects. The minority member said:

If I am correct in my assessment of credibility, I consider it most unfortunate that [Mr G.], who has apparently demonstrated himself to be a very competent teacher over the last twenty years, would choose to fabricate a story calculated to bring disgrace on two members of a community in which he was teaching.

Counsel for the school division attempted to argue that the board of reference should consider that homosexual activities were contrary to the moral values of the community and, by implication, that this justified the dismissal of the teacher. The board of reference refused to accept this concern as being within their jurisdiction and decided the case on the specific allegations made in the school division's letter of termination. The majority still chose to comment, however, on Mr G.'s homosexual activities in a way which suggests they could have been used as grounds for termination and that the community concern could have been given as part of these grounds. In our view, the comment, as it stands, is *obiter dicta*, but a broad hint nonetheless; at least for 1979.

Item 2 in the letter of termination was not discussed as such by the board of reference decision. Only the *obiter dicta* mentioned above can be construed as an oblique reference to it.

The facts cited in the board of reference decision leave unaddressed the degree to which homosexual activity was in fact contrary to community values. The quality of the testimony introduced by counsel for the school division concerning community values is not discussed. Homosexual activity was distasteful to some persons. Both the local school board and the divisional board of education thought it was contrary to the values of enough people in the community that Mr G. was thereby unfit to teach in that community. Since the issue of offending community values, however, was left largely unexamined, the question of how to ascertain those values was also left unexamined.

No criminal charge of 'indecent assault' is mentioned by the board of reference. At first glance, therefore, Mr G. seems to have lost his job as much for being a pest and disclosing his behaviour, tactlessly, as for actually committing homosexual acts.

Case 32: Gross Indecency in a Public Building

This case is a labour arbitration case and not actually a board of reference case. Although the case received some newspaper publicity, we shall say only that it occurred in Ontario. We shall call the teacher Mr X., and the town where the events occurred shall be called 'Nameless.'

Mr X. was one of thirty-one persons who in early September 1983 were charged under section 157 of the Criminal Code for homosexual incidents in the washroom of a public building in the town of Nameless. The charges were a result of police surveillance of the washroom (involving the use of video cameras) for some eighteen days in August. The thirty-one persons included three teachers. Besides Mr X., one of the teachers was Mr Y., who taught at the same school as Mr X. The three teachers were dismissed by the school board. Mr Y. grieved his dismissal and was subsequently reinstated. Following the charge, Mr X. went on sick leave until his trial in May 1984. During this period, Mr X. also underwent psychiatric counselling.

At his trial in criminal court, Mr X. admitted that he had committed the offence with which he was charged. The judge gave Mr X. a conditional discharge, which meant that according to the Criminal Code, Mr X. would be deemed not guilty. This trial took place on 16 May 1984.

The school board met on 23 May and decided to terminate Mr X.'s contract as of 31 August. The board's letter of dismissal said, among other things:

As a result of your conduct in connection with the [nameless public building] incident as a result of which you were convicted of gross indecency, the Board no longer has confidence in your ability to command the respect of students and therefore does not believe that you can function effectively as a teacher. Further, it is the opinion of the Board that parents would no longer find you acceptable as a teacher. Your admitted conduct is in violation of your duty as a teacher under section 235 of the Education Act and therefore the Board has no alternative but to terminate your teaching contract.

Mr X. duly grieved his dismissal.

The chairman of the board of arbitration reviewed the facts briefly and discussed Mr X.'s role in the community, and the response of the community to Mr X.'s offence. The explanation for the incident, said the chairman, was that Mr X. had experienced a period of deep depression caused by the death of a very close friend. A psychiatrist testified concerning this depression and recommended that Mr X., who had an otherwise 'unblemished record as a civilized and concerned citizen of his community,' should be restored to his familiar profession and 'to the stability of his community of friends, colleagues, and family.'

The remainder of the chairman's judgment, with suitable emendations to protect privacies, deserves to be quoted:

A number of witnesses were called on behalf of [Mr X.] all testifying to his standing in the community, the fact that he was very well known ... as an active community worker in a number of areas and, above all, was known as an excellent and committed teacher. Particularly relevant was the testimony of [Mr S., an administrative superior of Mr X. Mr S.] testified that he knows [Mr X.] well both as a friend and as a teacher. He spoke highly of him as a teacher and noted that he had contributed much outside the classroom as well as in the classroom in terms of organizing assemblies, shows and dramatic events. When asked whether there would be any difficulty with [Mr X.] returning to the classroom, [Mr S.] replied that he could not foresee any difficulties and that he would be willing to work with him. He noted that since [Mr Y.] had returned to the school, it had worked out well and there were no difficulties at all.

As noted, a number of other witnesses, all testified to [Mr X.'s] high standing in the community, his reputation for honesty and integrity and the fact that there was a good deal of sympathetic understanding for his problem.

Counsel for the Board produced only one letter from a parent with respect to the return of [Mr Y.] as a teacher at [the school]. In that letter, the citizen, whose son does not attend [the school], commented that if he did, that she would not permit him to be one of [Mr Y.'s] students. She added that her feelings 'are the same as in the case of [Mr X.].' As noted, this is the single letter indicating community feeling addressed to the Board that was produced to the hearing by counsel for the Board.

There is no question that the incident that occurred here occurred outside the hours of employment and off the employer's premises. However, this is a case where the conduct, although not directly concerned with the employment nor occurring at the place of employment, clearly reflects on the employee's ability to carry out his job. An essential element of a teacher's ability to effectively carry out his or her job, is personal reputation and standing. Conduct which goes to the heart of one's personal character may so damage that reputation that a teacher is rendered incapable of effectively carrying out his classroom function. The attitude of parents as well as of students must be seen to be relevant in this context. Moreover, section 235 of the Education Act, R.S.O. 1980, Chapter 129 sets out a number of duties that are laid upon a teacher. Section 235(1)(c) reads as follows:

(c) to inculcate by precept and example respect for religion and the principles of Judaeo-Christian morality and the highest regard for truth, justice, loyalty, love of country, humanity, benevolence, sobriety, industry, frugality, purity, temperance and all other virtues;

This was the section particularly referred to by counsel for the Board, the allegation being that [Mr X.'s] conduct as evidenced by the plea of guilty was clearly in breach of the standards set out in the Education Act. We agree with [the chairman's] comment in the [Y.] case, that given the circumstances of the guilty plea, [Mr X.] did not live up to the duty as set out in section 235(1)(c). It does not necessarily follow, however, that breach automatically leads to justification for discharge. We agree with [the chairman of the board of arbitration in Mr Y.'s case], that the circumstances of this case do not justify discharge in the sense that [Mr X.] will not be able to effectively carry out his functions as teacher nor will his employment be prejudicial to his employer's interests in that he will not be acceptable as a teacher to either students or parents.

Indeed, there is a singular lack of evidence in this case that the community would be hostile to [Mr X.'s] return to duty as a teacher at [the school]. The great weight of the evidence before this Board was one of respect and admiration for [Mr X.] both as an individual and contributor to community life in [nameless] and as an outstanding teacher. That evidence was not seriously challenged in cross-examination. The only contrary evidence is the single letter with respect to [Mr Y.] consequent upon his return to teaching at [the school]. Indeed, we would comment that we were impressed by the evidence with respect to the understanding shown by broad elements of the [nameless] community with regard to this single incident in an otherwise unblemished career as a teacher and active community participant ...

We are then left with the [nameless public building] incident and the evidence of community support and community reaction as noted above. In these circumstances, we fully agree with the disposition of [the chairman] in the [Y.] grievance. To quote him:

> 'What must be determinative of the instant case, in our view, is on the one hand the lack of evidence to show that the grievor's having been guilty of this offence would be likely adversely to affect his effectiveness and his role as a teacher, and on the other hand the wealth of positive evidence to show that he would remain an effective teacher and a benefit to the community if reinstated in employment. We are persuaded by the positive evidence in this case.'

We also agree with [that chairman] that some discipline was clearly appropriate. [Mr X.] was on sick leave since September, 1983 and was subsequently discharged as of August 31, 1984. To order him returned to work as of 1 September 1985 is to impose a substantial discipline upon him, apart from all else that has been visited upon him in personal terms.[39]

Accordingly, the grievance is allowed to the extent that [Mr X.] is ordered returned to work effective 1 September 1985.

The chairman's judgment was concurred in by the second member of the board of arbitration, but apparently not by the third.[40]

This case is noticeable for the arbitration board's attempt, through the testimony of witnesses, to assess how the community actually felt about Mr X. The paucity of evidence provided by the school board against Mr X. suggests either that the school board made no such careful attempt to assess the community, or else it did and the result was not to the liking of the school board. It would seem probable, therefore, that in this case, the school board's action did not reflect the attitudes of the community but, instead, chiefly the school board's own prejudices.

Case 33: The Teacher Who Met a Runaway

This is the story of a teacher who was convicted of the criminal offence of gross indecency and became an object of dismay and concern among the parents of pupils whom he might have occasion to teach. It involves questions of both employee and professional misconduct, as well as differences of opinion among persons in the community, the school board, the board of reference, the B.C. College of Teachers, and the courts. The case (a B.C. case) gained some notoriety and was publicized in local and Vancouver newspapers. For this reason, we have chosen not to use anonymous initials.

The following account is a much abbreviated summary of the longer and thoughtful report of the case done by one of our students, Mr Peter Ewens (see Ewens 1991).

The Triggering Incident

Shortly before midnight on 23 September 1987, Mr Gordon Ledinski, aged forty-five years, with twenty-five years experience as a public school teacher, was driving along the streets of Kelowna, B.C. He observed a male adolescent walking along the streets and rummaging through garbage cans looking for empty bottles. The two met in a neighbouring parking lot and drove away together. They agreed to go to a local hill known informally as 'Lovers' Mountain.' There they talked. The young man, Brad, told Mr Ledinski that he was a runaway from home and that he was sixteen years old. They revealed to each other that they both had strong homosexual inclinations. Then they drove to another part of the mountain and enjoyed a homosexual encounter, after which they started to return to the city.

Unfortunately, on the previous day, human remains had been discovered on the mountain and the RCMP were out in force. They stopped Mr Ledinski and his companion. The police constables suspected that there had been a homosexual encounter and may indeed already have been aware of Mr Ledinski's proclivities. The police took them to the police station and interrogated them. Finally, the two admitted that there had been a homosexual encounter. The police let Brad go to a friend's house where he was staying and duly charged Mr Ledinski with having committed an act of 'gross indecency' contrary to section 157 of the Criminal Code. This charge was sworn on 29 September 1987.

Suspension, Trial, Dismissal

On 29 September the Board of School Trustees of School District No. 23 (Central Okanagan) suspended Mr Ledinski at once without pay because of the criminal charge. They did so under the provision in the B.C.

School Act which empowers them to suspend or dismiss a teacher for *misconduct*.[41]

Mr Ledinski duly appeared in provincial court for the preliminary hearing and was ordered to stand trial for the charge of gross indecency.

A complication arose on 1 January 1988 when Parliament repealed the gross indecency section of the Criminal Code and replaced it with a section prohibiting sexual assault.

After some delays, Mr Ledinski's trial took place in Vernon, B.C., at the county court, and on 4 March the judge ruled him guilty as charged. On 21 March 1988, in Kamloops, B.C., Mr Ledinski was sentenced to a fine of $1,000 or six-months' jail for non-payment of the fine. Mr Ledinski applied to the B.C. Court of Appeal, but on 4 November he was denied leave to appeal.

On 23 November 1988, after hearing submissions by Mr Ledinski and his legal counsel, the school board resolved to dismiss Mr Ledinski under section 122(2)(b) of the School Act. This section allowed the school board, having suspended the teacher for misconduct, to dismiss him for the same reason.

Hearings, and More Hearings

On 6 December 1988 the B.C. College of Teachers[42] cited Mr Ledinski for 'conduct unbecoming' and set up a disciplinary hearing. This hearing was subsequently postponed until after the hearing of a board of reference. In January 1989 the College suspended his teaching certificate pending the outcome of the disciplinary hearing. Mr Ledinski also applied for a board of reference to review his dismissal.

The board of reference met in Kelowna and held its hearings on 2 and 3 May and 27–9 June 1989. On 20 July the board of reference varied the decision of the school board. Instead of dismissal, they imposed a twenty-three-month suspension without pay beginning 29 September 1987 (when the criminal charge had been laid and the school board suspended him) and ending 28 August 1989.

The school board filed a petition for judicial review and for a stay of execution with respect to the board of reference decision. The board got the stay of execution, and the judge further ruled that the school board was not obliged to assign Mr Ledinski to a teaching position until his teaching certificate was returned.

From 28 August to 6 October, the B.C. College of Teachers heard submissions concerning Mr Ledinski. Among other testimony, they heard a psychiatrist testify that Mr Ledinski is not a paedophile. On 19 October

1989 the Council of the B.C. College of Teachers met and passed motions concerning Mr Ledinski. These motions included a suspension of his certificate from 23 January 1989 (therefore retroactively) to 22 October 1989 and a ruling that his name be made public (as, in fact, it already was).

Back at Work ... Public Protests
On 22 October 1989, Mr Ledinski began to receive full salary and employee benefits from the Central Okanagan School Board. Shortly afterwards, the school board dropped the application for judicial review of the board of reference decision. On 15 November, Mr Ledinski was assigned to a grade 5–6 class at Glenrosa Elementary School in Westbank, just across Okanagan Lake from Kelowna, B.C. The school principal sent a letter to parents whose children would be in Mr Ledinski's class and informed them of the changes in school organization consequent upon Mr Ledinski's reappearance in school. He did not tell them that Mr Ledinski would be the new teacher.

On 16 November, however, three sets of parents requested that their children be allowed to transfer from Mr Ledinski's class. This request was refused. Other parents called the school superintendent to ask for more information and express concern about the presence of Mr Ledinski. On 17 November parents of twelve children in Mr Ledinski's class prevented their children from attending his class. On the evening of that day, parents held a public meeting in the gymnasium of Glenrosa School, which some 125–50 people attended.

Protest Heats Up
On 19 November a second meeting of parents was held. More than 200 were present with two camera crews and several reporters. The meeting voted to boycott school for a day (Monday, 20 November). Dr James Balderson, a professor of educational administration at the University of Alberta, lambasted Mr Ledinski and the school board and received a standing ovation.

On 20 November parents kept their children from school and sent form letters to the school principal informing him of their intentions. Of a total 490 children, 142 were absent that day, and in Mr Ledinski's class, only 13 out of 23 pupils attended. The principal of Glenrosa School complained of the distraction to staff and students caused by the presence of local, regional, and even national news media.

The school board held a special emergency meeting and concluded that the stay of execution of the board of reference decision was still in effect. The board resolved to instruct Mr Ledinski not to attend work pending the outcome of a judicial review of the board of reference decision.

On 21 November, Mr Ledinski was officially told not to report for work. He would, however, continue to receive salary and employment benefits. On the same day, Tony Brummet, then Minister of Education, said the matter was to be decided by the courts, not the provincial government. He expressed displeasure at the College of Teachers having reinstated Mr Ledinski's teaching certificate.

On 22 November a bomb scare caused the evacuation of part of Glenrosa School. At a regular public meeting of the Central Okanagan School Board, public questioning of the school board's actions extended over an hour.

On 23 November a forum was held, at which both supporters and opponents of Mr Ledinski appeared. In addition, Mr Ledinski received several death threats and was provided with a guard by the RCMP.

On 24 November sixteen parents organized a group in support of Mr Ledinski and proposed a home-study school where he could teach their children. Revelations concerning Mr Ledinski's previous teaching, however, later caused this proposal to be withdrawn.

Revelations

On 25 and 26 November, the Kelowna *Courier* and other media sources revealed that Mr Ledinski had previously taught intermittently in Saskatchewan between 1962 and 1976. In 1976 he had also taught at a school in Alberta but had resigned from this school following a complaint by a male student to the principal, alleging some form of misconduct. Dr James Balderson formally requested that the Saskatchewan Board of Teacher Education and Certification cancel Mr Ledinski's still valid Saskatchewan teaching certificate.

As a result of these revelations, the school superintendent of the Central Okanagan School District started to investigate Mr Ledinski's previous career in Alberta and Saskatchewan.

On 22 March 1990 the media reported that Crown Council in Saskatchewan was reviewing five RCMP files alleging sexual assault by Mr Ledinski.

Judicial Review

Finally, on 16 March 1990, the hearing for the judicial review of the board of reference decision occured. The judge's decision was not made public until 25 April. On the grounds that the board misinterpreted the provisions of the School Act and that it had no right to impose a lesser penalty, Mr Justice K.E. Meredith ordered the board of reference to reconsider its decision.[43] On 30 May he dismissed a request that the board of reference be given jurisdiction to hear new evidence.[44]

Before the board of reference could complete its reconsiderations, Mr Ledinski appeared in provincial court, North Battleford, Saskatchewan, to answer four charges of indecent assault dating back twenty years. He pled 'not guilty.'

On 28 July 1990 the board of reference released its decision. It followed the directions of Justice Meredith and confirmed the school board's dismissing of Mr Ledinski.

Mr Ledinski's counsel duly filed for judicial review of the board of reference decision. On 16 October 1990, Mr Justice Gow ruled that the board of reference had not answered the fundamental question of whether Mr Ledinski's dismissal by the Central Okanagan School Board was for just and reasonable cause.[45] He ordered the board of reference once again to reconsider its decision.

On 26 November 1990, Mr Ledinski appeared in provincial court in North Battleford. The judge ruled that there was enough evidence for Mr Ledinski to stand trial (this does *not* mean that Mr Ledinski was guilty of any crime). Trial was set for early 1991.

Considerations
This is not a simple case. To begin with, Mr Ledinski was charged with an offence that was criminal when it was alleged to have occurred, but was no longer in the Criminal Code when he came to trial. Accordingly, the judge finally concluded that because Brad was aged fifteen and 'in somewhat pathetic circumstances,' Mr Ledinski's behaviour amounted to sexual exploitation and was a marked departure from ordinary decent conduct. The charge of gross indecency was consequently upheld. The judge fined him $1,000 or six months in jail.

Since he had been convicted of a criminal offence, Mr Ledinski's job and teaching certificate were both in jeopardy. The school board had to consider whether this conviction amounted to misconduct deserving dismissal: if it did not, parents and other members of the public would certainly ask for his dismissal. The school board was also legally obliged to notify the College of Teachers. Once notified, the College had the option to investigate Mr Ledinski for 'conduct unbecoming.' Once the College cited him for investigation, it had the power to suspend him until the hearing was concluded. Once the College suspended his certificate, he would be unemployable by any school board in British Columbia.

Had the College's hearing been favourable to Mr Ledinski, the dismissal by the school board would still stand. The future of Mr Ledinski as a teacher in British Columbia depended heavily upon the finding of the board of reference.

After hearing evidence concerning the events and the characters of the persons involved, especially of Mr Ledinski, the board of reference concluded that Mr Ledinski did not constitute a potential threat to students. He had admitted to misconduct. The issue before the board was, therefore, whether he should be dismissed or whether an alternative penalty was preferable.

The board, after reviewing several cases, came to the conclusion that in Mr Ledinski's case, dismissal was too severe a penalty. The board did not think that Mr Ledinski was likely to repeat his offence and considered that the punishment of lengthy suspension with loss of pay was sufficient to deter recurrence and other potential offenders. The board also considered that Mr Ledinski would be able to be reintegrated into the community: the board thought that the school board was 'under-estimating the tolerance of the community.'

The College of Teachers, as was noticed earlier, decided that Mr Ledinski's criminal conviction justified the temporary suspension of his teaching certificate but not its permanent removal.

Both the board of reference and the discipline committee of the College of Teachers regarded Mr Ledinski's behaviour and subsequent criminal conviction as misconduct deserving punitive sanction but not the severity of dismissal and a permanent bar to teaching. The criminal court had assessed a fine of only $1,000 dollars. In the view of all three tribunals, Mr Ledinski had done wrong, but he had not shown a disposition unfitting him for teaching. The school board reluctantly accepted the decision of the board of reference.

Sections of the local community did not agree. Someone with a criminal conviction for gross indecency, for a homosexual encounter with a boy of school age (fifteen years), surely could not be trusted with children of still younger years. These persons protested and the protests accelerated. The media picked up the story. Professor James Balderson intervened and loudly castigated both Mr Ledinski and the school board. The community began to take sides, some for Mr Ledinksi and many against him. The school board reconsidered its stand and reopened its application for judicial review.

The judicial review by Justice Meredith turned on the interpretation of the statutes and the issue of whether the board of reference had the jurisdiction to make the decision which it had made. He held that the school board could dismiss *or* discipline the teacher and that it had elected to dismiss. He therefore concluded that the board of reference did not have jurisdiction to vary the school board's dismissal. He directed the board to reconsider its decision and either confirm the school board's dismissal or reject it.

The board of reference accepted the judge's direction and felt that they could, therefore, do nothing other than confirm the dismissal. The board still believed that its earlier decision was the correct one.

This second decision was appealed for judicial review and Mr Justice Gow directed the board of reference to reconsider whether or not Mr Ledinski had been dismissed for just and reasonable cause. He upheld Mr Justice Meredith's reading of the statutes that the board of reference could not legally substitute another penalty. He also confirmed that misconduct did not automatically justify dismissal. By the end of 1990, the board had not yet reached a decision.

The Community's Attitudes
The fuss began when the school board returned Mr Ledinski to teaching but not at the same school as he had formerly taught. He was moved to a school on the other side of the lake. The neighbourhood around Glenrosa Elementary is a middle- to low-income community. The objections made by various people from that neighbourhood indicate that Mr Ledinski's behaviour had sharply challenged their ideas of right and wrong. Ewens (1991: 111) summarizes their assertions as follows:

– Mr Ledinski was a good to excellent teacher;
– no one was willing to have their children taught by Mr Ledinski;
– Mr Ledinski took advantage of a weaker member of our society;
– teachers ought to be role models for children;
– Mr Ledinski has, by virtue of his actions, disqualified himself from ever being placed in the role of trust and responsibility which is that of a teacher;
– it makes no difference that the act which Mr Ledinski committed was with someone else who was not his student nor directly related to his duties as a teacher, i.e., that it was 'off the job' conduct;
– it makes no difference that Mr Ledinski's partner in the act consented to the act;
– it would not have made any difference if Mr Ledinski had committed the act

with someone who was 16 or 17, a child is a child;
- even if we could be sure that Mr Ledinski would never do anything like this again we would still not give him a second chance because there are too many situations available to teachers where they could deviate from the norm and take advantage of a child;
- even though the testimony of the psychiatrist stated that his behaviour was impulsive and out of character, psychiatry is an inexact science and its assertions are speculative, not fact;
- if the act were not homosexual in nature the repugnance by the community would be no less than it already is;
- Mr Ledinski would not be accepted into a school by either his peers, students or parents;
- if Mr Ledinski was to be reinstated as a teacher of my (our) children, then protests would be very, very strong.

In retrospect, the school board was uncertain what to do with Mr Ledinski. If the school board had been firm in its determination to dismiss Mr Ledinski, it would not have abandoned the judicial review, only to resume it after public outcry. On the other hand, once the public outcry began, resuming the judicial review was a way of deferring further decisions until the outcry subsided.

The parents of the students at Glenrosa were advised that a new teacher would be joining the staff. They were not advised who he was and were not consulted in advance. Most of the teachers at Glenrosa were female. Mr Ledinski was a considerable change. Further, when parents sought information from the school board, they found the school board and the school district administration rather uncommunicative.

The community felt that since Mr Ledinski was a convicted criminal, he was not 'one of us.' This view grew stronger as the affair proceeded.

The intervention of the media exacerbated matters. The media also led to the discovery of previous offences by Mr Ledinski in Alberta and Saskatchewan.

Conclusions
Once Mr Ledinski was labelled a convicted criminal and a sex offender and one whose offence involved a fifteen-year-old, he was in trouble. His character was in question, his sexual mores were in question, and his relationships with children were in question. His homosexuality offended some persons but perhaps not as many as it would have in earlier years. As the board of reference noted, community ideas concerning homosexual-

ity change. Paedophilia was not approved, and Mr Ledinski's defenders found it necessary to state that he was not a paedophile. In a new school, he was also a stranger. When people found out who he was, some became suspicious.

We see here how communities or school neighbourhoods can bring pressure on school boards. They can hold public protests, dramatize their concerns, and call in the media. The work of the school can be disrupted, the school board can receive unpleasant publicity, and the contentious teacher can become the lightning rod through whom the unpleasantness is discharged.

The teacher may be dismissed and the affair may subside. It leaves a bad feeling behind, however, as trust among the school board, community, and teachers is weakened and will be regained only with difficulty.

Transvestism and Transsexuality

If homosexuality contradicts the notion that proper sexual behaviour is between male and female, transvestism and transsexuality contradict the notion that male and female are separate identities which should not be mixed. Transvestism and transsexuality confuse and complicate gender categories. In transvestism, one sex takes on the clothing and the outward appearance of the other. The transvestite is not the gender he or she appears to be. In transsexuality (which is different from transvestism),[46] one sex changes his/her body until it fits the bodily form of the other sex. Along with the bodily change is a change there in social roles. The boundaries between gender roles thereby become permeable while still maintained. To persons unsure of their own sexual identities, such changes can be challenging and unsettling.

If the schools and teachers are expected to teach children, especially adolescents in a time of sexual transition, how they should behave as males or females, then a certain concern by the schools for the gender roles displayed by teachers may reasonably also be expected. Much depends, therefore, on how gender roles are conceived and modelled by the school boards and the communities which they presumably represent.

Case 34: The Teacher Who Stole Women's Clothes

The following case, which occurred in a rural town of Alberta in 1979, involves both transvestism and the crime of stealing. It was the stealing which brought the teacher's transvestism to public knowledge; and it was the effect of the criminal conviction which led the board of reference to uphold the dismissal of the teacher.

Mr A. was dismissed by the school board on the grounds that (a) he had pled guilty to the criminal charge of possession of stolen property; and (b) he had manifested abnormal behaviour, which included storing women's clothing and accessories in his classroom and wearing women's clothes in the school building, albeit during off-hours when the building was closed to the public. He had acquired the clothes through theft over a number of years. He was discovered on two occasions cross-dressing in the school. After the first incident, he was met with sympathy by school authorities and directed to take special counselling, which he did. Some time later, however, 'the stolen property was discovered in the school, the situation became general knowledge in the [named] district and obviously the Respondent was obligated by public pressure to deal with the question.'

Mr A. was first suspended and then dismissed. He appealed to the board of reference and asked for damages for wrongful dismissal:

One issue to be determined by the Board of Reference is whether the Board of Education acted reasonably in the circumstances. Counsel for the Appellant suggested that the Respondent may have yielded mainly to public pressure, whereas the public did not understand the matter, and it is the Appellant's counsel's view that the Board of Education should have given more consideration to such factors as the information available indicating that the offence arose because of a medical problem. He also thought as there was no danger to the children in the actions, that should have been taken into consideration as well as the fact that a solution to the problem was at hand by means of medical treatment. The counsel for the Appellant went on to suggest that the action of the Board of Education at the time might have taken the form of sick leave having beeen granted to the Appellant. Also, counsel for the Appellant alluded to the fact that the offence charged, that is, the offence of having stolen property in his possession, was dealt with by the Court, and that the Board of Education really should not have concerned itself further with that factor or the matters behind the charge. He pointed out that no real harm was done; that the thefts were not for commercial gain.

It is my conclusion, from considering the facts as brought out in the evidence, that the Board of Education did act reasonably under the circumstances. I make this finding on the basis of the criminal offence alone. And, notwithstanding that the possession of stolen property arose out of the Appellant's medical problem, the Board had as its primary duty the responsibility for the operation of the local school system. Whether the students were justified or not, knowledge of the thefts and related conviction precluded the Appellant from reasonably carrying out his duties in the [named] area. This consideration overrides any suggestion of a leave of absence for medical reasons of [*sic*] he relatively minor nature of the crime, and the fact that the Court saw fit to give the Appellant a conditional discharge.

The judge, however, held that in light of Mr A.'s medical problem, the one month's pay in lieu of notice was insufficient and awarded him an extra three months.

In this case, the combination of Mr A.'s being charged with a criminal offence and the public knowledge of his sexual deviation made it impossible for him to continue teaching in the school district. The board of reference decision, however, does not describe the kind of public pressures directed at the school board or against Mr A.

This case was decided, not under the rubric of misconduct, but under the rubric of reasonable cause.

Other

Under this heading, we include a case of sexual assault. The case is noteworthy for the board of reference's remarks on teachers being in a position of trust. This is a Saskatchewan case.

Case 35: A Criminal Charge of Sexual Assault

On 29 September 1986 the board of education was informed that criminal charges were to be laid against Mr X. On 1 October 1986, the charges were laid and Mr X. was accordingly notified by the board in writing that he was suspended without pay until the charges were confirmed or dismissed. On 8 October, Mr X. pled guilty to the criminal charge of sexual assault. On 14 October the board of education decided to terminate Mr X.'s contract as a teacher effective 13 November 1986. The board's grounds were that (a) Mr X. had pled guilty to a charge of sexual assault and the complainant was less than eighteen years old and in Mr X.'s care at the time;[47] (b) this conduct was inconsistent with Mr X.'s teaching role and responsibilities; (c) Mr X.'s conduct reflected 'negatively' on the board's reputation; and (d) the teaching staff in consequence were reluctant to work with Mr X.

The board of reference decided that the board of education had been acting in good faith and that the board had good reason for arriving at its decision to terminate Mr X.'s contract. The reasons of the board of reference seem worth quoting:

Evidence submitted indicated the importance of the teacher being in a position of trust and a role model for the children. The community must respect the teacher and feel that their children can be entrusted to the teacher. There must also be trust and harmony on a teaching staff. This is especially true in a small rural community.

The other teachers in the — School, the Local Board of Trustees and a number of parents in the community had indicated to the Board of Education, that [Mr X.] was not an acceptable teacher after his plea of guilty to the charge of sexual assault.

Evidence presented indicated that administration, fellow teachers and parents felt that [Mr X.'s] effectiveness as a teacher was seriously impaired.

The Board of Reference agree that the Board of Education had good reason to arrive at its decision.

The board of reference upheld the termination of contract and refused to make an order for compensation for loss of pay for the period of time during which Mr X. was suspended.

Discussion

What can we learn from these cases? The effect of the teacher's sexual conduct upon the reputation of the school in the community is – sometimes clearly, sometimes obscurely – indeed a concern for the board of reference to address. Case 32 deals expressly with this issue. Case 34 refers to 'public pressure,' but the judge's decision does not reveal what that public pressure was nor, for the purposes of his judgment, did he need to discuss the matter. In case 27, community response was an issue, and the requirement that teachers adhere to community standards was emphasized by the court which rejected the decision of the majority of the board of reference. Nowhere in the case, however, is there a discussion of what those values were nor how they might have been ascertained. In case 28, the board of arbitration noted that there was no public outcry but implied that the board's decision might have been different if there had been such an outcry.

In cases 21, 22, 23, 24, and 26, the effect of the teacher's behaviour on the community was not an issue and did not need to be. In case 25, the actual effect on the community was also not an issue. What was at issue was whether or not the school board had the right to be concerned about possible effects and to direct the teacher accordingly.

Cases 30, 32, 34, and 35 were complicated by the presence of criminal charges followed by convictions, even though in two cases there was a conditional discharge, according to which, for the purposes of criminal record, the conviction is deemed not to have occurred. Criminal conviction is itself *prima facie* evidence of misconduct since teachers are also expected to uphold the law. (In case 21, the teacher, though charged, was acquitted.)

The cases, therefore, do tell us something about how communities may, through school boards, control the behaviour of teachers and correct the unconventional. They tell us more perhaps about the way school boards fear community disapproval and accordingly control teachers' conduct. They also show boards of reference and courts controlling the actions of school boards and communities, thus limiting and directing the 'community control effect.'

The process of board of reference hearings and appeals to the courts smoothes out the dispute and obscures the community dynamics. Like a court of law, a board of reference must render its decision on the basis of the evidence which is placed before it, and only on that evidence. The disputants necessarily select what evidence they present and try to control what evidence the other disputants bring forth or elicit. This evidence may or may not reveal the pressures from the community. When the board makes its decision, it too must decide what evidence is relevant and what is not. The board of reference decisions provide only a hint of the community debate and dissension which may have actually occurred.

The cases represent the 'tip of an iceberg,' while most of the iceberg is hidden from view. Many contentions are settled between school boards and teachers by means of resignations and minor suspensions, without suspensions and dismissals, that is, which involve boards of reference. Many suspensions and dismissals go uncontested, and many applications for boards of reference are withdrawn or abandoned. Increasingly, in some provinces, disputes go to labour arbitration rather than to boards of reference. The cases which do reach boards of reference, therefore, are often not average cases but involve some ambiguity in the issues, some legal issue, or a special degree of bitterness in the dispute. The above cases have been chosen to show the issues and to reveal evidence of the 'community control effect.' They represent the *types* of conflict quite well, but they are not necessarily average cases. Sometimes, indeed, they are quite unique (for example, cases 27 and 34).[48]

Some principles clearly emerge from the board of reference decisions and from subsequent judgments by the courts:

(1) Public school teachers are in postions of trust vis-à-vis the school-children, older or younger, entrusted to their care. Within the school and the classroom, they must of course do nothing which abuses this trust. Outside the school and classroom, however, teachers must also do nothing which would lead other persons to believe that the teachers might abuse their trust. They must, twenty-four hours a day, display a trustworthy character. Hence paedophilia and sexual assault, whether with the teacher's own pupils, own children, or other young people or adults, whether in school or out of school, become putative evidence of a disposition dangerous to children and so may require the teacher's dismissal. Teaching is *not* 'just a job.'

(2) Sexual liaisons between teachers and their students are forbidden. This is because the loyalties engendered by an *honest* sexual relationship are in conflict with the teacher's obligations to the school system. Sexual liaisons between a teacher and a student in the school system, but not a student of the teacher, are not obviously wrong but are regarded with disfavour by boards of reference. However, sexual liaisons between teachers and persons who were, but at the time of the liaison are not, students, are acceptable, even if the teacher met the other while the other was a student.

(3) Teachers are expected to serve as role models for their students and to maintain the reputation of the school in the community. This expectation includes 'off-the-job' behaviour. If the school upholds certain religious values (for example, Roman Catholic schools supporting the idea that divorce is wrong, at least for Roman Catholics), the teachers at that school are expected to uphold those values in their behaviour.

(4) This expectation that teachers serve as role models is prescriptive, not descriptive. By 'prescriptive,' we mean that teachers would be required to be role models even if there were evidence that students (and other people) do not model their behaviours after their teachers.

(5) Sexual exhibition and lewdness, extramarital and non-marital heterosexual relationships, homosexuality, transvestism, and transsexuality are proscribed because the school or community considers these behaviours wrong or immoral and requires teachers to be exemplars of right or moral behaviour. Such proscriptions are not required by the necessities intrinsic to teaching *qua* teaching. However, the proscriptions may follow

from the *content* of what the school expects the teacher to teach. This content portrays and inculcates a particular view of human nature and its potentialities.

In the introduction to this chapter, we proposed a distinction between the 'inherent necessities' of teaching and the requirements imposed by the content of what is taught. We think these cases of sexual misconducts underline the usefulness of this distinction. Applied to board of reference concerns, this distinction would (we think) sharpen and clarify the arguments before and by the boards.

In a changing and multicultural world and in a society which officially accepts some degree of cultural pluralism, the moral values which schools and teachers are expected to exemplify become problematic. Different moralities contend for dominance. Persons with opposing interests wield different moral claims as part of their armament (just as they wield different legal claims). This conflict and debate is reflected in the arguments presented to boards of reference and is sometimes discussed in their decisions. Sexual misconduct is only one occasion for such debate.

The Question of Gender Bias: Some Quebec Cases

Looking back over the cases, we are struck that thirteen of these fifteen cases concerned male teachers, one (case 29) concerned a female teacher, and one (case 27) concerned both male and female teachers. Why this preponderance of men? Was it merely an accident of our selection, or does it represent a real difference in sexual offences by men and women and in the way school boards, teachers, and communities react to them? It is not just an accident of our selection, for in the review of board of reference cases which we have done, we have encountered very few cases of sexual misconducts by women teachers. Apart from a few involving women teachers in Roman Catholic schools who have divorced and remarried and so contravened Roman Catholic doctrine, case 29 is the only one. Perhaps we are touching on a real difference in the sexual offences of men and women. Note, for instance, that we found no cases of female homosexuality or female paedophilia. Any such difference, however, is also masked by (a) possible differences in the way school boards react to the offences of male and female teachers; and (b) differences in the readiness of male and female teachers to appeal their cases to boards of reference and beyond.

The preponderance of men in sexual misconduct cases is a phenomenon Elizabeth Grace discusses in her article 'Professional Misconduct or

Moral Pronouncement: A Study of "Contentious" Teacher Behaviour in Quebec.' Grace examines the situation in Quebec regarding the disciplining of teachers for moral misconduct. The article outlines Quebec's legislative and administrative machinery for dealing with misconduct and examines several arbitration awards to identify the kinds of behaviour likely to qualify as teacher misconduct warranting discipline. The author focuses particularly on allegations involving physical and psychological forms of sexual misconduct, concluding that the legal concept of 'immorality' is an inappropriate yardstick for gauging the propriety of conduct involving serious abuses of power and trust. The appropriateness of grievance arbitration as an adjudication mechanism in such cases is also questioned.

Last Words

Aside from the Quebec cases studied by Elizabeth Grace, most of the cases described in this chapter are board of reference or board of arbitration cases. The teacher has chosen to fight the dismissal or suspension. This implies that the teacher thought that the school board's grounds for that suspension or dismissal are either morally or legally wrong or else unsupportable.[49] The teacher's reputation and income are at stake and a simple withdrawal is not enough. How many similar cases were dealt with quietly by an agreement between the teacher and the school board that the teacher should resign and go elsewhere and the school board write a letter of reference politely avoiding the real reasons for the resignation? We do not know. How many cases were settled by some other agreement between teacher and school board? We do not know.

Note that most of these cases came to public attention, so that the school board not only had to do something but had to be *seen* to do something. The public's image of the school and of teachers was at stake and had to be maintained.

Teachers are expected to teach by example as well as by classroom instruction. These examples require a certain consistency between in-school and out-of-school behaviours. When the lessons that teachers are required to present include models of sexual or gender roles, teachers are required themselves to refrain from those behaviours which are disapproved. What these behaviours might be depends largely on the comuunity's or state's notion of what they ought to be. Only paedophilia and sexual liaisons between teachers and their students actually offend against the inherent necessities of teaching as such.

Some of these behaviours, such as homosexuality, transsexuality, transvestism, and appearing nude in photographs in nudist publications, might be argued to be part of the rights of citizens to do whatever they wish so long as they harm no one.[50] This thought raises the question: what happens when teachers exercise their rights as citizens – such as the rights of free association and free speech – and so offend influential members of the community, or even members of the school board? Or what if the teacher is a member of an unpopular minority or expresses opinions disapproved of by established authority? We look at these questions in the next chapter.

5

Unorthodox Teachings and Unquiet Citizens

Introduction

While issues relating to 'character' and sexual misconducts are important both to teachers in particular and to school systems in general, the most important concerns are freedom of opinion and the rights of the citizen. These issues concern liberty, and without a careful regard for liberty, education can be nothing but servile. This liberty includes the right of the citizen to criticize the institutions of society. These institutions include the educational institutions and especially the public schools.

The common law of master and servant allows an employer to dismiss, without notice, an employee in whose continued service the employer has reasonable cause to no longer be confident. There must be a certain degree of trust between employer and employee if the employer's enterprise is to be faithfully conducted. If an employee criticizes the employer either publicly or among co-workers, this criticism *may* be taken as evidence of a loss of that faithfulness that an employer is entitled to expect of employees. This is especially so if the employee criticizes the employer *in public*. Public criticism, by one who presumably knows the enterprise from the inside, damages the reputation of the employer among his customers.

If the criticism is false, the employer presumably also has grounds to sue the employee for slander or libel, especially if the employer can prove that he or she has lost business because of the criticism. If the criticism is true, however, the employer can still dismiss the employee because the essential trust between them has been broken.[1]

Public schools are not ordinary economic enterprises; they are monopolies. Because people do not pay special fees for their children to attend the school (only taxes that even the childless must pay) and must send their children to *some* school, the public schools have an essential monopoloy on educational services. Those private schools that are not supported by taxation must offer something very special if they are to compete successfully with the tax-supported public schools.

Monopolies, especially of essential services, are not subject to the ordinary discipline of the market. Their customers go to them or go without – there are no alternative suppliers. The monopolies, therefore, need to be subject to public *political* criticism. The public educational system needs to thus be open to such criticism.

Furthermore, the public educational system is an arm of the community or of the state (in Canada, both of these at once) and therefore ought to be open to public inquiry and criticism, just as the rest of the government and its agencies. The right to criticize is part of the rights of citizenship in a liberal, democratic state. Should citizens be deprived of this right because they are employees of the government (at whatever level)? Remember that the government as an employer is also entitled to be confident in its employees' loyalty. Add to this the complication that the public school system as a whole is, in effect, a monopoly *employer* as well as a monopoly provider of educational services. If one wishes to make one's living as a teacher, there is basically only one employer. Criticism of this employer, therefore, can lead not only to loss of a job but loss of one's entire occupation. One cannot effectively set up one's own private educational system. The sanction for a teacher's criticism of the public school system is, therefore, more severe than for an ordinary employee's criticism of his or her employer.[2]

When teachers have alternative job possibilities and other incomes, this economic sanction may not be unduly severe. When they do not, however, the economic sanction is effectively punitive. There is nothing like the threat of loss of income to encourage docile acquiescence in a system going bad. Under these circumstances, we would argue that teachers have both the right and the duty to criticize the school system. This right needs protection from overly sensitive school boards and educational ministries.

There still remains the problem of distinguishing responsible, truth-seeking criticism (whether well grounded or ignorant) from reckless and malicious criticism. The latter, coming from an employee, is still sufficient grounds for dismissing him or her.

Beyond the criticism of the school system is the general exercise of citizens' rights. In smaller communities especially, the teacher who belongs to an unpopular group or expresses opinions that upset the majority or an influential minority of the community is open to the economic sanction of dismissal by an employer who is afraid of that majority or influential minority (or even belongs to them).

In chapter 1, we listed 'unauthorized teaching activities' and 'contentious conduct as citizens' as two sets of behaviours that are sometimes grounds for allegations of misconduct. Among the first set, which includes teaching activities conducted outside the classroom, we distinguished:

a) use of unauthorized material (e.g., sex- or religion-related books, magazines, and films)
b) use of unauthorized strategies or methods of teaching
c) unauthorized teaching of controversial topics, issues, or subject matter
d) ideological teaching, including partisan politicking and partisan support for candidates
e) religious teaching for proselytizing purposes

'Contentious conduct as citizens' includes political, religious, academic, and social-personal activities, and involves actions related to the following issues:

a) free expression (written, oral, or symbolic; e.g., public espousal of controversial ideas or lifestyle; wearing symbolic material and religious material; criticism of school policy, colleagues, or superiors)
b) affiliation or association (e.g., membership in controversial political, religious, or social groups such as the Communist Party of Canada, the KKK, neo-Nazi organizations, and cultic societies; marriage to a notorious person)
c) public activities (e.g., partisan speeches for a party or its candidate; refusal to take patriotic oaths or to participate in patriotic activities; participation in activities, such as demonstrations and petitions, of controversial groups)

These two categories tend to overlap. The same behaviour may fall into both at once. In particular, unauthorized teaching activities, whether inside or outside the school, are much involved with freedom of expression and freedom of opinion.

Let us now trace a number of cases under these general headings.

These are affairs that have actually occurred in Canada within the past twenty years.

Unauthorized Teaching Activities, in School and out of School

Case 36: The Teacher Who Taught Anti-Semitism in His Classes

This Alberta case, the Keegstra affair, touches on the use of unauthorized teaching material, the unauthorized teaching of controversial subjects, ideological teaching, and free expression. Of course, this case became a national *cause célèbre*. It has been described in detail and some of its implications are discussed in David Bercuson's and Douglas Wertheimer's *A Trust Betrayed: The Keegstra Affair* (1987). This book is our chief source for what follows.

In 1968, Jim Keegstra commenced a permanent teaching position at Eckville High School in the County of Lacombe School District. At first, he taught industrial arts but soon was teaching a diversity of subjects, including social studies. As he taught social studies, he introduced his own ideas about history. These ideas included the notion that the French and Russian Revolutions, socialism, communism, and a great many other things of which he disapproved, were the result of an ancient and pernicious Jewish conspiracy. By 1980 this conspiracy was the exclusive content of his social studies courses. He also showed prejudices against Roman Catholics, and some Catholic parents removed their children from Eckville High School. He did not tolerate dissent from his views by his students, and he rewarded them for repeating back to him the ideas and 'facts' that he presented in class. Though various complaints were made to the school principals and to the superintendent of schools for the school district about Keegstra's teachings, these complaints were not attended to seriously until R.K. David became superintendent in June 1981 (Bercuson and Wertheimer 1987: 67).

In 1974 and 1977, Jim Keegstra was elected by acclamation to the Eckville town council, and in 1980 he was elected (also by acclamation) mayor of Eckville.

In September 1981, Superintendent David received complaints from parents about Keegstra's teaching social studies and again in December. On 18 December 1981 he met Keegstra and the school principal and learned directly of what Keegstra was teaching. Later that same day, David wrote to Keegstra reviewing the issues and instructing Keegstra not to present the 'Jewish conspiracy' as a proven fact of history. The procedural sequence of events thereafter went as follows (Bercuson and Wertheimer 1987: 92).

12 January 1982: The school board meets to consider David's letter to Keegstra. The board agrees to call Keegstra in for a termination hearing at its 9th of February meeting.

9 February 1982: The school board meets with Keegstra. Keith Harrison of the Alberta Teachers' Association (A.T.A.) is among those present.

9 March 1982: David, on behalf of the school board, writes to Keegstra. The letter requires Keegstra to comply with the Alberta social studies curriculum and to refrain from teaching discriminatory theories as if they were facts. The letter advises Keegstra that failure to comply with these directives will result in the termination of his contract.

17 May 1982: David's deputy visits Keegstra's classes and finds Keegstra still teaching the international Jewish conspiracy.

7 October 1982: Susan Maddox tells Superintendent David what Keegstra has been teaching her son Paul and then prepares a detailed written statement that she gives to David on 11 October 1982.

12 October 1982: The school board meets and directs David to prepare for a hearing on the termination of Keegstra's contract.

7 December 1982: The school board holds its hearing. Keegstra is present and states his beliefs at length. In consequence, the board decides to terminate his contract.

14 December 1982: Keegstra appeals his dismissal to the board of reference.

22–8 March 1983: A hearing is held before the board of reference.

14 April 1983: Judge McFadyen, of the board of reference, hands down her judgment.

Judge McFadyen held that Keegstra had taught the theory of the world Jewish conspiracy as a fact and, in so doing, had failed to comply with 'the lawful and reasonable direction of his employer' and with the Alberta social studies curriculum. Keegstra's appeal was dismissed and the termination was upheld (Bercuson and Wertheimer 1987: 114).

The A.T.A.'s discipline process was not activated concerning Keegstra until some months later when the A.T.A. received a complaint, in writing, about him. A hearing by the discipline committee was held at the beginning of October 1983. The committee recommended that Keegstra's teaching certificate be suspended (not cancelled) and that his membership in the A.T.A. be revoked. Keegstra was informed of this decision on 8 October 1983. On 10 October, Dave King, Alberta's minister of education, who had been waiting for the A.T.A. to act, announced that he would cancel Keegstra's teaching certificate. In early 1984, Keegstra appealed the revocation of his membership in the A.T.A. to the Teaching Profession Appeal Board. The latter upheld the A.T.A.'s decision.

During April to July of 1985, Jim Keegstra was tried in criminal court on the charge of wilfully fomenting hatred against an identifiable minority group and was convicted. This conviction was appealed to the Alberta Court of Appeal. On 6 July 1988 that court allowed the appeal and quashed the conviction. The court held that section 281.2(2) of the Criminal Code, under which Keegstra was charged, both offended the presumption of innocence and was an unconstitutional violation of the guarantee of freedom of expression given by section 2(b) of the Charter of Rights and Freedoms.[3] The Crown appealed to the Supreme Court of Canada. On 13 December 1990 the Supreme Court, in a four-to-three decision, allowed the appeal, rejected the reasoning of the Alberta Court of Appeal, and returned the case to the Court of Appeal for reconsideration.[4] On 3 March 1991 the Court of Appeal confirmed Keegstra's appeal and ordered a new trial. Their grounds were that the publicity before, during, and after the original trial gave good reason to believe that the impartiality of the jurors might have been irretrievably affected and also that the judge had misdirected the jury in a matter of proof.[5]

The Keegstra affair was more complex, more public, and more important than this bare recital of selected events indicates. For this wider context, see Bercuson and Wertheimer's book-length account.

Keegstra held and advocated doctrines that offended the viewpoint of the majority of Canadians but certainly did not offend a large minority in the immediate local community. The town council of Eckville did not censure Keegstra, and he was not defeated in the election for mayor until the news concerning Keegstra's dismissal had become a national issue and Eckville had become the object of unpleasant publicity. As Keegstra's views became better known and Eckville's reputation suffered, the town reacted. He lost the mayoralty contest on 17 October 1983 by a vote of 273 against him and 123 for him (Bercuson and Wertheimer 1987: 174). He still had supporters in Eckville and elsewhere in Alberta and in Canada. His dismissal from teaching was not, as such, dismissal for advocating unconventional opinions or pursuing unconventional behaviour. He was not dismissed for introducing his ideas in the classroom. He was dismissed for introducing his ideas into the classroom to the *exclusion* of the materials required by the Alberta social studies curriculum and for going contrary to a school board directive that he treat his ideas as 'theory' and not as 'fact.' We could say that he was *technically* dismissed for using unconventional teaching materials. He was not *technically* dismissed for his off-the-job conduct or for holding the wrong opinions.

In our view, Keegstra's theory about the international Jewish conspiracy and his notion that the Holocaust did not happen show him to be ignorant and paranoid. Such views do not belong in a public school curriculum. As a citizen, however, he has a public right to espouse his beliefs and to present them in a public forum where they may be examined (and hopefully refuted).[6] In our view, the procedure of the school superintendent and the school board, once the nature of Keegstra's teaching was brought to their attention, was correct, namely 'Desist, or be dismissed.' *Note that Keegstra did not tolerate dissent.* There was, therefore, no rational way in which Keegstra's opinions *could* be proven wrong to him. In this sense, he could be regarded as an indoctrinator, who has no place in the classroom.

Case 37: The Teacher Who Brought Georgia Straight to Class

This is a Saskatchewan case that was widely publicized when it occurred and twice involved appeals to the Saskatchewan Court of Appeal. We therefore again depart from our usual practice of keeping the cases anonymous. Our facts are chiefly taken from *Margaret Temple Gordon v. The Board of the Moosomin School Unit No. 9*, a board of reference decision dated 10 April 1973. The case involved the use of unauthorized teaching materials that upset some members of the community and the school board.

On 4 October 1971 the school board dismissed Ms Margaret Gordon for 'gross misconduct.' On 28 October 1971, following a letter from Margaret Gordon, the minister of education ordered a committee of inquiry. On 31 December 1971, following receipt of the committee's report, the minister directed that the charge of gross misconduct be withdrawn and that the termination of contract be set aside.

The school board was upset. The board appealed to the Saskatchewan Court of Queen's Bench asking for an order of *certiorari* quashing the minister's order. The court dismissed the appeal on 21 February 1972. The school board appealed to the Court of Appeal. On 23 May 1972 the Court of Appeal upheld the decision of the lower court.

On 15 June 1972 the minister of education ordered that a board of reference be convened. The board made a preliminary finding that it had jurisdiction to determine if Margaret Gordon had a contract.

On 11 July 1972 the Court of Queen's Bench dismissed an appeal by the school board asking the court to overturn the preliminary finding of the board of reference. The school board appealed this dismissal to the Court of Appeal. On 23 November 1972 the Court of Appeal dismissed this appeal.

Finally, on 10 April 1973, the board of reference rendered its decision. The board held that Margaret Gordon was not guilty of gross misconduct but of 'a serious misjudgment as to what were acceptable standards in the community.' The board ordered that she be paid her salary from the date of dismissal to the date when her contract would otherwise have ended (31 December 1971).

What caused the dispute? Margaret Gordon had taught in the school district during 1970–1 and was hired again on a probationary certificate for the school year beginning in September 1971, although the certificate would have expired on 31 December 1971. Sometime during the first half of September, Ms Gordon brought to her grade 9 class a number of copies of *Georgia Straight*.[7] One of her pupils took a copy home, and the pupil's parents found in it an article entitled 'Dear Abby.' This article is named but not described in the board of reference decision, which gives no indication why this article should have been considered unsuitable for grade 9 boys to look at or read. (In the 'Dear Abby' article, a young woman described her sexual awakening, and some boys in Ms Gordon's class, naturally enough, boasted of reading it.) Parents in the community complained to the principal, the principal complained to the school superintendent, and in due course the school board passed a resolution (on 4 October 1971) dismissing Ms Gordon for 'gross misconduct.'

The statute under which she was dismissed was section 118(34) of the then School Act, which gives the school board power: 'to suspend or dismiss any teacher for gross misconduct, neglect of duty or refusal or neglect to obey any lawful order of the Board, and to forthwith transmit a written statement of the facts to the department.' The school board, in deciding that Ms Gordon was guilty of 'gross misconduct,' were following, as they thought, the definition of 'gross misconduct' given in *The Board of Trustees of the Edmonton School District v. Malati* (1970), 74 W.W.R. 435. In that case, the judge had stated that in the relevant section of the then Alberta School Act, '... the words "gross misconduct" mean conduct that involves a marked departure from the standards by which responsible and competent teachers habitually conduct themselves.' The school board considered that Ms Gordon's conduct was gross misconduct in this sense.

The minister of education, while holding that the article was not gross misconduct, still considered that the 'Dear Abby' article was not in good taste. The board of reference quoted his statement that the article overstepped the limits of good taste and suitability for school use. The board of reference agreed with his estimate. Perhaps it should be added that Ms Gordon had not received any instructions not to use *Georgia Straight* for discussion material in her class.

There might have been another element in the affair which also is not reflected in the board of reference and court decisions. The community where the school was located was a conservative community, while Ms Gordon lived in a neighbouring community that was regarded by the first community as 'dangerously radical.' Ms Gordon's use of *Georgia Straight* would have confirmed their suspicions!

Case 38: The Teacher Who Promoted Critical Enquiry

This case touches on the use of both unauthorized teaching material and unauthorized teaching methods, as well as the unauthorized teaching of controversial topics. It occurred in Prince Edward Island and did not reach the board of reference stage. It did become a public matter, although the then education minister rejected calls for a public inquiry.

In this affair, Mr Rick Morin, a language arts teacher, showed to his class a PBS documentary titled *Thy Kingdom Come, Thy Will Be Done*. It examined the fundamentalist movement in the United States. Morin asked his students to carry out a project involving each student interviewing someone concerning what religion meant to that person. Subsequently, he was prevented from continuing his teaching on the topic by the vice-principal. In due time, there was a public outcry and the school administrators, as well as the school board, supported the vice-principal's action. Prevented from dealing with the subject matter in class, Morin decided voluntarily to take a leave of absence until the controversy died down. His return to teaching was greeted by a student boycott, and he was given another leave of absence. A special committee was consequently appointed to study his teaching of religious subject matter. The committee reported that although the documentary was age-appropriate, the presentation was not. The school board placed him on extended leave for the rest of the school year as a non-disciplinary measure in the best interests of the students. Still unhappy about the censorship, Morin announced that he was leaving the province. It appears, however, that Morin has gone to court for a redress of his grievances and that his case remains unsettled.

Case 39: The Teacher Who Published Books

This case reveals the necessity for the teaching *profession* in each province to develop and enforce a clear set of professional standards. Such standards should govern the behaviour of schoolteachers in both public and private schools,[8] outside the classroom as well as in it. Malcolm Ross's behaviour in this case is much more a question of professional misconduct than it is of employee misconduct (Hill 1992; Givan 1992).

In this study, we have been looking primarily at how a certain idea in the law governing employee discipline allows communities, by way of locally elected school boards, to discipline public school teachers who deviate from local community standards of conduct. The legal link is, of course, the idea that the 'off-the-job' behaviour of an employee must not jeopardize the reputation of the employer among the employer's customers (who, for the school board, are the community that sends its children to the school). Much depends on whether or not the school board, as the employer, perceives that the teacher's behaviour threatens the reputation of the school board or the school system.

The school board has jurisdiction over the teacher only insofar as the teacher is an employee of the school board. The teacher's behaviour 'outside school' can thus properly come under the school board's jurisdiction only if (a) the teacher is acting on behalf of the school (for example, taking students on a field trip or representing the school at a conference or on a radio talk show); or (b) the teacher's action is such that it affects the reputation of the school or the school board's faith in the teacher's ability and willingness to perform his or her duties.

In denominational schools, the teacher's out-of-school behaviour must clearly be consistent with the values and doctrines of the school. The rule that the employee's conduct must not detract from the employer's reputation has been applied by the courts to permit denominational school boards (within limits) to dismiss teachers who violate the denomination's doctrines.

For public schools, this application of the rule is much less certain. Can, or ought, a school board censure or dismiss a public school teacher who publishes, on his own time, books whose form and content are repugnant or contrary to the values and ideals of the school curriculum that the school board is legally obliged to teach its students? Keegstra was fired eventually and cautiously by the school board for teaching *in class* contrary to the curriculum. But Malcolm Ross did not teach his doctrines in class.

If we do conclude that the school board had the right, or even the duty, to remove Ross on these grounds from his teaching position, then we have to face the question. Does this right or duty constitute a reasonable exception to the entrenched Charter right to freedom of expression of opinions? If it is not such a reasonable exception, then the dissident teacher has a defence against dismissal and there are limits to the expectation that the teacher be a role model for students.[9]

If a teacher is found guilty of *professional* misconduct, of course, such a finding gives a school board reasonable grounds to censure, perhaps even to dismiss, the teacher. If, further, the teacher loses his or her teaching certificate, the school board (pursuant to provincial legislation) is legally obliged to dismiss the teacher. School boards, however, are not themselves competent to assess professional misconduct; only the professional association (or, if there is none, the ministry of education) can do this. Decertification is also outside the competence of the school board.

The Offence, and Reactions Thereto[10]

Malcolm Ross, a teacher of mathematics at a Moncton, N.B., high school in School District/Division No. 15, with seventeen years' experience, published a series of books and pamphlets in which he argues that there exists an ancient and pervasive Jewish/Zionist plot against Christian civilization and Western values. This plot, he argues, is responsible for a dilution and corruption of Christian values even within the Christian church; an attack on the historicity of the Gospels; supporting the right of women to have abortion on demand; a socialist and communist attack on the rights of private property; a thrust towards collectivism and statism; the promotion of loose sexual habits leading to promiscuity and the spread of AIDS; and for a steady erosion of traditional family values. He blames all of this on a 'Jewish/Zionist' conspiracy. In defence of this view, he quotes from the tradition of anti-Judaism in Christianity itself. He begins with the Gospel writer who blamed 'the Jews' for the death of Jesus and proceeds through anti-Jewish statements of Saint John Chrysostom and Martin Luther to present-day anti-Semitic outbursts.[11] It is plain from the manner of his quotations that he accepts and approves this anti-Jewish tradition.[12]

His pamphlet against abortion is called *The Real Holocaust – the Attack on Unborn Children and Life Itself*. The title implies that the abortion campaign is more serious than the Nazis' mass destruction of European Jews, which is now referred to as 'The Holocaust.' The cover of this pamphlet has a picture worthy of the Nazi newspapers *Die Stuermer* and *Volkische Beobachtung*. A thickly bearded and big-nosed figure is shown advancing towards a place labelled 'Herod's abortion clinic.' The figure looks like a cross between Dr Morgentaler (the well-known advocate of abortion clinics) and the crafty Jews of Nazi propaganda. The reference to Herod alludes to the story of the massacre of the innocents in the Gospel according to Saint Matthew.

Ross documents his assertions by picking out those passages from his sources that confirm his ideas. His sources are mostly secondary or even tertiary; they are often 'anti-Semitic,' as we have noted above. He also cites passages from 'the enemy' (Jewish, Christian, and secular writers advocating ideas that Ross hates). Thus he weaves his tapestry of conspiracy (or what he calls 'the web of deceit'). Though his accusations are severe, he makes no attempt to examine the quality of his sources. He cites, for instance, 'The Protocols of the Elders of Zion' (Ross 1978: 43) but sidles around the evidence that this document is a Czarist-Russian adaptation of a document forged by a nineteenth-century Russian agent in France. The document is based on a satirical criticism of the regime of Napoleon III (Cohn 1967: 73). Given the severity of Ross's accusations, one would expect a fair and critical inquirer to consider the quality and history of the evidence. Ross's passion, however, does not allow him to do this.

Indeed, in chapter 7 of *Spectre of Power*, Ross goes beyond accusation to advocate a policy of systematic expulsion of Jews from society. He does this by citing with apparent approval various Christian writings, from anti-Jewish sayings in the Gospels to the anti-Jewish ravings of Saint John Chrysostom and Martin Luther, who advocated severe measures to punish the Jewish people for murdering Christ. These measures included forbidding Jews to hold any public office, requiring Jews to wear special distinguishing marks, publicly burning the Talmud, and deporting Jews (Ross 1987: 77). Cleverly, Ross does not openly recommend these actions, but the manner in which he writes gives the impression that he would eagerly take the opportunity to implement them, and would approve anyone who did. In short, Ross is advocating genocide.

The sequence of events are as follows:

In 1978, following Malcolm Ross's publication of *The Web of Deceit*, Mr Julius Israeli requested the District 15 School Board to fire Ross from his position as a teacher because of his anti-Jewish writings. In the same year, the Rev. Gary MacAuley also requested that Ross be dismissed. Noel Kinsella, chair of the Human Rights Commission, requested that

Ross's classroom teaching be supervised. The chair of the District 15 School Board stated that Ross could 'do what he wanted on his own time.' Time passed.

In 1983, Ross wrote a letter to the Fredericton newspaper, the *Daily Gleaner.* This letter evokes complaints that appeared in the public media. Ross also published *The Real Holocaust.* The school board again discussed Ross's publication.

1986: On 22 October, Ross wrote a letter outlining his views and it was published in the *Miramichi Leader.* The school board 'monitored' Ross's teaching and reviewed the materials that he used in his teaching. The New Brunswick attorney-general refused to lay a charge against Ross under the hate-literature sections of the Criminal Code; he thought that a conviction was unlikely.

1987: On 28 January the school board set up a review committee 'to review the possible impact of this issue upon the learning environment in school programs.' After fifty-nine interviews in four days, the committee reported in February to the school board. There was no evidence that Ross was teaching his beliefs or discussing them with staff or students. There was also no evidence that the publicity had an adverse effect on human relations in the school or between the school and the community. On 22 April 1987 (Hill 1992: 281; Mackenzie 1992: 349), Audrey Lampert, the only Jewish member of the school board, introduced two motions, one dealing with the public release of the review committee's report and one asking the school board to make a public statement rejecting all forms of racism and hate-mongering. No one seconded either motion and they failed. One school board member described Ross's opinions as well documented and accepted that Ross 'had done his homework' (Hill 1992: 281). In 1987, Ross also published *Spectre of Power.* The first part of this book describes the opposition to Ross and also cites persons in the Moncton area who Ross believed supported him and his views. According to Ross, some members of the local Roman Catholic establishment supported him.

The community was divided concerning Ross. The minister of Ross's own church records that some of the congregation supported Ross and that some wanted the minister to censure Ross (Steele 1992: 295). More persons publicly opposed Ross than supported him.

1988: On 16 March the school board sent a letter to Ross stating that his writings were 'controversial' and that any further publication or public discussions of his works would lead to greater disciplinary action, including the possibility of dismissal. The school board had finally concluded that Ross's behaviour was detrimentally affecting the school board's reputation.

On 21 April 1988, David Attis and others filed a complaint with the New Brunswick Human Rights Commission. The burden of the complaint was that the school board had deprived Jewish and other minority students of equal opportunity within the educational system. Through its inaction with regards to Ross, said the complainants, the school board had publicly condoned a racist and anti-Jewish role model and had fostered a climate in which students might more easily express anti-Jewish views. The complainants said that some students had made Nazi salutes to tease Jewish fellow students in the school playgrounds. Some Jewish students had begun to be afraid to go to school.

From April through September 1988, the school board denied the Human Rights Commission access to the District 15 files that were relevant to the affair. The commission also made two settlement offers to the school board; the school board rejected both.

1989: On 22 March, School District 15 adopted Policy 5006. This policy required school trustees and staff to provide an acceptable learning environment and to tolerate individual differences. On 20 September the reprimand was removed from Ross's file, and he was asked to abide by Policy 5006. In November, Ross appeared on a local television program to explain his views. On 30 November, the school board sent Ross a severe reprimand.

It seems also that 'at least one teacher' in New Brunswick attempted to file a charge against Ross under the New Brunswick Teachers' Association code of conduct but was told that there were no grounds for such a charge (Mackenzie 1992: 351). Indeed, the New Brunswick Teachers' Association was conspicuously inactive in this affair.

The Board of Inquiry
After its preliminary inquiry, the New Brunswick Human Rights Commission recommended that a full board of inquiry be appointed to investigate the complaint. The minister of labour followed this recommendation and appointed Professor Brian Bruce.

Ross (who was not formally a disputant in the case) tried to stop the inquiry. He argued that the board was biased. The courts rejected his arguments.[13]

In August 1991 the board of inquiry found in favour of the complainants.[14] Professor Bruce found that Ross's writings were anti-Semitic and that though Ross had not expressed his views in class, the result had been to foster an anti-Jewish climate. He therefore:

- ruled that School District 15 had discriminated against the complainants (the students, not David Attis) contrary to subsection 5(1) of the Human Rights Act;
- directed the school board to place Malcolm Ross on immediate leave without pay for eighteen months, appointing him to a non-teaching position if within that period one became available for which he was qualified, and terminating his employment at the end of the eighteen months if no non-teaching position were found;
- directed the school board to terminate Malcolm Ross's employment immediately if during his leave of absence or during his employment in a non-teaching position, he continued his publications or publicly mentioned a Jewish Zionist conspiracy or attacked followers of the Jewish religion; and
- made certain directions to the Department of Education.

The Appeal to the Courts
In December 1991 the decision of the board of inquiry was appealed for judicial review to the Court of Queen's Bench. Justice Paul S. Creaghan held:[15]

- that removing Malcolm Ross from the classroom did in fact impinge on his freedom of conscience and religion and his freedom of thought, belief, opinion, and expression, contrary to section 2 of the Charter of Rights and Freedoms;
- that these limitations on Ross's freedoms were demonstrably justifiable in a free and democratic society and were therefore saved by section 1 of the Charter;
- that the order requiring Ross's employment to be terminated if he published his views was beyond the jurisdiction of the board of inquiry and could not be saved by section 1; and
- that the directions to the Department of Education be removed.

In a word, Mr Justice Creaghan held that Ross's views and publications justified his removal from his teaching position. He did not decide whether or not Ross should be dismissed from a non-teaching position with the school board.

The decision of the Court of Queen's Bench was duly appealed to the New Brunswick Court of Appeal. On 20 December 1993, in a two-to-one decision, the court reversed all of the board's instructions and upheld Ross's right to publish his books without losing his teaching position.[16]

Chief Justice Hoyt, with Justice Angers concurring, held that the board

of inquiry's order requiring Ross to be removed from teaching and further forbidding him to publish his views while employed by the school
board violated his rights under subsections 2(a) and 2(b) of the Charter.
As Hoyt put it:

The issue is somewhat easier to state than to resolve. Is this sanction demonstrably
justifiable in a free and democratic society? The issue is whether an individual's
freedom of expression can prevail against the fear that there will be a public perception that Mr Ross' discriminatory remarks directed against a religious or eth-
nic minority are being condoned. The discrimination here is aggravated because
the minority is one that has been historically targeted for discrimination and
because the author of the discrimination is a teacher, who might be considered a
role model to students.[17]

Chief Justice Hoyt argued that it is well established in law that teachers may be disciplined for off-duty activities. None of the cases cited
raised any allegations of Charter violation. Applying the test set out in
R. v. Oakes,[18] the court must determine whether or not 'the silencing of
Mr Ross' anti-Semitic views is such an important public objective that
his constitutional rights to freedom of expression and speech can be
overridden.'[19] Ross did not attempt to further his views in the classroom. The board of inquiry made no connection between Ross's
expressed views and any offensive remarks directed to the student complainants:

Remarks made by school-children in the playground of another school are, in my
opinion, too tenuous to found such a restriction. If the evidence disclosed that Mr
Ross' remarks sparked or even were used to legitimize the offensive remarks made
in the schoolyard, perhaps the sanction in the order would be appropriate.[20]

Though teachers 'do indeed enjoy a high status in our society and have a
unique opportunity to influence youthful minds,' there is nothing to suggest that Ross used his teaching position to advance his views.
    Chief Justice Hoyt concluded, therefore, the violation of Ross's consti-
tutional freedoms did not meet the requirement of being 'a specific purpose so pressing and substantial' and that the constitutional guarantee
should not be overridden:

To hold otherwise would, in my view, have the effect of condoning the suppression of views that are not politically popular at any given time. Perhaps I am giving

too much weight to the 'slippery slope' fear expressed by Dickson C.J.C. in *R. v. Keegstra* (1990), 61 C.C.C. (3d) 1 at p. 51, [1990] 3 S.C.R. 697, 1 C.R. (4th) 129. In my opinion, however, the denial of an individual's freedom of expression can only occur in the clearest of cases. In my view, the evidence does not disclose that this case meets that test.[21]

Mr Justice Ryan emphatically dissented. He drew attention to the board's findings that Ross's views were prejudicial and discriminatory. He emphasized the public school teacher as a public servant who has a duty to be a role model of tolerance in accordance with the values of the Charter. He decided that not only should the board's order dismissing Ross from employment as a teacher be upheld but that the order forbidding him while in public employment to publish his views should be restored. Justice Ryan argued as follows:[22]

Ross, as a schoolteacher, is a role model to pupils in an elementary school, inside and outside the classroom. He teaches developing minds. He is a role model to children and yet, outside the classroom, he advocates prejudice. He urges discrimination. He publicly proclaims outside the class room that which would not be tolerable if said in the class-room. He is a servant of the public. In my opinion, a teacher cannot discriminate, in the sense of show bias, inside the class-room or publicly, in such an important area as is this target in the *Human Rights Act* of this province.

Though the right of freedom of expression is deeply rooted in the Canadian constitution and rooted even more deeply by the Charter, that right is not absolute. The right to freedom from discrimination is also implicit in section 2 of the Charter:

Is the competing value, that of prohibiting discrimination, sufficiently consequential in this case that the rights of free speech and freedom of religion should be qualified as ordered by the board of enquiry? I am of the opinion that they can be and should be, similar to situations where the right runs head-on into laws dealing with libel and slander, sedition and blasphemy, restrictions on the press in order to ensure a fair trial or to protect minors or victims of sexual assault.

He thought that the Court of Queen's Bench should have also retained the ban on Ross's publishing his views. He referred to the potential cumulative effect of Ross's public statements made outside the classroom. Then he continued:

A balance must be struck between Ross' freedoms, the victims' freedoms and an educational system which teaches impartiality and does not espouse prejudice, bigotry or bias. A teacher teaches. He is a role model. He also teaches by example. Children learn by example. Malcolm Ross teaches by example. He is a role model who publishes and promotes prejudice. This is wrong ...

As contended by the Human Rights Commission, the rights and freedoms specifically guaranteed by the *Charter*, including those of speech and religion, may be measured against the underlying values and principles of a free and democratic society which are their very genesis, and limited where to do so furthers those values and principles. Included in these are the inherent dignity of the human being, commitment to social justice and equality, and respect for cultural and group identity. To give free reign to the asserted freedom of speech and religion of Ross would be to trample upon these underlying values and principles, themselves having the status of entrenched rights under the *Charter* and in international law.

Ross remains free to leave public employment and engage fully in the exercise of his freedom of speech and religion without restraint. A restriction, therefore, that he cease his discriminatory conduct is a justifiable infringement. It is not absolute.

Justice Ryan, therefore, would dismiss Ross's appeal and would allow, in part, the cross-appeal by David Attis et al. and reinstate the ban on Ross's publishing his views while employed by the school board.

Aftermath

In 1992 (after the decision of the Court of Queen's Bench but before the appeal to the New Brunswick Court of Appeal), the *University of New Brunswick Law Journal* devoted a special issue to the Ross case. The various articles explore the complexity of the case and set Ross's books within the historical context of Western and Christian anti-Semitism.

Some comments by Leonidas Hill (1992: 282) in that *Journal* seem very apposite here. On the evidence of the board of inquiry's own summary of Ross's views, these views are not merely 'controversial or discriminatory' (as the board had characterized them). Hill says flatly, 'They are false.' Then he goes on:

It is nonsense, then, to say that he [Ross] had documented his views and done his homework. Such a claim is based on the view that reading the writings of anyone and citation of their works is as good as reading and citing anyone else. That is the method of Keegstra and Zundel. Critical scholarly method makes it possible to separate legitimate and credible sources from falsifiers and liars. Ross did not and does not do this. Because he does not, he violates the canons of his profession. Professionals have qualified and are licenced for a job, but the license can be taken away, or they can be fired without losing their license. A teacher may be controversial for many reasons. But if a teacher propagates manifestly vicious falsehoods, that is not controversial. It is unprofessional.

He goes on to observe:

[The board of inquiry] report illustrates nicely the danger of confusing professional conduct with the conduct possibly expected by the community. A teacher's falsification of what is known to be true is rather different from the argument in the report that teachers are role models and that their off-duty behaviour should be consonant with the values of the community.

Hill's comment highlights an ambiguity in the notion that teachers should be role models. Should the teacher be a role model of the values *of* the community, namely of those values to which the community supposedly adheres? The notion that a teacher should uphold the reputation of the school in the community tends to emphasize the teacher's role as a model of the community's values. Or, should the teacher be a role model *for* the community of values that the community ought to uphold, though in fact it does not? A teacher should uphold ideals of truthfulness, rationality, and critical scholarship even though no one else in the community, including the school board, is aware of such ideals. The profession, as a whole, should support each teacher in supporting these values.

Appeal to the Supreme Court of Canada
The Ross dispute was finally dealt with by the Supreme Court of Canada, whose judgment was delivered on 3 April 1996.[23] In this judgment, the Supreme Court firmly took the responsibility of a public school teacher for his or her out-of-school conduct well beyond the duties of an employee to the employer, to the very nature of the role of the teacher as a servant of society. The employer/employee relationship remains relevant: it provides the occasion which activates the role of the public school teacher, and may set some of the expectations of that role. However, the role of schoolteacher is not circumscribed by the employer/employee relationship. It carries with it duties to the general society as well. In particular, a schoolteacher who is hired by an agency of public education established by provincial legislation is clearly expected to act at all times,

in school and out of school, in a manner consistent with the values of the Canadian Charter of Rights and Freedoms. Such, at least, this decision seems to us to imply.

The legal issues discussed in the judgment concerned civil rights, judicial review, administrative law, the Charter, and freedom of religion, but we need not examine all this here. The Supreme Court restored the judgment of the New Brunswick Court of Queen's Bench, which had upheld clauses 2(a), 2(b), and 2(c) of the order of the board of inquiry. These clauses had required the school board to place Ross on a leave of absence without pay for eighteen months, appoint him to a non-teaching position if one became available during that period, and terminate his employment if at the end of the eighteen-month period he had not been offered and accepted a non-teaching position. Clause 2(d) of the order had been quashed by the Court of Queen's Bench. This clause had required the school board to fire Ross if he published or wrote anti-Semitic materials either during the 18-month period or while employed in a non-teaching position. The Supreme Court agreed with the Court of Queen's Bench that this clause violated the Charter of Rights and Freedoms and could not be justified as a reasonable limitation on those rights in a free and democratic society. The Supreme Court thus did *not* agree with the dissenting judge of the Court of Appeal, who had held that Ross should not be employed even in a non-teaching position.

The Supreme Court began by dealing with various issues of administrative law and judicial review, including the scope of the board of inquiry's jurisdiction. The outcome of this part of the judgment was to confirm the jurisdiction of the board of inquiry except where the board's order was incompatible with the Charter of Rights and Freedoms – for then the board would be exceeding its jurisdiction and its order would be null and void.

The Supreme Court also upheld the finding of the board that Ross's conduct out of school had 'poisoned the educational environment at the school and created an environment in which Jewish students were forced to confront racist sentiment,' and that Ross's continued employment had 'signalled the School Board's toleration of his anti-Semitic conduct and compromised its ability to provide discrimination-free educational services' (para. 34). The Supreme Court held that such a finding was a finding of fact well within the competence of the board and not patently unreasonable on the face of the evidence presented to the board.

In discussing the board's finding, the court had much to say about the role of teachers as exemplars of the moral values of the school system and of the community (paras. 42–5):

A school is a communication centre for a whole range of values and aspirations of a society. In large part, it defines the values that transcend society through the educational medium. The school is an arena for the exchange of ideas and must, therefore, be premised upon principles of tolerance and impartiality so that all persons within the school environment feel equally free to participate ...

Teachers are inextricably linked to the integrity of the school system. Teachers occupy positions of trust and influence, and exert considerable influence over their students as a result of their positions. The conduct of a teacher bears directly upon the community's perception of the ability of the teacher to fulfill such a position of trust and influence, and upon the community's confidence in the public school system as a whole ...

By their conduct, teachers ... must be perceived to uphold the values, beliefs and knowledge sought to be transmitted by the school system. The conduct of a teacher is evaluated on the basis of his or her position, rather than whether the conduct occurs within the classroom or beyond. Teachers are seen by the community to be the medium for the educational message and because of the community position they occupy, they are not able to 'choose which hat they will wear on what occasion' ...[24]

It is on the basis of the position of trust and influence that we hold the teacher to high standards both on and off duty, and it is an erosion of these standards that may lead to a loss in the community of confidence in the public school system. I do not wish to be understood as advocating an approach that subjects the entire lives of teachers to inordinate scrutiny on the basis of more onerous moral standards of behaviour. This could lead to a substantial invasion of the privacy rights and fundamental freedoms of teachers. However, where a 'poisoned' environment within the school system is traceable to the off-duty conduct of a teacher that is likely to produce a corresponding loss of confidence in the teacher and the system as a whole, then the off-duty conduct of the teacher is relevant.

These are strong and important words.

The Supreme Court held that the order of the board had genuinely infringed the Charter rights to freedom of expression and freedom of religion to which Ross was entitled. However, both these rights are subject to such reasonable limitations as are demonstrably justifiable in a free and democratic society (section 1 of the Charter). In deciding what such reasonable limitations are, the court should be guided (para. 77)

... by the values and principles essential to a free and democratic society which I believe embody, to name but a few, respect for the inherent dignity of the human person, commitment to social justice and equality, accommodation of a wide variety of beliefs, respect for cultural and group identity, and faith in social and political institutions which enhance the participation of individuals and groups in society. The underlying values and principles of a free and democratic society are the genesis of the rights and freedoms guaranteed by the charter and the ultimate standard against which a limit on a right or freedom must be shown, despite its effect, to be reasonable and demonstrably justified.

These are the words of Chief Justice Dicson in *R. v. Oakes*, [1986] 1 S.C.R. 103, at. p. 136.

In assessing the circumstances within which the limits on Ross's rights are to be considered, Mr Justice La Forest distinguished three contexts, the 'educational context,' the 'employment context,' and the 'anti-Semitism context.' The educational context included the important fact that the schools at which Ross taught were elementary schools (paras. 82–3):

Young children are especially vulnerable to the messages conveyed by their teachers. They are less likely to make an intellectual distinction between comments a teacher makes in the school and those the teacher makes outside the school. They are, therefore, more likely to feel threatened and isolated by a teacher who makes comments that denigrate personal characteristics of a group to which they belong. Furthermore, they are unlikely to distinguish between falsehoods and truth and more likely to accept derogatory views espoused by a teacher. The importance of ensuring an equal and discrimination free educational environment, and the perception of fairness and tolerance in the classroom are paramount in the education of young children. This helps foster self-respect and acceptance by others.

It is this context that must be invoked when balancing the respondent's freedom to make discriminatory statements against the right of the children in the School Board 'to be educated in a school system that is free from bias, prejudice and intolerance,' a right that is underscored by s. 5(1) of the Act and entrenched in s. 15 of the Charter.

The employment context, said the judge, is relevant to the degree that the employer, in this case the state and the school board, has the duty to ensure that public functions are carried out in ways which do not undermine public trust and confidence. Hence there is an obligation on the teacher, as an employee, to act so as to avoid such undermining.

The anti-Semitism context was the third context which the New Brunswick Human Rights Commission had invited the court to consider. La Forest J. quoted from the commission's factum (para. 86):

After Auschwitz it is simply not feasible to consider the constitutional values of freedom of expression and freedom of religion where these are proclaimed to shield anti-Semitic conduct, without contemplating the centrality of that ideology to the scourge of death and destruction which swept across Europe during the era of the Third Reich.

The judge considered that Ross's publications, having been assessed by the board as attacking the truthfulness, integrity, dignity, and motives of Jewish persons, hardly (para. 91)

... reflect an adherence to the principle of equality, valuing all divergent views equally and recognizing the contribution that a wide range of beliefs may make in the search for truth. [Therefore] to give protection to views that attack and condemn the views, beliefs, and practices of others is to undermine the principle that all views deserve equal protection and muzzles the voice of truth.

The judge concluded that Ross's views also undermined democratic process and denied to Jews the respect for dignity and equality which upheld the ideal of freedom of religion. He concluded (para. 94):

Where the manifestations of an individual's right or freedom are incompatible with the very values sought to be upheld in the process of undertaking a s. 1 analysis, then, an attenuated level of s. 1 justification is appropriate.

In other words, since Ross's ideas menaced the very freedom of expression and freedom of religion which he was calling upon to defend his right to advocate his ideas, limitations on his rights required very little justification in order to be upheld as legal. If there were any reasonable grounds for terminating his employment as a teacher, such termination would be upheld.

Was there a reasonable connection between Ross's publication of his anti-Semitic tracts and the harm which would result from such publication if Ross were allowed to continue as a teacher? The judge said (para. 101):

... it is sufficient that the Board found it 'reasonable to anticipate' that there was a causal relationship between the respondent's conduct and the harm – the poisoned educational environment. In my view, this finding must depend upon the respondent's maintaining a teaching position. The reason that it is possible to 'reasonably anticipate' the causal relationship in this appeal is because of the significant influence teachers exert on their students and the stature associated with the role of a teacher. It is thus necessary to remove the respondent from his teaching position to ensure that no influence of this kind is exerted by him upon his students and to ensure that the educational services are discrimination-free. The Order seeks to remove the respondent from his teaching position through clauses 2(a), (b) and (c). These clauses are rationally connected to the objective of the Order.

The judge found, however, that this rational connection did not support clause 2(d) of the Order. The school board's employment of Ross in a non-teaching position would not endorse Ross's views.

The judge's final summary was the following (para. 111):

In my assessment, the evidence reveals that the School Board discriminated within the meaning of sec. 5(1) of the Act, with respect to educational services available to the public. The continued employment of the respondent contributed to an invidiously discriminatory or 'poisoned' educational environment, as established by the evidence and the Board's finding that it was 'reasonable to anticipate' that the respondent's writings and statements influenced the anti-Semitic sentiment. In my opinion, this finding is necessarily linked to the finding that the respondent's statements are 'highly public' and that he is a notorious anti-Semite, as well as the supported view that public school teachers assume a position of influence and trust over their students and must be seen to be impartial and tolerant.

This last sentence is important. Besides being a teacher, Ross was 'notorious' and 'highly public.' Had he published nothing, not appeared on TV, or written to the newspapers, the entire dispute would never have arisen. However, would it have arisen if he had been a school janitor rather than a schoolteacher?

In Summary: The Basic Issue
There are two basic issues here. One is the issue raised by Hill, namely the professional duty of a teacher to uphold standards of truthfulness, rationality, and critical scholarship. This puts the onus of judgment on the professional association. School boards are not competent either

factually or juridically to assess professional standards. Only the profession can do this.

The second issue is that Ross, unlike Keegstra, seems to have kept his views out of the classroom. Do public school teachers have the right to advance whatever opinions they wish, even bigoted ones that could trigger public hostility against a minority group? Do they have this right even if those opinions and putative effects are contrary to the values and beliefs they are expected to inculcate in class, provided that they advance those opinions only outside the school on their own time, as private individuals? Does the position of public school teachers as role models require that their opinions and behaviours *outside* school be consistent with the values and beliefs that they are expected to teach *in* school?

Does dismissing such a deviant teacher as Ross offend against the basic principle of freedom of opinion that allows dissent to be expressed without penalty? Is such dismissal a reasonable limit (such as the laws against defamation and hate propaganda) on freedom of expression? If it is a reasonable limit in Ross's case, are there distinctions that should be made regarding differences between the teacher's opinions and the curriculum? Ross's views tie into a tradition of anti-Semitism which has had the outcome of systematized mass murder on a very wide scale.[25] What if Ross were a mathematics teacher who outside school published books advocating the hypothesis of special creation, while the school curriculum required the teaching of evolutionary biology? Would Ross's dissent then require him to be censured or dismissed? We do not think so.[26]

Given the nature of Ross's uncritical and paranoid belief in an international Jewish/Zionist conspiracy, the affinities of his belief to anti-Semitism as a political ideology, and the incompatibility of that ideology with the fundamental values set out in the Charter of Rights and Freedoms (which public schools may be expected to uphold), we judge that Ross should be dismissed from his position as a public school teacher. Furthermore, he should lose his teacher's certificate. His world-view and the manner in which he holds and advocates his world-view deprive him of any moral right to claim professional standing as an educator *in a society committed to the values set out in the Charter.*

In fact, Ross has done worse than the previous paragraph indicates. In chapter 7 of *Spectre of Power*, as we have already noted, he has in effect approved and advocated a policy of social denigration and deportation, if not quite extermination, of Jews. If this does not fall into the crime of wilfully promoting hatred against an identifiable group (Criminal Code, sec. 319[2]), it escapes doing so only by a hair's breadth.

Removing Ross from his teaching position would not prevent Ross from continuing to advocate his views. It would, however, prevent the school board *and the school system* from appearing to condone views at such variance with the basic values of the Charter.[27]

Because Ross's publications are inconsistent with the basic values which the public school is expected to inculcate and support, the school board in this case is competent justly to dismiss Ross. The board of inquiry, in our view, did rightly in censuring the District 15 School Board and ordering it to dismiss Ross from his teaching position. The New Brunswick Teachers' Association, as the professional association for anglophone teachers in New Brunswick, ought to have investigated Ross and removed his professional standing.

Ross's views are permeated by anti-Semitism. Anti-Semitism, especially the myth of the pervasive Jewish world conspiracy to subvert true values (i.e., whatever the person asserting the existence of the conspiracy holds dear), is not an ordinary political opinion nor an ordinary criticism of present-day society. It is a persistent idea that has led again and again to pogroms, to mass murder, and to acts of extreme and vicious cruelty (Cohn 1967: 251). Along with similar demonologies, it dehumanizes its victims and allows its believers to vent their own viciousness upon those victims. It is, indeed, a malignant cultural virus that should be suffered to exist only in such small amounts as are necessary to immunize the body politic against it. We need, therefore, some persons like Ross to remind us of the existence of this virus and to prompt us to protect ourselves against it by recalling its falsity.

Case 6, 'A Conflict of Values and Community Factions,' described in chapter 3 as an affair involving the teacher's character, also falls under the present heading. Since Mr M. had conducted Bible readings in his classroom without the school board's approval and in spite of the principal's instruction that he desist until such approval had been obtained, this Saskatchewan case falls under the categories of unauthorized teaching of controversial subjects and ideological teaching. This does not seem, however, from the board of reference decision, to have been more than a symptom of the 'character' issue.

Contentious Conduct as Citizens

The next set of cases involves teachers who exercised their usual rights as citizens in ways that some people, including the school board, found contentious in some manner. Some of these are serious, others are not. Each involves a balancing of the teacher's rights as a citizen against the teacher's duties as an employee.

Two cases from chapter 3 should first be noted: case 4, 'The Teacher Who Disagreed'; and case 7, 'The Teacher Who Supported a Student Strike.' Both of these involved questions of freedom of expression, especially the criticism of school policy. In case 4, the board of reference observed that the teacher had attempted to present his opinions through all of the proper channels and that alleged misconducts of insubordination and non-cooperation had not occurred. The judge did chide the teacher, however, for the public outburst which he had given. In case 7, the board of reference, in a two-to-one decision, held that the teacher's actions had destroyed the essential trust in his advice required by the school board and therefore justified his dismissal.

Case 40: The Teacher Who Wrote a Letter

This case from British Columbia involves the question of freedom of expression in the criticism of school policy. There were special conditions in the community, however, that made the teacher's action especially sensitive. Since describing these special conditions in detail would identify the community, we shall have to be rather vague concerning them.

Ms N. taught art during the 1977–8 school year. Because of personnel problems at the school, the principal advised her on 31 May 1978 that she would no longer be the art teacher but would be given the position of full-time substitute teacher in both elementary and secondary schools. Ms N. was very upset at this, promptly wrote a strong and defamatory letter to the chairman of the school board, and sent copies of this letter to, among others, the British Columbia Teachers' Federation, members of the local government, and other local notables.

The school board suspended and then dismissed Ms N. for misconduct on the grounds that her letter would adversely affect public confidence in the school board and the school administration, a confidence that the schools in this particular community had worked hard to gain and to maintain. The school board had to act on the issue and had to be *seen* to be acting on the issue.

Ms N. appealed the dismissal. Eighteen teachers petitioned the school board to reconsider the dismissal on compassionate grounds.

The board of reference (decision dated 10 August 1978) heard the case during 8–9 August 1978. The board of reference concluded, without giving reasons, that Ms N. had committed misconduct but that dismissal was too severe and that other disciplinary action should have been taken. They allowed the appeal and ordered reinstatement. At this time, the board of reference did not have jurisdiction to vary the decision of the school board.

The school board appealed this decision to the B.C. Supreme Court. On 24 November 1978 the Supreme Court found that the board of reference's decision was within the jurisdiction of the board of reference and that the evidence heard by the board of reference had been admissible. The appeal by the school board was accordingly dismissed.

Case 41: The Teacher Who Posted a Notice

This board of arbitration decision from Newfoundland involves the issue of freedom of expression and criticism of the school board by one of its employees during a labour negotiation.

The school board imposed on the teacher a three-day suspension for posting a letter in teachers' common-rooms in a number of schools within the school district. The letter was intended to stir up fellow teachers regarding their union's efforts to have a greater say in the assignment of specific teacher duties. The employer alleged that, although any teacher has the right to communicate with fellow members of his or her bargaining unit concerning working conditions, such communication does not have to be inflammatory and beyond the bounds of propriety, nor need it ridicule or sweepingly denounce the competence of the school board.

In examining the allegations, the board of arbitration noted that the case arose at a time when the employer and the teachers were engaged in negotiation. During this process, each side of the adversarial process must be as free as possible, though there would necessarily be some constraints. Within this context, the letter could not be regarded in a way that justified disciplinary measures. Though mildly pejorative, it did not damage the effectiveness of the school board and merely pointed out what was true. The employer had the onus to establish misconduct on the part of grievor. Having failed to show that the letter was offensive, inflammatory, embarrassing or improper, the employer had breached the collective agreement which allowed the imposition of discipline only for just cause. Accordingly, the board of arbitration ordered that the grievor be reinstated with reimbursement for salary and benefits lost.

Case 42: The Principal Who Became an M.L.A.

This case, from Alberta, concerns the public activities of the teacher. These public activities were both legal and commendable. They gave rise to a conflict between the teacher's roles as employee of the school board and as citizen.

In this case, the appellant, Mr P., a principal and a teacher, had been elected Member of the Legislative Assembly. On the grounds that as an M.L.A., he could not do his job as principal, the school board desired to terminate his designation.[28] Mr P. appealed.

The school board did have a written policy requiring a principal elected as an M.L.A. to forfeit or terminate a designation as principal. This policy, however, had not been adopted before Mr P. was nominated as a candidate for the M.L.A.'s position and duly elected.

The judge held that a policy requiring a principal elected as an M.L.A. to forfeit or terminate a *designation* as principal did not violate the Charter of Rights. The principal still enjoyed the status of a teacher on leave without pay and would regain his full pay as a teacher when the leave ended, namely when his time as M.L.A. was over and he returned to full-time teaching.

Had the school board's policy been in place before Mr P. had been nominated, the school board would have acted reasonably in terminating the designation (though not the contract). As it was, however, the facts revealed a failure of understanding between Mr P. and the school board.

The judge, therefore, ordered that Mr P. be reinstated as principal and that he be given leave of absence without pay for the duration of his current term of office as M.L.A.. The judge observed, approvingly, that Mr P. was not asking for pay.

The judge also held that the board of reference was competent to decide whether or not school board policies infringed the Charter of Rights: the board of reference was a 'court of competent jurisdiction' within the meaning of section 24(1) of the Charter.

This judgment contains an extensive discussion of the role of a principal, and how this role is affected by the principal's work outside the school, including being an M.L.A.

Case 43: The Teacher Who Bought a House from an Old Believer and Upset the Community

This case[29] is particularly interesting because it deals with the degree of responsibility that a school board owes to the local electorate, and the degree to which a school board may reasonably bend to community pressures. Within the class of 'Contentious Conduct as Citizens,' we could put it under the subclass of 'Other.'

Mr Riabov was hired in October 1983 to teach a Russian-language program at a school in Plamondon, Alberta. This was done in response to a request by members of a nearby community of Old Believers who had decided that Mr Riabov (himself not an Old Believer) was a fit person to conduct the program. His contract ran from October 1983 to the end of June 1984. At the end of July 1984, the school superintendent, believing that all was well between Mr Riabov and the Old Believers, offered Mr Riabov another contract, this time for a full school year from 30 August 1984 to 26 June 1985.

About two hours after the new contract was executed, the superintendent learned that Mr Riabov was no longer acceptable to the Old Believer community. On the first day of school, instead of the expected enrolment of 65 to 70 children in Mr Riabov's class, only 20 to 25 children were enrolled. Several Old Believers gave the school principal a list of 41 children who were not to attend Mr Riabov's classes. The school board met on 5 September 1985 and decided that if the enrolment reached 60 per cent of the Old Believer children attending the school, the board would continue the program. (During the previous year, the enrolment had been 100 per cent.)

At the time of the school board's meeting, the board apparently knew only that there was some dissension within the Old Believer community but did not know the details of the dispute.

At the next meeting of the board, on 1 October 1984, the board learned that only 24 or 25 out of a possible 67 students were enrolled in Mr Riabov's class. The board decided, following the superintendent's recommendation, to terminate the Russian-language program at Plamondon School. The school board's reasons were that continuing the program for so few children would be too expensive and that placing the other Old Believer pupils elsewhere in the school would be too disruptive. The board also resolved to eliminate Mr Riabov's teaching position on the grounds that the Russian-language program was being discontinued.

The board, through the superintendent, then wrote to Mr Riabov suspending him from 3 October to 3 November 1984 and paying his salary for that period only. The letter stated:

The reason for termination of your contract is that the Board has determined your position is redundant to the needs of the system due to discontinuance of the Russian Language Program at Plamondon School.[30]

The letter did not refer to the reasons for the discontinuance.

The dispute in the community arose when Mr Riabov, in March 1984, purchased a house in the community from an Old Believer, Mr Karayel. Mr Karayel insisted that the purchase be kept secret because (as Mr Riabov, according to his own testimony, was unaware) the Old Believers prohibited sale of their houses to persons who were not Old Believers. When it came time for Mr Riabov to take possession of the house, Mr Karayel had to be ejected under the threat of legal proceedings. When the sale of the house became known in the village, during July 1984, there was an uproar and a series of meetings. The community demanded that Mr Karayel repurchase the house, but he did not. Mr Karayel threatened that Mr Riabov would lose his job.

The Old Believer community was divided, but the majority came to believe that it was undesirable that Mr Riabov teach their children.

The judge said:

Essentially the situation was one which could be reproduced, with appropriate changes in the facts, so that any group of parents in any school district, determined without any reason related to the teacher's competence to cause him to be dismissed from his teaching position, could achieve that result by refusing to allow their children to attend his classes.

In my view, a board in terminating a teacher's contract of employment in those circumstances, and specifically in the circumstances of this case, cannot be said to comply with its duty, imposed by s. 89(2) of the Act, to 'act reasonably' ...

In my view, redundancy is a relevant consideration that would justify a school board in deciding that at the end of the school year the contract of employment with a teacher does not, despite s. 84, continue in force from year to year. But, during the course of the 'complete school year' represented by 'a contract that terminates at the conclusion of that school year' (s. 87)(1), it would be an abuse of statutory power if a school board were to terminate such a contract on the basis of an irrelevant consideration such as a redundancy created by a decision of the school board itself, particularly a redundancy for which the teacher is not responsible and which is in no way a product of his own teaching incompetence. Termination in such circumstances cannot be said to be reasonable. Nor may the Board of Reference confirm a termination decided upon in such circumstances.

I reach the same conclusion for a second reason. A board which declares redundancy and terminates a teacher's employment because a group of parents have withdrawn their children from the teacher's classes cannot be said to have acted reasonably unless that withdrawal is based on a belief of the parents that the teacher is incompetent *as a teacher*, and the school board is satisfied of the existence of such incompetence, as is the Board of Reference in the event of an appeal. When I speak of 'incompetence' I include not only the inability to impart knowledge but also immorality in relation to students and other conduct in the classroom that adversely affects the ability to teach children. If the position of the parents is based on their disapproval of some aspect of the teacher's private life, such as his lawful commercial dealings with another person, his marital status or his politics or if their disapproval is based on any of the grounds of discrimination prohibited by s. 15 of the *Canadian Charter of Rights and Freedoms*, the termination by the school board in such circumstances could not be said to be reasonable, and a Board of Reference could not be expected to condone the termination. Any other view of the matter would tolerate rule of the school by the mob, and tyranny over teachers by unelected groups, rather than administration by a school board duly elected by democratic process, with certain express powers and duties provided for in s. 72 of the *School Act* and the overarching implied duty to administer the affairs of the school system rationally and fairly.

The judge held that the just remedy was to terminate the contract (which was, after all, only for the one year) at 30 June 1985 and to pay Mr Riabov for that period. Reinstatement was by now impossible, so that the money award was the appropriate remedy.

The board of reference decision was delivered on 10 July 1985.

Note that the issue here was not whether the teacher had misconducted himself but whether the school board's action was reasonable. The judge did not think it reasonable that a competent teacher should lose his job merely because parents in the community disapproved of his private actions outside the classroom. 'Mob rule' was not acceptable.

Case 44: The Teacher Who Defied a Worldly Court

In our study of teacher discipline in Manitoba, we found only one board of arbitration case involving contentious conduct as a citizen (though we did find several ministerial disciplinary committee cases involving anti-war or pro-German expressions in class and out of class during 1939–45). The single case that we did find occurred during the years 1980–5 and involved religious arguments. This case could be said to involve questions of freedom of expression and freedom of association, as well as being in the class of 'Other.'

Mr M.'s employment was terminated by the school board after his second thirty-day imprisonment for contempt of court. Mr M. had violated a court order forbidding him to visit his wife and children in their residence following a serious marital dispute and subsequent divorce. After the first imprisonment, Mr M. was informed officially that he could return to class on the condition that the incident did not recur. Mr M. violated the order allegedly on religious grounds – that he had a God-given right to visit his wife and children and that a worldly court could not dissolve a holy marriage. The board of arbitration found dismissal an overly severe penalty but imposed suspension without pay for about nine months. The case was then brought before the Manitoba Court of Appeal, where Mr M. was exonerated and reinstated with full pay.

Case 45: The Teacher Who Had AIDS

This case also falls under the label of 'Other.'[31] It has been reported in the newspapers.

Eric Smith, a Nova Scotia teacher who carries the AIDS virus, was reassigned out of his grade 6 class to a non-teaching job. His condition became public because of an information leak at a medical clinic near his home. It was this breach of confidentiality that prompted him to advise his teaching supervisors of his condition. When news of his condition became public, parents in the county threatened a boycott until finally the Nova Scotia government hired Smith as an AIDS consultant. Subsequently, he prepared for litigation until he was advised by his medical doctor to take a year's sick leave because of stress-related migraine headaches. Apparently, he received threats of violence, and though parents understand that there is no likelihood of children contracting AIDS from Smith, they remain opposed to his return to the classroom. A further consideration is that as a homosexual he is not acceptable to them as a teacher for their children. Because of his illness, Smith has given up his battle to return to teaching.

For Denominational Cause

The question of denominational rights or denominational cause produces special concerns. It arises when teachers at a denominational school act in ways that are legal, according to the general society, but offend special tenets of the religious denomination for whose school the teachers are working. Denominational rights are specially protected in the Constitution Act (formerly the British North America Act), 1867.

In case 46, denominational rights challenged the jurisdiction of the board of reference. In case 47, denominational rights were brought under the jurisdiction of labour arbitration boards because of provisions in the collective contract. The occasions for both these cases were provided by teachers at Roman Catholic separate schools in Ontario who embarked on civil marriages contrary to Roman Catholic canon law. These marriages were, of course, legal. Is the teachers' exercise of this legal right consistent with their continued employment as teachers in the Roman Catholic separate schools? The school boards did not think so.

Case 46: The Teachers Who Had Civil Marriages

This case was reported in the newspapers and went to the Ontario Court of Appeal. It involved important constitutional issues and has become an important precedent. There is, therefore, no point in attempting to preserve the anonymity of the two teachers or the school board. In our view, none of the parties to the dispute did anything wrong. The two teachers simply did something which rendered it difficult for the denominational school board to continue to employ them. The facts of the case and the decision of the Court of Appeal are briefly and neatly set out in the 'reasons for judgment' of the Court of Appeal, and we therefore quote it in full:

Susan Porter and Patricia Podgorski v. The Essex County Roman Catholic Separate School Board, in the Supreme Court of Ontario, Court of Appeal, heard 13 September 1978, reasons for judgment, *per* Zuber, J. A., released 28 September 1978[32]

This is an appeal by Susan Porter and Patricia Podgorski (the teachers) from a judgment of the Divisional Court setting aside decisions of a Board of Reference. The appeal raises an important issue respecting denominational rights and privileges.

The facts which give rise to the issue are as follows. Susan Porter and Patricia Podgorski (the teachers) were both employed by the school board pursuant to permanent teachers' contracts in the form prescribed in the regulations passed under *The Department of Education Act,* R.S.O. 1970, c. 111 (now *The Education Act,* 1974). Both teachers are Roman Catholics and for reasons that are not disclosed, each elected to enter into a civil marriage. As a result of so doing, they were dismissed from their positions as teachers by the school board by resolutions passed by the school board on November 12th, 1974. The relevant portions of the resolution dealing with Susan Porter read as follows:

'WHEREAS a Roman Catholic Separate School has the right under the British North America Act to select, employ or dismiss otherwise qualified teachers in accordance with the denominational requirements of such school, and

WHEREAS Mrs Susan Porter, by entering into a civil marriage has publicly and seriously infringed upon such requirements,

THEREFORE BE IT RESOLVED THAT in virtue of the said right of The Essex County Roman Catholic Separate School Board, the said Mrs Susan Porter be hereby declared disqualified for employment as a teacher by this separate school board within its jurisdiction and consequently dismissed.'

The resolution relating to Patricia Podgorski was identical in terms. Counsel agree that the school board was acting in good faith in treating the dismissal as a denominational matter.

The dismissals were effective forthwith. Both teachers applied to the Minister of Education for a Board of Reference which was granted pursuant to section 24 et seq. of *The Schools' Administration Act*, R.S.O. 1970, c. 424 (now section 233 et seq. of *The Education Act, 1974*). The teachers took the position before the Board that they had not been properly dismissed, i.e. they had been given insufficient notice. It is a part of this argument that the terms of the permanent contract dealing with the notice of termination of the agreement when read with section 24 of *The Education Act* must be observed even in the case of dismissal for cause.

The school board took the position that the Board of Reference had no jurisdiction to deal with the matter at all on the grounds that their action was based upon rights and privileges reserved to it as a Separate school board by the *British North America Act*, 1867, 30 and 31 Victoria, c. 3, s. 93. The Board of Reference felt that it could not deal with the issue raised by the school board and went on to find that the notice given the teachers did not comply with the teachers' contract and directed that the contract of each of the teachers be continued. The school board applied to the Divisional Court for judicial review of these decisions of the Board. On June 7, 1977, the decisions of the Board were set aside by the Divisional Court and it is from the order of the Divisional Court that the teachers now appeal.

The relevant portions of section 93 of the *British North America Act, 1867*, are as follows:

93. In and for each Province the Legislature may exclusively make Laws in relation to Education, subject and according to the following Provisions:

(1) Nothing in any such Law shall prejudicially affect any Right or Privilege with respect to Denominational Schools which any Class of Persons have by Law in the Province at the Union.

It is apparent that the starting point must be an inquiry into the rights and privileges with respect to separate schools in Ontario as of 1867. Section 7 of the *Separate Schools Act*, 1863, 22 Vic. c. 5 provided that the trustees of separate schools should have the same powers in respect of separate schools that the trustees of common schools had with respect to common schools. As employers, the trustees of common schools had the power to hire and dismiss teachers. I find nothing in the *Common Schools Act*, 1859, 22 Vic. c. 65 which takes away or diminishes the trustees' common law rights as employer. If authority is needed to support this proposition, it can be found in *Raymond v. School Trustees of the Village of Cardinal* (1887), 14 O.A.R. 562. I take it to be obvious, that if a school board can dismiss for cause, then in the case of a denominational school cause must include denominational cause. Serious departures from denominational standards by a teacher cannot be isolated from his or her teaching duties since within the denominational school religious instruction, influence and example form an important part of the educational process. (Cf. Roman Catholic Separate School Trustees for *Tiny v. The King* [1928], A.C. 363 at 390.) I therefore conclude that as of 1867, separate school trustees in Ontario possessed the power to dismiss teachers for denominational cause. In my view, it follows that the power of the trustees to dismiss for denominational cause is a 'right or privilege with respect to denominational schools' possessed by separate school supporters and by virtue of s. 93 of the *British North America Act*, 1867 nothing in the legislation of the Province of Ontario can prejudicially affect this right. It seems apparent that to subject the right to dismiss for denominational reasons to a review by a Board of Reference would prejudicially affect the right.

Mr Markle in his argument reviewed in great detail Ontario legislation affecting the operation of both public and separate schools and argued that the right of any school board to dismiss a teacher for cause has been substantially eroded. Mr Smith argued in turn (and I agree) that this proposition simply emphasizes the fact that the subsequent provincial legislation would prejudicially affect the pre-confederation right to dismiss a teacher for denominational cause.

The Board of Reference which dealt with this matter is a creature of *The Schools Administration Act*, R.S. 1970, c. 424 (now *The Education Act*, 1974). In my view the Board of Reference had no jurisdiction to deal with the dismissals in this case simply because the Ontario legislature had no power to give it that jurisdiction.

It remains only to say that the teachers are not without recourse. They have a right to resort to the courts and ask for damages that they were wrongfully dismissed if such was the case.

This appeal is dismissed with costs.

Let us now backtrack to the Divisional Court. The appeal by the school board, asking that the decision of the board of reference be set aside, was heard 4 May 1977 before three judges. The judges released their decision on 17 June 1977. Two judges allowed the appeal, and one dismissed it.[33]

The majority judgment (*per* Weatherston, J.) examined relevant clauses of the Schools' Administration Act, and concluded:

The Act, therefore, recognizes the right of a school board to dismiss a teacher for cause, notwithstanding provisions in the contract for its termination on notice. In either case, the Board of Reference has power to direct the continuance of the contract. In this case, the Board of Reference did not recognize the distinction between 'dismissal' and 'termination of the contract' but treated the terms as synonymous. It said:

'In these circumstances, the Board of Reference finds that a binding contract existed between the parties and that the Board could not unilaterally terminate the contract other than in accordance with the terms of the contract. This the Board did not do.

Accordingly, this Board of Reference reports to the minister and directs the continuance of the contract.'

A dismissal is not something that occurs 'in accordance with the terms of the contract.' It is either a repudiation of the contract of employment by the employer, or an acceptance by the employer of some breach of contract by the employee which is sufficient cause for dismissal.

The school board argued that its right to dismiss for denominational reasons, 'whether or not those reasons were a sufficient cause in law,' is a right that existed at Confederation and is preserved by section 93 of the B.N.A. Act, 1867. Reviewing the legislation that operated in Ontario in that year, the judges concluded that the trustees of separate schools had the power to dismiss for cause:

It is quite clear that the trustees of separate schools had the power to dismiss for cause; See *Raymond v School Trustees of Cardinal* (1887) 14 O.A.R. 502. And, even if the provisions for arbitration applied to separate schools, the arbitrators had power only to make money awards, not to order the reinstatement of a teacher who had been wrongfully dismissed. The trustees, therefore, had the right to dismiss for denominational reasons, and, if sufficient cause could not be established, they were liable only to the usual damages in lieu of notice ...

The judges reviewed a number of cases concerning legislation with respect to denominational schools. Section 93(1) of the B.N.A. Act was not intended to preclude all legislation concerning denominational schools:

It is, I think, clear from these authorities that the right or privilege preserved by s. 93 must be a right or privilege which, if lost, would impair the integrity of the separate school. For counsel to argue that Boards of Trustees of Separate Schools had the power to dismiss without cause, and to pay damages in lieu of notice, and that is such a right or privilege, is to state the matter too broadly. The legislature surely has the power to give to teachers in separate schools the same security of tenure as teachers in public schools enjoy. But it seems to me that there may be cases where a teacher in a separate school, although not guilty of conduct sufficient in law to justify dismissal for cause, may, by his conduct or teaching, make his continued employment on the teaching staff intolerable. In the Tiny case, Anglin, C.J.C. said (1927) S.C.R. 637 at page 656:

'The idea that the denominational school is to be differentiated from the common school purely by the character of its religious exercise or religious studies is erroneous. Common and separate schools are based on fundamentally different conceptions of education. Undenominational schools are based on the idea that the separation of secular from religious education is advantageous. Supporters of denominational schools, on the other hand, maintain that religious instruction and influence should always accompany secular training.'

This difference in concept was recognized by MacPherson, J. in *Board of Education for Moose Jaw School District No 1 et al v. Attorney General of Saskatchewan et al.* (1975) 14 D.L.R. (3d) 732. He held to be invalid a provision for binding arbitration in the Teacher Collective Bargaining Act, 1973 (Sask.) because it involved one of the rights and privileges of a separate school board elsewhere preserved to it, namely the regulation of the selection of teachers, the administrative and instructional duties of teachers, or the nature or quality of an instructional program, including religious instruction.

S. 29 of The Schools Administration Act, now s. 238(1) of The Department of Education Act, gives to a Board of Reference the power only to direct a continuance or a discontinuance of a contract. If there is not sufficient cause for dismissal, it must direct a continuance of the contract, notwithstanding that the teaching or conduct of the teacher is incompatible with his continued employment as a teacher in his school. This, I think, is an infringement on a right preserved by s. 93, and it must therefore be held that it is *ultra vires* the legislation to empower a Board of Reference to direct the continuance of a teacher's contract in cases when the teacher has been dismissed for reasons which have a denominational validity and value to justify termination of his employment, even though not of sufficient cause in law. The direction of the Board of Reference is therefore set aside, but this order is without prejudice to any rights the respondents may have at law.

This line of reasoning was clearly confirmed by the decision of the Court of Appeal.

The minority judgment, given by Judge Steele, went a different route. The judge observed that the action by the school board in terminating the teachers' contracts on 12 November was not in accordance with the provisions of the permanent teachers' contract. Because of this, the board of reference had directed continuance of the contracts.

The issue, however, was whether or not the board of reference had jurisdiction, since section 93 of the B.N.A. Act preserved certain special rights and privileges of separate or denominational schools.

At the time of Confederation, the separate school trustees had the same rights as trustees of common schools. They had no rights over and above the rights that the latter had. The rights protected by section 93 must be ones that the relevant class of persons had 'by law' at the time of Union. There was, at that time, no right or privilege in law to dismiss teachers who entered into civil marriages or married outside the Roman Catholic Church.[34] There were, therefore, no rights or privileges in law that were applicable to the appeal by the school board and that were preserved to the trustees of separate schools under section 93 of the B.N.A. Act. The judge, therefore, held that the board of reference was acting within its jurisdiction in ordering the continuance of the contracts.

We observe that the minority judgment did *not* find that the teachers had been improperly or wrongfully dismissed. It held only that the board of reference decision could not be set aside on the grounds that the board of reference had no jurisdiction because of denominational rights.

When we turn to the board of reference decision, dated 25 April 1975, we find that the board of reference declined to discuss the constitutional issue and agreed with the school board's counsel that the board of reference did not have the 'right to deal with matters of constitutional law.' The board of reference found only

... that a binding contract existed between the parties and that the board [i.e., the school board] could not unilaterally terminate the contract other than in accordance with the terms of the contract. This the Board did not do.

The board of reference gave no reasons for this decision, other than that by the terms of the contract, the school board was not entitled to dismiss the teachers on 12 November. The board of reference did not discuss at all whether or not the teachers' entering civil marriages constituted valid reason (denominational or otherwise) for the teachers' dismissal. Perhaps it was because only denominational reasons could justify their being dismissed on these grounds.

Case 47: Another Teacher Contracting a Civil Marriage[35]

Denise Tremblay-Webster was a teacher employed on a permanent contract by the Roman Catholic separate school board. On 4 February 1980 the school board terminated her contract for denominational cause, namely, that in December 1979 she married outside the requirements of the Roman Catholic Church.

Ms Tremblay-Webster applied for a board of reference. The minister refused the application on the grounds that the minister had no jurisdiction to enquire into dismissals for denominational cause. The minister cited the judgment of the Court of Appeal in the *Porter* case.

Ms Tremblay-Webster also filed a grievance alleging that the dismissal was contrary to the collective agreement in force between the school board and the teachers. The school board argued that the board of arbitration had no jurisdiction. The majority of the board of arbitration concluded that it had jurisdiction. The school board appealed to the Divisional Court for judicial review. The Divisional Court held unanimously that the board of arbitration had jurisdiction. The school board appealed to the Court of Appeal.

The same arguments were before the Court of Appeal as had been placed before the board of arbitration and the Divisional Court. The first argument was that the dismissal was not arbitrable under the terms of the collective agreement. The second argument was that to subject the school board's rights to dismiss for denominational cause to a review by a board of arbitration, which had been constituted pursuant to a compulsory dispute-resolving mechanism imposed by provincial legislation, prejudicially affected the school board's rights and privileges with respect to denominational schools. There was, the school board held, no difference between a board of reference imposed by statute and a board of arbitration imposed by statute.

In answer to the first argument, the Court of Appeal held that although the collective agreement had clauses providing that any matter in which the teacher might have a right to a board of reference should not be arbitrable, in matters of denominational cause, for which the board of reference had no right of jurisdiction, such clauses could not apply.

Furthermore, the collective agreement provided that no teacher should be dismissed without just cause, and it also provided that the arbitrator may arbitrate when an allegation was made that the agreement had been contravened. Just cause included denominational cause:

The school board agreed that no teacher would be discharged without just cause: in the case of a denominational school, cause includes denominational cause ... It then follows that dismissals for cause in cases where there is no right to seek a board of reference can be the subject of arbitration if the teacher elects to invoke this procedure.

In the second argument, the court in the *Porter* case had held that the board of reference had no jurisdiction. The case was easily distinguishable from the present case. Conferring upon school boards and teachers the capacity to bargain collectively does not prejudicially affect the rights and privileges of denominational schools. Since the legislation imposed no obligation on the school board to agree with the teachers in any matter, there was no prejudicial effect upon denominational rights.

The source of the arbitration board's jurisdiction in this matter was the 'just cause' provision in the collective agreement. The parties had no statutory obligation to include this clause:

In this case, the parties agreed to include in the collective agreement a clause that prohibited the discharge of teachers without just cause. There was no statutory obligation to include such a clause. But once this clause was included, it attracted the operation of the arbitration mechanism in the event of a dispute.

The chairman of the arbitration board, in his reasons said:

The jurisdiction of our Board is determined by the collective agreement between the parties. The parties are free ... to vary the specific jurisdiction given to an arbitrator under the collective agreement as, for example, to expressly exclude specific disputes from the grievance and arbitration procedures.

The collective agreement, as we have stated earlier, provides us with the necessary jurisdiction to proceed in this matter.

With respect, I agree with this statement by the chairman.

The judge of the Court of Appeal went on to say:

Section 93 of the *Constitution Act* prohibits the provincial legislature from making laws which prejudicially affect any right or privilege with respect to denominational schools but does not prohibit voluntary collective agreements with respect to those rights and privileges.

The reasoning of the Divisional Court was similar.[36] This court held that a right to apply for a board of reference that would not be granted is not a right to a board of reference:

I agree with the view of the majority [of the board of arbitration] that it would be 'pure sophistry' to interpret the words 'may have a right to a Board of Reference' in Article 2:02 [of the collective agreement] as referring only to a right to apply for a Board of Reference. As the learned Chairman put it: 'The ability to ask for something which will not or cannot be granted does not in our opinion amount to a right.' In my judgment, the majority gave to Article 2:02(n) a reasonable interpretation, and the decision that the words of the collective agreement did not prevent the grievance from being arbitrable should not be disturbed.

The Divisional Court held that the chairman of the board of arbitration was correct in concluding that the provisions of the School Boards and Teachers Collective Negotatiations Act, 1975, did not compel school boards to submit dismissals for denominational reasons to arbitration. The majority of the board of arbitration had held that the parties to the agreement had agreed to submit their differences to arbitration. This agreement, together with the provision about 'just cause,' gave jurisdiction to the board of arbitration. The Divisional Court held that this interpretation of the agreement was reasonably based on the words of the collective agreement and was not an error in law, justifying a writ of *certiorari*. The reasoning of the board of arbitration was upheld by the Divisional Court and reaffirmed by the Court of Appeal.

Beyond the fact that, after the decision of the Court of Appeal, negotiations continued (or were resumed) between the teacher and the school board, we do not know what happened next.

These two cases came from Ontario, which has a secular public school system and a denominational (mostly Roman Catholic) separate school system, both well established in law. The next case comes from Newfoundland, where the entire school system is denominational. The choice for most people is between a Roman Catholic school and a Protestant school, not a secular one.

Case 48: The Teacher Who Joined the Salvation Army

In Newfoundland, denominational school boards have understandably insisted that their teachers conform to the religious doctrines of the denomination (see Magsino 1986). The teacher in this case was a Roman Catholic hired to teach in a Roman Catholic school. He later converted, however, to the Salvation Army and married a member of the Army. Upon hearing this, the school board dismissed him without notice. The teacher applied for a board of arbitration and was successful. The case duly reached the Newfoundland Court of Appeal. Let us review the facts and the arguments at each stage.[37]

When Mr Walsh accepted the teaching position, he was a practising Roman Catholic, although he was reassessing his religious affiliation because of a family tragedy. The letter offering Walsh the position included the following statement:

In view of your responsibilities as a teacher at this Catholic School, this position is offered to you on the understanding that you are a practising Catholic and are willing to participate in the religious education programme at the school.

The letter also included a copy of the school by-law that is quoted below. Before accepting the offer of a position, however, Walsh was assured by the assistant superintendent of the school district that Walsh's attending non-Catholic religious services would not be a problem. Walsh proved to be a competent, caring, and conscientious teacher.

In November 1982, Walsh joined the Salvation Army, and in July 1983 he married a non-Catholic in the Salvation Army Church in St John's. When the school principal in September 1983 asked Walsh where he had been married, Walsh said merely, 'In St John's.' In January 1984, Walsh readily admitted that he had joined the Salvation Army and married a non-Catholic.

Shortly afterwards, the school superintendent sent Walsh a formal notification. It said: 'Your employment is terminated immediately. This is done in accordance with s. 12:01(e) as stated in your collective agreement.' Section 12:01(e) of the 1984 collective agreement between the Newfoundland and Labrador Trustees Association and the Newfoundland Teachers' Association permitted a contract of employment to be terminated 'without notice, by the school board, where there is gross misconduct, insubordination or neglect of duty on the part of the teacher, or any similar just cause.' Note the phrase 'or any similar just cause.'

Walsh grieved before the board of arbitration that his firing was not in accordance with section 12:01(e). The school board said that it was and argued that Walsh had broken a school by-law. The by-law, which the

Newfoundland Teachers' Association had refused to have included in the collective agreement, read as follows:

6. A Roman Catholic Teacher in the Schools operated by this Board is expected to abide by the laws and regulations common to all members of the Catholic Church and by word and example to encourage pupils to do likewise. When such a teacher employed by this Board acts in flagrant and explicit contradiction with fundamental Roman Catholic values or with the official teachings of the Magisterium or with the educational objectives of the Roman Catholic Church, that action is incompatible with the continued exercise of the teacher's function in a school operated by this Board.

At the board of arbitration hearing, which began 7 January 1985, the Newfoundland Teachers' Association argued that the by-law in question was null and void. The by-law had been approved by the director of school services on behalf of the minister and should have been approved (according to statute) by the minister himself.

The board of arbitration agreed that the by-law was null and void. It also agreed with the school board, however, that ordinary contract law (i.e., the master-and-servant law which we have reviewed in chapter 2) was relevant, in which the contract set out the conditions of employment and the context determined what other requirements were implied therein. The Board also considered that it was bound by an earlier Newfoundland case[38] and by a decision of the Supreme Court of Canada,[39] both of which held that adherence to Roman Catholic teachings by a teacher in a Roman Catholic school was relevant to a dismissal for just cause. The board, therefore, ruled that being and remaining a practising Catholic while being employed by the Roman Catholic school board was a *bona fide* occupational qualification for teaching in a school run by that board; that by joining the Salvation Army, Walsh had thereby eliminated his own qualification; and that the loss of this qualification constituted just cause for his dismissal.

Walsh and the Newfoundland Teachers' Association applied to the Trial Division of the Newfoundland Supreme Court for an order to set aside the decision of the board of arbitration. The judge held that both the school board and the board of arbitration had been right in law. He stated:

While the words master and servant may have faded from popular use, the principles stated by Lord Esher remain as fresh as ever. A teacher, in the employ of a school board, who, by his own act, puts himself into the position of not being able to perform, in a due manner, his duties, or of not being able to perform his duty in a faithful manner, so that his continued employment is intolerable, may be dismissed for just cause pursuant to s. 12:01(e). Whether or not he has done so is, in the first instance, a question to be determined by the school board and, in the event of a grievance, finally, by the arbitration board. In this instance, both boards found that Walsh's conduct justified his dismissal.

Mr Justice Noel thus held that the arbitration board had not erred in law and that the determination of fact was therefore within the jurisdiction of the arbitration board.

Mr Justice Noel had been the judge in the Newfoundland case cited by the arbitration board, and he was thus also reaffirming his reasoning in that case.

The Newfoundland Teachers' Association also argued that the arbitration board's decision had denied Walsh the fundamental freedom of conscience and religion that was guaranteed by the Charter of Rights and Freedoms and that it had given the school board the right, contrary to the collective agreement, to prohibit its Roman Catholic teachers from changing their religious faith. Mr Justice Noel noted this argument but refused to accept it.

Walsh and the Newfoundland Teachers' Association, therefore, appealed to the Newfoundland Court of Appeal. The court affirmed the decision of the Trial Division.

The court first examined the grounds upon which an arbitration board's decision may be appealed for judicial review:

The criterion ... for judicial review of an arbitration board's decision which hangs entirely upon construction of a collective agreement is whether the interpretation determined by the board was patently unreasonable or one which the words of the agreement could not reasonably bear.

In other words, the arbitration board had made a decision about the meaning of the phrase 'or similar just cause,' and had held that the denomination cause reflected in the by-law constituted such just cause. The appeal court's judicial review would be only to determine if the arbitration board's decision was reasonable.

The transaction between Walsh and the school board had been consummated with the intent to function within the established denominational system of education. Within this system, said the court per Mr Justice Marshall, amongst the rights existing at Confederation was the right conferred upon a denominational Board of Education to appoint and dismiss teachers (*The Education Act*, S.N. 1927, C. 14, s. 11[d]) ... it is evident that it must encompass the right to hire and dismiss teachers for denominational cause. It follows that in a school system founded upon denominational instruction and witness to a particular faith, school boards should have the concomitant right to require that teachers who were adherents to that denomination when employed will continue to respect and abide by the basic precepts of that faith.

The wording of section 12:01(e) of the collective agreement, therefore, may rationally be construed to include denominational cause. The essential nature and character of the denominational system could not render unreasonable the upholding of a Roman Catholic school board's decision to dismiss a teacher who had been unfaithful to the terms of a reasonable contractual understanding.

The Court of Appeal then considered the argument concerning the Charter. Section 29 of the Charter protected the legitimate exercise of denominational educational rights from challenges under the Charter. These rights had been constitutionally established at the date of Union of Newfoundland and Canada by term 17 (the equivalent of section 93[1] of the British North America Act, now the Constitution Act, 1867):

That is not to say, as intimated by appellants' counsel, that requiring religious conformance as a condition of employment renders Mr Walsh's rights to freedom of conscience and religion illusory. These rights exist. However, they cannot be exercised to impair the right of the school board to operate its denominational school in accordance with its bona fide religious beliefs and practices for the benefit of all members of that faith. Where a conflict exists, s. 29 of the *Charter* clearly requires the scale to be tipped in favour of the general right.

The Court of Appeal upheld the decision of the arbitration board, which in turn upheld the decision of the school board to dismiss Mr Walsh for having left the Roman Catholic Church for another denomination, making him unfit to teach in a Roman Catholic school.

Other Cases: Case 29: The Teacher Who Pursued an Incompatible Lifestyle

This case, from chapter 4, also applies here. Roman Catholic teachings concerning permissible sexual behaviour had been contravened by the teacher, although she had been warned about this behaviour before-hand, and the school board therefore dismissed her. 'Denominational cause,' together with a concern for maintaining the reputation of the school in the eyes of the relevant community, were accepted by the board of reference and the court as just and reasonable cause permitting the school board to dismiss her.

These cases illustrate 'denominational cause' sufficiently for our purposes. Let us sum up what these cases show.

Denominational cause is effectively already allowed by the common law of master and servant. A denominational school may properly expect its teachers to uphold and display the particular moral and religious values to which the school adheres. If the teachers do not show these values, the school may predictably lose its reputation in the eyes of the constituency to which the school appeals, namely the denomination that supports the school. Membership in the denomination may also be required as a precondition for teaching in such a school.

If the school is a public school and tax-supported, however, this denominational connection becomes partisan and questionable. Furthermore, if there are statutes, such as provincial or federal human rights codes, not to mention the Charter of Rights and Freedoms anchored in the very constitution of Canada, the common law of master and servant may be overruled by these statutes.

Denominational cause, however, has been given special status in the Charter. The way is clear for any school with a denominational connection to call upon the principles already well laid down in master-and-servant law in order to require its schoolteachers to abide by the denomination's standards. Denominational cause, protected by the Charter, can override federal and provincial statutes that would otherwise limit denominational school boards' powers over their employees. It can also qualify the enjoyment of other rights protected by the Charter.

Discussion

Looking back over the cases, two tensions or oppositions seem to be at work. The first is the tension between the role of the teacher as a loyal servant of an employer and the role of the teacher as a citizen. The second is the tension between the teacher as someone loyal to a larger cause and the teacher as merely a job-holder. The interplay of these two tensions is represented in the following diagram:

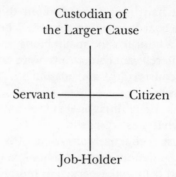

Custodian of
the Larger Cause

Servant ———————— Citizen

Job-Holder

In the first opposition, the teacher has to balance the obligations imposed by the teacher's role as an employee with the rights and duties incumbent on the teacher as a citizen of the larger society. As an employee, the teacher is expected to support the enterprise that employs him or her. This includes abstaining from adverse criticism that, being made 'off the job,' may destroy the reputation of the employer in the eyes of the general public or of the community that the enterprise ostensibly serves. If the enterprise is a commercial one, the reputation of the business is an asset that the employee is expected to conserve. The same principle is extended to public enterprises and their employees by the law of master and servant.

As a citizen, however, the teacher's duty is to expose corruption and inefficiency, especially in enterprises supported by public funds for public purposes. Indeed, we argue that any employee has a public duty to expose those acts by the employer that would harm the public.

Of course, the employee who exposes the employer's practices is not a person in whom the employer can have any confidence – unless both employer and employee are persons of integrity and honesty, in which case, the occasion for public criticism will not arise!

The kind of criticism that the law seems to envisage, however, is irresponsible and untrue criticism by a disgruntled and insubordinate employee. Such criticism may, indeed, be an exercise of citizen's rights of freedom of opinion, but it also warrants the employer's dismissing the employee in whom the employer can no longer have confidence. Naturally, when the criticism *is* justified, the unjust or fearful employer tries to define the criticism as irresponsible and untrue and the employee as an insubordinate liar.

The teacher, caught in such a conflict, will (like any other employee) be invited to resign. If he or she can no longer have confidence in his or her employer, then resignation is the honourable action. The economic sanction involved shows that the teacher is seriously making the criticism. For persons dependent on the teaching profession in order to support themselves and their families, however, a proud and principled resignation may be too costly.

There are situations when the forced resignation or dismissal of the disloyal teacher is appropriate. There are situations when the teacher is entitled to criticize the public school system in public for the failings of its policy or administration, without fear of dismissal. There are also borderline situations, in which neither alternative is correct. Given the nature of public education as an enterprise that employs teachers who (at least in a democratic polity) are also citizens, the tension between the employee's role and the citizen's role is inevitable.

Denominational cause for dismissing teachers who are exercising their legal rights is a different kind of this same tension. If adherence to the beliefs and practices of the denomination is a known precondition for employment, however, and the maintenance of those beliefs and practices is an avowed purpose of the denominational school, then there is no injustice in requiring the employee who has departed from those beliefs and practices to depart the school. For in the liberal democratic state, the religious denomination also has the freedom to engage in its own common enterprises and to set certain requirements for membership or employment in those enterprises.

The second tension concerns how the role of the teacher is conceived. If public school teaching is merely a job, then the teacher is teaching because he or she *can* and receives from it a certain satisfaction with an adequate compensation. The motives of teaching may be quite limited, with loyalties only to the teacher's own self and to the employer. There is no larger perspective or mission to the teacher's task. The teacher follows the curriculum that he or she is hired to teach and that is all.

For many teachers, however, teaching is not just a job. It is something more. It is a set of ideals into which the students are supposed to be initiated. It may be a religion, as in a denominational school. It may be an ideal of human development or an ideal of national mission. It may be an ideal of civilization or of a tradition of learning. For such ideals, the teacher is a 'cultural custodian' whose task is to conserve and transmit those ideals to coming generations, so that the ideals of religion, human growth, national mission, civilization, learning, or what have you, may continue.

Given such ideals shared by the teacher, the school that employs the teacher, and the larger community of which both the teacher and the school trustees are citizens, the two sets of oppositions should be reconcilable. Teacher, school, and community are, in essence, of like mind, and that mind is mutually agreeable among its parts.

Where there is no such shared ideal, there will be conflicts, even between people of good intentions. Out of these conflicts, working compromises will evolve. Some of these working compromises will be satisfactory for many years. Others will be less stable, and new compromises will have to be made.

When intentions are corrupt and even malicious, however, shared ideals will only be tools for the Hobbesian war of all against all. In such a society, the public school teacher will become only an employee and a job-holder, and the public schools themselves will decay into custodial institutions of another sort.

6

The Normative Character of Teaching

Reprise

This study focused on cases of trouble in which local communities put pressure on school boards to penalize and correct 'unconventional' or 'contentious' behaviour by teachers; it is clear from the instances reported here that this community pressure does sometimes exist. The law relating to employee misconduct, both in general and as applied in board of reference cases, clearly permits school boards to discipline or even to dismiss teachers whose acts *cast into disrepute* the school and the education system. This rubric covers on- and off-the-job conduct that seriously upsets the community or constituency whose parents send their children to the school and whose taxes pay for it; hence an expression of 'public indignation' and a concern for the reputation of the school system would be reasonable grounds for disciplining and sometimes dismissing a teacher.

At the same time, however, community control seems to be reduced, and itself forced to be reasonable, by the board of reference appeal procedures and the decisions of these boards. School boards must not be too responsive to public pressures, so that the role of the community is muted in the board of reference decisions; indeed, it is generally not mentioned. The role of the community appears when a teacher is considered by his or her behaviour to cast the school and the education system into disrepute, when a teacher is considered not to be a good role model for children (off-the-job conduct is relevant here), and when denominational rights are in issue. Criminal charges and convictions are relevant to the first two of these concerns.

Apart from these three concerns, however, unconventional or contentious behaviour, provided it is legal, does not seem as such to have played much part at the board of reference level, at least over the past twenty–odd years. If the teacher's behaviour, whether conventional or unconventional, has directly interfered with performance of his or her teaching duties, or has threatened the welfare of the children in the teacher's care, then boards of reference have expected the school board to act. Incompetence, disabling conduct, and insubordination are the most common reasons for dismissal proffered by school boards.

The predominant value supported by these decisions, indeed, seems to be respect for and obedience to authority. Provided an order or policy can be shown to be within the school board's jurisdiction, a teacher is expected to obey it without publicly criticizing or otherwise obstructing the school board. If a teacher believes that an order or policy is wrong, he or she is expected to follow official procedures, to go through proper channels, in making objection to the order or policy. Complaining to the public media is not regarded as a proper procedure.

Given the strong presence of this value, we hypothesize that the unconventional or contentious teacher, that is, the person who for better or for worse upsets the local community by following different standards, would be nudged out of the teaching profession or job by subtle pressures long before the dismissal became a matter for a board of reference. The obstreperous would be unhappy in the job and would depart for more congenial occupations anyway. In addition, the down-playing of public criticism encourages teachers and administrators to 'let sleeping dogs lie' and to avoid stirring up matters to the point that the public becomes involved and excited. Hence, a fair amount of 'deviation' will be allowed to occur, provided that it is discreetly and quietly done and respect for authority is at least apparently preserved. 'Don't rock the boat' thus becomes an operative value, followed by teachers and principals as much as by anyone.

Boards of reference serve primarily to ensure that school boards follow fair procedures when they choose to dismiss teachers. School boards must have good reasons – not mere whimsy or fear of public criticism – for their decisions, and they must give the teacher a full chance to present his or her side of the story. If a teacher is alleged to have misbehaved in a certain way, he or she must really have acted as alleged. School boards are expected to err on the side of generosity to the teacher but to put first the welfare of the students. If the school boards do all this, their decisions to suspend or to dismiss a teacher are more than likely to be upheld by the board of reference. In practice, the statistics gathered to date for British Columbia, Alberta, and Ontario suggest a preponderance of outcomes roughly two in favour of the school board to one in favour of the teacher. In Saskatchewan, by contrast, board of reference decisions were about half for the school board and half for the teacher, with some of those for the school board also being modified in favour of the teacher. These proportions suggest, incidentally, that boards of reference are both necessary to ensure fairness and fairly successful in doing so, at least in terms of the values of the law. Central to these values – and to the attendant disputes – is the character of the teacher.

The Teacher as a 'Character'

So far, in referring to the teacher's 'character,' we have meant the moral and psychological disposition of the teacher, namely what he or she is like as a human being who chooses to act in some way or another. 'Character' also means a role in a play – a social drama – and the teacher may well be a character in this meaning. (We use a capital *C* to distinguish this meaning of 'Character' from 'character' as disposition.)

The moral philosopher Alasdair Macintyre (1984: 27) has noticed that there are some social roles that are like stock Characters in plays of a fairly standard sort. These plays are often morality plays. The Characters symbolize and exemplify social roles loaded with some kind of moral values, such that the roles *together with the persons occupying those roles* become examples of these values, whether of good or evil – they become moral exemplars. Persons who occupy these roles are expected by other persons in the society to live up (or, on occasion, down) to the roles they occupy. Macintyre cites as examples of such Characters the Public School Headmaster, the Explorer, and the Engineer in Victorian England, and the Prussian Officer, the Professor, and the Social Democrat in Wilhelmine Germany. We would add the role of the Gentleman in Edwardian England as another such Character.

According to Macintyre (1984: 28), these Characters sum up sets of moral values and beliefs about the nature of the human world:

Characters have one other notable dimension. They are, so to speak, the moral representatives of their culture and they are so because of the way in which moral and metaphysical ideas and theories assume through them an embodied existence in the social world. *Characters* are the masks worn by moral philosophies. Such theories, such philosophies, do of course enter into social life in numerous ways: most obviously perhaps as explicit ideas in books or sermons or conversations, or as symbolic themes in paintings or plays or dreams. But the distinctive way in which they inform the lives of *characters* can be illuminated by considering how *characters* merge what usually is thought to belong to the individual man or woman and what is usually thought to belong to social roles. Both individuals and roles can, and do, like *characters*, embody moral beliefs, doctrines and theories, but each does so in its own way. And the way in which *characters* do so can only be sketched by contrast with these.

Consider the difference between the Priest, the Teacher, or the Explorer, on the one side, and the butcher, the garbage collector, or the stenographer, on the other. The latter roles are not usually regarded as standing for values beyond themselves, while the former roles are. The Priest epitomizes the values of the Church (especially a Church with an ecclesiastical and sacramental system), the Teacher stands for the values of Education, and the Explorer for the mission of exploring and expanding civilization into the wider world (consider the astronauts as modern examples of Explorers). What are the institutions and values butchers, garbage collectors, and stenographers are expected to epitomize?[1]

Characters, in a word, become moral exemplars, models for others to look up to and imitate. In them, the personality of the individual and the stock character of the social role are fused. When a person imitates such a Character, that person also adopts and adheres to the social order the Character symbolizes. Macintyre (1984: 29) singles out another feature of Characters, as he defines them:

There are then many cases where there is a certain distance between role and individual and where consequently a variety of degrees of doubt, compromise, interpretation or cynicism may mediate the relationship of individual to role. With what I have called *characters* it is quite otherwise; and the difference arises from the fact that the requirements of a *character* are imposed from the outside, from the way in which others regard and use *characters* to understand and to evaluate themselves. With other types of social role the role may be adequately specified in terms of the institutions of whose structures it is a part and the relation to those institutions of the individuals who fill the roles. In the case of a *character* this is not enough. A *character* is an object of regard by the members of the culture generally or by some significant segment of them. He furnishes them with a cultural and moral ideal. Hence the demand is that in this type of case role and personality be fused. Social type and psychological type are required to coincide. The *character* morally legitimates a mode of social existence.

The Character is *expected* by other people to adhere to the official definitions and to *be* what these expectations prescribe. 'Social type and psychological type are required to coincide.'

Consider the role of the Public School Teacher or the Priest or Minister/Pastor of a church. These persons are expected to show in their words and deeds the values one should uphold. They are expected to have the inner character and thoughts that produce those words and deeds. These expectations are imposed upon the Characters by the other people who regard those Characters with respect and approval. Woe betide the role-player who betrays those expectations by some kind of human frailty.

The idea of the teacher as a role model effectively appoints the teacher to a sort of secular priesthood as an exemplar of the values which the community, state, or society officially promulgates. When the teacher fails to live up to these ideals, the resulting downfall is felt to be criminal or even blasphemous, and the teacher becomes a sacrifice to the values thus challenged. The offence may be called 'misconduct,' but it has taken on overtones bordering on sacrilege. This is evident in the school board's reaction to the Shewans.

Such offences may be classified under the labels of 'employee' or 'professional' misconduct. Indeed, professional misconduct for any profession takes on an aura of breach of the sacred. The professional is in charge of a 'mystery' of which the ordinary person – revealingly called a 'layperson' or a 'client' or 'patient' – is supposedly ignorant. The reputation of the profession and its worthiness to be trusted by the lay (i.e., the people) must be preserved at all costs. This entails that any member of the profession who is caught in some activity detrimental to this public trust must be publicly and severely chastised. This sanctioning is the logical corollary of the claim to special knowledge or to exemplary status which the members of the profession have made or accepted – even if through social ascription.

Teachers, however, are more than merely persons in whom a public trust has been reposed. They are held up as exemplars of good behaviour. In this respect, they are like clergy rather than doctors or lawyers or fire-fighters or architects. (Police officers are similar to teachers in this respect.) Hence the overtones of sacrilege which tend to creep into considerations of teachers' misconduct. However, being a Character is not an 'all-or-nothing' phenomenon. Social roles may be moved towards or away from such Characterization. The Lawyer or Teacher in one society or one era may be a Character, but in another society or another era may not be so. In other words, he or she may be much more ordinary in the eyes of ordinary people and less of an example. In still other times and places, these roles may hover on the brink of being a Character or not. We might ask, what moves a social role in one direction or the other?

Geoffrey Gorer's study (1956) of the social role of the English policeman describes the policeman as such a Character (in Macintyre's meaning) and suggests that the policeman, being selected for his character (in the ordinary meaning), became a role model shaping the national character of most of the English (for a time at least). There are other examples as well:

In this paper, I wish to explore the hypothesis that the national character of a society may be modified or transformed over a given period through the selection of the personnel for institutions that are in constant contact with the mass of the population and in a somewhat superordinate position, in a position of some authority. If the personnel of the institution are selected chiefly for their approximation to a certain type of character, rather than for specific intellectual or physical skills; if persons of this type of character have not hitherto been consistently given positions of authority; and if the authority of the institution is generally felt to be benevolent, protective, or succoring; then the character exemplified by the personnel of this institution will to a certain degree become part of the ego ideal of the mass of the population. The mass of the population will then tend to mold their own behavior in conformity with this ideal, and will reward and punish their children in conformity to this adopted pattern. As generations pass, the attempt to approximate this ideal will become less and less conscious, and increasingly part of the unconscious mechanisms that determine the content of the superego; with the ultimate consequence that a type of character that may have been relatively very uncommon when the institution was first manned will subsequently become relatively common, even perhaps typical of the society as a whole, or of those portions of it with which the members of the institution are in most continuous contact.

The English police forces are the institution that I propose to examine in detail; but the evidence that is available to me suggests that strictly analogous functions were performed by the public school teachers in the United States, particularly during the period of the great immigrations of the half century ending in 1914, when classes of immigrants' children were transformed into 'hundred per cent Americans' and given new models of the parental roles. It also appears that a similar attempt is being made in the U.S.S.R. (and presumably in China), where the members of the Communist Party are consciously presented as models for the mass of the population. (Gorer 1956: 330-1)

After describing the policeman's role and some of the regulations and other expectations concerning it and citing public opinion studies about the general population's view of the police, Gorer concludes:

I should like to suggest that, increasingly during the past century, the English policeman has been for his fellow-citizens not only an object of respect but also a model of the ideal male character, self-controlled, possessing more strength than he ever has to call into use except in the gravest emergency, fair and impartial, serving the abstractions of Peace and Justice rather than any personal allegiance or sectional advantage. This model, distributed throughout the population (in 1949 there were 59,000 police officers, averaging one police officer for every 720 inhabitants) has, I suggest, had an appreciable influence on the character of most of the population during recent decades, so that the bulk of the population has, so to speak, incorporated the police man or woman as an ideal and become progressively more 'self-policing'; and with this incorporation there has been an increasing amount of identification, so that today, in the words of one typical respondent:

I believe the police stand for all we English are, maybe at first appearances slow perhaps, but reliable stout and kindly. I have the greatest admiration for our police force and I am proud they are renowned abroad.

If this hypothesis be correct, then what started as an expedient to control the very great criminality and violence of large sections of the English urban population has resulted in a profound modification of the character of this urban population. In a somewhat similar fashion, the need to provide a common language and literacy for the children of immigrants to the United States placed the American public school teacher in a position of prestige that was not shared by her colleagues in any European society and turned her into a model of ideal American conduct. If the metaphor be allowed, the American has an incorporated schoolteacher as part of his or her superego, the English man or woman an incorporated policeman.

There is not yet sufficient evidence to show whether the Communist Party member in the U.S.S.R. is producing analogous results in the mass of the Soviet population. The Communist Party is a much more recent institution than the two others hitherto discussed, but its personnel are distributed throughout the population in much the same proportions and similar relationship as the policeman or the schoolteacher. The major contrasts are that the policy is quite self-conscious on the part of the regime, and that Communist Party members are publicly connected with the whole apparatus of state power, in a way that neither the police nor the teachers, both under the control of local authorities, are. This public connection with state power may interfere with the processes of identification by the powerless; and, it would seem, it is by means of the more-or-less complete and more-or-less conscious identification with the members of an admired and succoring institution that the characters of the mass of the population and the ways in which they interpret their roles as parents are gradually modified or transformed. (Gorer 1956: 337–8)

The character-forming role of the American public school teacher was described, for the years before 1942 at least, by the anthropologist Margaret Mead in the following words:

The teacher, in the American school, is teaching the child something which the parents don't know. If not in sober fact, giving the child a mastery of English grammar of which the parents have never heard, or a facility with fractions which the mother never mastered, still in spirit the teacher is the representative of the changing world in which the children must succeed. The teacher symbolizes a gulf between parents and children which will grow year by year – not the inevitable gulf between old and young, for that, like the seasons, is a circumstance to which man can bow with dignity, but the more dishonorable gulf which results from the parents getting out of date. The children are fast outstripping the parents, and handling daylight saving time with no mistakes at all while the parents are still missing trains. It is hard to find in such a breach between youth and age a place for pride in the young who outstrip the old, not because of greater ability but merely because of being born in a different year. Only those who have made a point of pride out of the very pace of our lives, out of the very fact that those who are born in 1920 start off wiser than those born in 1910, can find pride in such a circumstance. For the majority it is galling to slip behind, for it was one's place in the race which gave one dignity. And the teacher, often younger than the parents, becomes the symbol of this indignity. Children come home from school, anxious to put their parents in their place, and quote the teacher's word against theirs. It is small wonder that American parents retaliate by taking a savage interest in the teacher's character, by surveying her morals with a scrutiny accorded no one else except the minister's wife and the characters of political opponents. In a sense she is the enemy. They have given in, they have turned their children over to her to be made smarter than themselves and to learn a lot of things they, the parents, never needed to know. But just let them find her wanting in some way, failing to teach the children what the parents do know – that sacred symbol of the little bit of the Past which is worthy of respect, the Three R's – and they become merciless.

The situation, although difficult for the teacher, can be used to good purpose, if she makes herself the child's ally, the person who helps him take home to his parents the success which they so eagerly demand and upon which their love is contingent. If she is merely the dispenser of grades, she becomes to the child the person who, when she gives out a low grade, is denying him his passport to his parents' love. If she is helping the child to learn, she is helping him gain the coveted approval. She is in no sense a parent, but always she is professionally concerned with success, and this concern may be phrased in various ways. She may give or withhold, or she may turn with the child by her side to some impersonal power, which says whether the task was well done, and, if it was not, help again. In more static societies where there are schools, it is the duty of teachers merely to represent the parents, teaching what the parents would have the children learn. The teachers are the custodians of the past, the preservers of tradition. In America, the teacher is, in fact, never the representative of the parents – hardly even in those Eastern schools and colleges which attempt to imitate English institutions – she is always the representative of the future into which the parents are anxious that the children should enter, and enter well prepared. (Mead 1965: 96–8)

Note the reference to the scrutiny of the teacher's character and of her morals.

The schoolteacher, whether the representative of the future as among Margaret Mead's Americans or the representative of the parents as Mead suggests for more traditional societies, is in either case a cultural custodian. As such, the teacher's role implies a certain claim to authority and thus demands a degree of trust from the pupils and their parents. This requirement of trust makes the character of the teacher important and so encourages other people to make the teacher's role into a Character in Macintyre's meaning.

The Teacher as a Professional

By treating the teacher as a 'character' whose character is at issue, the community or the society nudges the teacher towards claiming a 'professional' status. 'Professionals,' having esoteric knowledge and specialized skills that outsiders, being ignorant, cannot properly judge, must be given a good deal of autonomy and must be trusted to use their knowledge in ways beneficial to their 'clients.' The character of professionals becomes an issue. There is, therefore, an analogy between the 'characterization' of teachers and that of professionals, and this analogy permits teachers to think of themselves as professionals.

This professionalization of teaching will be enhanced if the teacher is part of a national or state-wide system of education with little or no control by the local community, but increasingly subject to regulation by peers. Eric Hoyle drew this conclusion in comparing the British and American educational systems of the 1960s:

The American teacher is much more susceptible to community control than his British counterpart. This applies to what he does as well as what he is as a person. The community seeks to exert control over the teacher both in school and out. There are a number of reasons for this, but basically the difference stems from historical factors which have led to different structures of control. In America schools were often founded at grass roots level in small communities and the influence of the local community is still very great. In Britain on the other hand, universal elementary education evolved as a national system with a nation-wide salary structure and standard of entry to the profession. The local authorities themselves tend to be large administrative units controlling densely populated urban areas or large counties. As a result, the British teacher tends to be much more removed than his American counterpart from even local centres of administrative control. He is also insulated from parental pressure since he functions on behalf of society as a whole and not simply of the local community. Baron and Tropp (1961), in their interesting discussion of these contrasts have written:

The essential difference is perhaps to be summed up as follows: whereas in England it is the teacher who represents to the community in which he works 'nationally' accepted values, in America it is the community that interprets to the teacher the task he is to perform.

A further source of insulation for the British teacher is that his education will have removed him from the non-selected mass, and he will have spent far longer in full-time education than the majority of the parents of his pupils. He therefore maintains an intellectual authority over parents, and the confidence which comes from this habit enables him to deal with parents who are his intellectual equals in an authoritative manner. In America, on the other hand, a far higher proportion of parents will have been educated to college level where they are more likely to challenge the authority of the teacher.

The high degree of control which the American small community exerts over all aspects of the lives of its teachers is notorious. The leisure activities of the teacher, especially women teachers, have, in the past, been closely controlled, although these pressures are decreasing with the growing urbanization of American society. In a similar way the local community has been able to control what was taught in the schools. The British teacher, on the other hand, experiences very little community control over his professional activities or his leisure pursuits. (Hoyle 1969: 70–2)

Teachers in Canada aspire to the professional model but exist within the community-control model of organization, with emphases varying from place to place and time to time. The peers of the teacher, in the professional model, are his or her fellow teachers, and they will be concerned to maintain 'professional conduct.' This includes maintaining the autonomy of the profession. In the community-control model, the teacher's peers are the other members of the community, and they will be more interested in the teacher being a proper servant of the community and the school. In both cases, however, character will be an issue. The sanctions and the sanction-agents will differ.

Our cases focused on the control of teachers by school boards elected by and responsible to school districts. Sometimes these school districts corresponded to local communities, and sometimes they incorporated several local communities. We have not explored in any great detail the control of teachers by their professional organizations or by the provincial ministries of education. We have noticed these two other control systems, however, and it is clear that these are important.

The board of reference decisions show that there is a degree of community control over the conduct of teachers and that this control is achieved through school boards' power to dismiss or suspend teachers for conduct regarded as tending to throw into disrepute the schools and the educational system. Boards of reference, and the courts to which board of reference decisions may be appealed, recognize this power and also variously define and limit it. School boards may even have the power to dismiss teachers for 'unprofessional conduct' (since it tends to reduce the employer's reputation). School boards, however, are not professional associations and are not competent to decide what is or is not unprofessional conduct. Recall case 14, 'The Teacher Who Laid on the Lath,' and case 39, 'The Teacher Who Published Books.'

The Norms of Teaching

Whatever view of public school teaching emerges, with national or local control or a combination of these, the teacher is going to be 'on the job' twenty-four hours a day. Time in school is when the teacher's behaviour is especially scrutinized but there will be a 'halo effect' to out-of-school activities. This 'halo effect' will be dictated by two distinct (though connected) concerns. First, the teacher will be expected to be a person whose character justifies trust by parents and/or school authorities. Second, the teacher will be expected (to a variable degree) to exemplify a certain morality that fits him or her in the judgment of 'society' to instruct the young. For both of these concerns, the teacher's behaviour out of school is relevant. How relevant it will be depends, of course, on the values of the society and *how narrowly or widely society defines the tasks of the teacher.*

Teaching in the public schools is a distinct kind of purposive social action. It is *institutionalized.* That is to say, public school teaching follows the outline or form of an institution set out in 1944 by the anthropologist Bronislaw Malinowski in his search to find a natural unit of culture. An *institution* has a defining *purpose* expressed in a variety of statements. Malinowski called these statements the *'charter'* of the institution. Public pronouncements about the purpose and value of the public schools would be examples of such chartering statements. The valedictory speeches given at high-school graduation ceremonies, as well as such ceremonies themselves, are other examples. Next, institutions have *personnel,* namely the human beings who enact the institution and more or less carry out the purpose. For the public school, the personnel are the pupils, the teachers, administrators, school trustees, secretarial and janitorial staff, parents, taxpayers and feepayers, and other involved persons. The school itself is set within another institution, namely, the state and its department of education. These too have their charters and personnel. Third, the personnel are guided by *norms.* These norms are the personnel's ideas about what must be done or ought to be done if the purpose is to be realized and achieved. Norms in this meaning refer to ideal norms rather than statistical norms (which should be called 'behavioural modes'). The ideal norms are expectations, rules, prescriptions. They include both knowledges (i.e., expectations about what is or will be the case), expectations about what ought or ought not to happen, and imperatives or commands. Some norms are quite general; others (such as schedules for classes) are quite specific and detailed. The fourth part of an institution, according to Malinowski's scheme, is the *material apparatus* used by the personnel in enacting the norms that prescribe how the purpose expressed in the charter is to be achieved. For the public school, this material apparatus includes such things as books, papers, blackboards, chalk, pens and ink, typewriters, computers, athletic equipment, electric light bulbs, school buildings, school buses, and perhaps even school uniforms for the pupils. These four elements (purpose/charter, personnel, norms, and material apparatus) come together in the fifth, which Malinowski called the *activities.* The activities are what the personnel actually do – the behaviours or conduct that actually happen. Some of these activities follow or comply with the norms. Some activities do not follow the norms and may even contradict them. A great deal happens that the norms do not touch upon at all: indeed, much happens that the norms *cannot* anticipate. Through these activities, the purpose is (or is not) achieved. The teaching, the meeting of the teachers in the teachers' coffee room, and sports day are all activities – but so is a student fainting in the classroom, or students reading comic books in the back rows of the classroom when they should be doing their homework.

The sixth element distinguished by Malinowski is the *function*. The function is the *actual* consequences of the institution for the society or culture that contains it and for the individuals who enact it. These consequences may be intended by the actors (i.e., they may be the realization of the purpose) or they may be quite unintended.[2]

The norms, then, are a necessary part of the implementing or actualizing of the purpose. They bring the purpose 'down to earth.' The norms present in any institution may be distinguished into (a) the *necessary or essential* and (b) the *accidental or adventitious*. The necessary norms follow from the purpose and may be deduced, at least partly, from the idea of the purpose. The accidental norms cannot be so deduced, even partially, from the idea of the purpose, and their presence indicates the intrusion of other purposes into the institution.

In public school teaching, the necessary norms are those that are 'built in' to the role of teacher and the idea of the public school. They are the norms teachers *must* follow if they are to be described as 'public school teachers.' A person who consistently acts differently from these necessary norms is simply not a teacher but some other kind of actor. The accidental norms are those not inherent either in the generic role of teacher or in the idea of a public school but imposed upon the teacher by the rest of the society (including the teaching actor's other roles). The accidental norms may be part of the lessons the teacher is required to teach – 'course content,' as it were – or they may not. They are not given in the necessities of public school teaching as such.

The *necessary* norms of public school teaching comprise three sets, corresponding to three normative sources. The first set consists of those inherent *in the generic teacher-student relationship itself* and are tied to the intrinsic purpose, namely teaching. The second set consists of those norms related to the role of the teacher as an *employee* of the school. The third set consists of those norms connected to the *professional* aspect of the teacher's role.

(a) Norms Inherent in the Teacher-Student Relationship

The teacher's task is to communicate to students knowledge, skills, and values of some kind or another. (1) The first requirement, therefore, is that the teacher *know* the subject(s) to be communicated. (2) The second requirement is that the teacher *have the pedagogical expertise to teach* this subject to students. (3) As a corollary of this, the third requirement is that the teacher *create and maintain an environment conducive to learning* by the students. (4) The fourth requirement, if the learning is to continue, is that the teacher *must not allow other concerns to interfere* with the teaching and learning. These other concerns (whatever they may be) act like 'noise' to block and distract the communications by the teacher. (5) The fifth requirement is fundamental: if the teacher is to be listened to and accepted as an authority by the students, the teacher must be *known to be reliable and truthful.* If the teacher is considered to be unreliable and even a liar, whatever the teacher communicates will be discounted accordingly by the students. (6) If the teacher gives and marks examinations and other assignments, the teacher must *mark exams and assignments fairly* according to some standard known and accepted by the students.

We would add a seventh requirement, especially if what the teacher is supposed to communicate are the values of a liberal education. (7) The teacher must *love and respect* the subject he or she is trying to communicate, the characters or natures of the students who are supposed to learn the subject, and the engagement in the teaching act itself.

When these requirements are *not met,* the teacher may be described as 'ignorant,' 'incompetent,' 'dis-committed' or 'distracted,'[3] 'dishonest' (even 'mendacious'), and 'thoughtless' (or, at worst, even 'exploitative' and 'malicious'). Behaviours deserving these labels must be corrected.

(b) Norms Related to the Role of the Public School Teacher as an Employee

As an employee, the teacher is an agent and not a principal actor. The content and much of the methods of the teaching have been set by a higher authority, and the teacher has undertaken to teach this content to the students according to the approved methods. From this undertaking, the following norms may be deduced:

(1) The teacher must teach the assigned curriculum. (2) The teacher must abide by the rules of the public school and must not disrupt the administration. (3) The teacher must respect the authority structure of the organization. (4) The teacher must generally cooperate with col-

leagues and co-workers and at least not disrupt their work. (5) The teacher must perform the assigned tasks reliably and should not be absent without leave. (6) The teacher's activities off the job must not be such as to discredit the organization or cast doubt either upon the organization or upon the teacher's performance of his or her tasks. (7) The teacher has a duty to bring to the attention of the authorities in the organization any defects in the organization that hinder the teaching purpose that justifies the existence of the organization and for which the teacher has been hired. (This seventh norm does not always fit comfortably with the sixth.)

When the teacher fails to meet these norms, the teacher may be described as 'negligent,' 'insubordinate,' 'uncooperative,' 'disruptive,' 'unreliable,' 'absent without leave' (AWOL), 'disloyal,' 'misconducting self off the job,' 'disreputable,' or 'complacent.'

While criticism is a duty, unwelcome criticism may all too often be labelled 'disloyal,' 'disruptive,' 'insubordinate,' and 'adverse to the good reputation of the school or of the educational system.' A rather delicate line must be trod by any member of an organization between due and undue criticism. The authorities in any organization, furthermore, are apt to regard *any* adverse criticism as 'undue.' An organization that cannot take and profit by adverse criticism is in a most unhealthy condition.

*(c) Norms Arising from the Developing Professional Status of
     Public School Teaching*

The public school teacher usually is in charge of pupils whose status in the society is that of minors. These pupils are considered not to be fully responsible for their own well-being because of tender years, ignorance or lack of experience, lack of judgment, or various mental and physical impairments (even though, in fact, some may be fully responsible for their lives). Someone else is officially responsible for overseeing and ensuring their well-being. During school-time, this responsibility is delegated to the public school teacher. In the classroom, however, the teacher may be alone with the students and otherwise unsupervised. It therefore becomes necessary that the teacher be the sort of person who can be trusted with this responsibility: *trusted to act properly when no one is watching.*

From this basic requirement of trustworthiness, the following norms emerge: (1) The teacher must not *exploit or mistreat the students* entrusted to his or her care. This may be called the basic 'fiduciary duty' of the teacher or a basic 'duty of care.' As part of a profession, the teacher has two further obligations: (2) The teacher must act so as to uphold the dignity of the profession and the trust people (supposedly) have in the members of the profession. (3) The teacher has the duty to duly criticize the profession and its members when they fail to abide by the profession's own proper standards.

When a teacher fails to meet these professional norms, the teacher may be described as 'negligent,' 'breaching the duty of care,' 'failing to uphold professional standards,' 'unprofessional,' or 'guilty of professional misconduct.'

Beyond these three major concerns, however, the norms *necessary* to public school teaching do not go. To find other norms public school teachers may (or may not) be obliged to obey, we must introduce other purposes and other concerns extrinsic to the structure of public school teaching.

The Teacher in Society

The accidental or adventitious norms of the public school teacher's role arise from the further demands the society or community makes upon the teacher. They are not inherent in the social action of public school teaching itself.

In particular, the social status the community ascribes to the teacher's role reflects the value the community places upon teaching. Is the schoolteacher a respected member of the community, a person looked up to because of his or her knowledge and responsibility? Or is the schoolteacher regarded merely as an employee of the school, doing teaching perhaps as a secondary occupation because he or she can find nothing better to do? A similar contrast occurs in the way religious congregations regard their clergymen: are the ministers respected guides or somewhat disregarded servants of the congregation?

This ambivalence arises in part from the nature of teaching in human society, though not within the role itself. The teacher is one who knows and who imparts that knowledge. To recognize the teacher as a knower of some sort is to give the teacher authority and to cloak the teacher in a sort of mystery. The teacher thus (potentially at least) becomes a sort of *guru* and the other people potential *chelas*. Like blacksmiths and shamans amongst some 'primitive' peoples, and scientists and doctors amongst some 'civilized' ones, the teacher's possession of knowledge makes the teacher both valued and suspect. The public school teacher is also an employee or servant paid by the community or the state to do a certain job. Servants have to take orders and are expected to show a certain deference to their masters and to those who pay them. Servants with special knowledge may interpret and change their orders and may even know that the orders are foolish, so that another ambiguity enters the relationship.

The ambivalence surrounding the teacher's role, in addition to the availability of the teacher, makes the teacher apt to be used as a 'lightning rod' to divert and receive the discharge of the community's anxieties and projections. The teacher becomes scrutinized, his or her conduct is interpreted, judged, and misinterpreted. When troubles come to the community, the teacher is there to be potentially blamed for the community's, or the individual's, ills and unease and accordingly suspended or dismissed. This may happen, as well, within that small partial community that is the school itself.

In this relationship, the kind of knowledge imparted by the schoolteacher becomes important. Teaching reading and writing to schoolchildren in a society in which parents cannot themselves read and write is different from teaching these skills in a society in which parents are literate: the latter teaching involves no mystery from the parents' viewpoint. Teaching reading and writing (perhaps by government fiat) to children whose parents perceive no value in reading or writing is different from teaching these skills to children whose parents regard reading and writing as important. The value placed by the society upon the teacher's role will vary with the value placed by the society upon what the teacher teaches. The knowledge possessed and imparted by the teacher, and the emergent *professional* status of the teacher, take the role of teacher into the role-types called 'characters' by Macintyre and surround the 'job' with a 'halo' that spreads to encompass off-the-job conduct.

Another set of values that may be imported into the teacher's role comprises those connected with gender and age. Are teachers usually men or usually women? The status of the gender will affect (and be affected by) the status of the teacher's role. Are teachers usually older persons, presumably with maturity and experience, or are they young persons, presumably with little life-experience? Does the society respect age, or idolize youth? These factors interact with the teacher's role to shape its status in the society.

The social status of the public school teacher may vary from society to society or from community to community, while the norms necessarily intrinsic to the role remain much the same whatever community the teacher is in. It is entirely possible that the necessary norms conflict with the accidental norms imposed upon the teacher by the particular society or community.

If teaching really has the generic nature that we propose here, then we should discover this generic nature in particular teaching activities, including disputes about whether teachers are doing a 'good job,' even if the participants are not aware of this generic nature. We should find this generic form in the particular cases as an invisible centre around which the debaters circle and circle again.

Our 'invisible centre,' however, is actually threefold. There are (1) the norms inherent in the teacher-student relationship; (2) the norms related to the role of the public school teacher as an employee of the school board (representing the state or the community); and (3) the norms relative to the role of the teacher as a professional. These three sets of norms are not necessarily concordant with one another.

This inquiry has focused on the control of teachers' out-of-classroom and out-of-school behaviour by school boards who react to actual or anticipated pressures from the community. When such behaviours become contentious, they may be labelled 'misconduct.' This label then justifies the school board in suspending or dismissing the teacher. (Teachers, in turn, may resist the description of their behaviour as 'misconduct' and characterize their suspension or dismissal as 'unjust,' 'unreasonable,' 'unfair,' even 'illegal.') Employees are expected (reasonably enough) to do nothing on or off the job that would unfairly diminish the reputation of their employer in the community or constituency the employer serves. This principle has been used to justify suspending or dismissing teachers departing from community standards in ways that upset important sections of the community.

Professional misconduct is not employee misconduct. Employers are not qualified, as employers, to judge whether or not a particular behaviour contravenes the standards of the employee's profession. That judgment belongs to the employee's professional peers. By the same token, the profession is not qualified, as a profession, to judge when the employee's behaviour threatens the successful conduct of the employer's business or activity.

Sometimes this distinction may be blurred. It is blurred in teaching. The profession of teaching, surely, is competent to judge whether or not the teacher's teaching conforms to the proper norms of teaching. The employer, namely the school board and its administrators, must also be able to assess whether teaching is adequate or not, or else the school board cannot do its proper job. Here, the domains of professional and employee misconduct overlap.

Furthermore, professional standards must include providing a proper service to schools and school boards. If this were not so, school boards would necessarily be less sure of the good services of the teachers whom they employ. Professional ideals draw into themselves some consideration, at least, of the roles of employer and employee and hence the idea of employee misconduct.

Our cases are primarily concerned with employee misconduct. Notions of professional misconduct, however, are hovering over them in the background.

Misconducts of 'Character'

(a) The Abuse or Misuse of Alcohol and Other 'Drugs'
Alcohol misuse, especially involving alcoholism, seems in the board of reference decisions to be regarded chiefly as an illness, rather than as a moral failing or as an offence against rationality. If it interferes with the teacher's performance as a teacher or with the teacher's administrative duties, then the school board is entitled to dismiss the teacher. The teacher should be given some chance, however, to mend his or her ways. At the board of reference level, such abuse is therefore treated as an offence against the duties of an employee as employee.

(b) Insubordination or Contrary-Minded Behaviour
The cases described actions by teachers in and outside school that went against and hindered policies or decisions of school boards and school administrators. Protest through proper channels was acceptable to the board of reference (not always to the school board). Sometimes this protest went beyond what the board of reference would accept. The board of reference was concerned, amongst other matters, whether or not trust and cooperation between the teacher and the school could continue.

(c) Behaviour Showing Signs of Cruelty
The cases reveal that whether in school or out of school, such behaviour is unacceptable. Such behaviour reveals a disposition in the teacher making the teacher untrustworthy as a person responsible for the care and safety of children. Intemperate behaviour and verbal abuse interfere with a proper teaching relationship and are therefore unacceptable.

Corporal punishment and similar forms of physical discipline may be permitted but have been increasingly narrowly defined and restricted.

(d) Using Obscene or Vulgar Language
The cases before boards of reference show that this is not considered a serious offence in itself. It may, however, be evidence of insubordination, and the insubordination may justify dismissal.

(e) Dishonest Behaviour
Dishonest behaviour goes to the heart both of teaching and of employer-employee relationship. It is grounds for dismissal. The criminal offence of stealing, however, may not always be evidence of dishonesty.

Sexual Misconducts

(a) Paedophilia
Boards of reference correctly consider this a most serious offence. It destroys the trust that ought to exist between teacher and pupil, and it violates the teacher's duty of care towards the children in the teacher's charge. The cases turn on the question of proof (according to the balance of probabilities) whether this offence has or has not occurred. The cases described all occurred in school. We found no instances of paedophilia outside the school among our board of reference cases.

(b) Sexual Liaisons with Students
When such liaisons could interfere with the teacher's responsibilities to the student and to the school, they are forbidden. The teacher is in a position of authority and judgment over the student, and this position is incompatible with sexual relationships between them. If the teacher's behaviour flouts community expectations (or denominational expectations) concerning extramarital intercourse and adultery, the teacher may also be liable to dismissal. It depends on what standards the school is expected to endorse.

(c) Sexual Exhibition and Lewdness
This *may* be grounds for dismissal or suspension *if* the behaviour is judged to offend community values and demean the reputation of the school board and the educational system in the community. The cases showed no evidence that this behaviour had hindered the teachers' abili-

ties to teach effectively in their schools, but this question was touched upon in the cases.

(d) Extramarital and Non-marital Heterosexual Relationships
These become a concern only when such relationships are contrary to the values that the school (a denominational school) is expected to teach. They do not seem to be a concern of the public schools unless they also involve students. These behaviours in themselves do not offend against the inherent necessities either of the teacher-student relationship or the employer-employee relationship.

(e) Homosexual (Gay or Lesbian) Relationships
All of the cases involved men. All entailed criminal charges of gross indecency. All but one were between consenting adults. The earlier cases included an argument that homosexuality offended community standards. The later cases did not. The one case involving a minor (but not a student) included the idea that the teacher's behaviour evidenced a disposition making him a person who should not be trusted with students.

These cases show the degree to which teachers may be expected to abide by certain community ideals that *may or may not* also be part of what teachers are expected to teach, but are not inherent in the roles of teacher-student or employer-employee.

(f) Transvestism and Transsexuality
The one case discovered shows the importance of a teacher in a small community being respected by the people of that community. Sexual deviation destroying that respect makes the teacher's position untenable in the community and may, therefore, entail dismissal by the school board. In such a case, the values of the community may become an interference in what otherwise is a satisfactory teacher's performance.

Unorthodox Teachings and Unquiet Citizens

These cases illustrate collisions between the duties of an employee to his or her employer and the rights of the teacher as a citizen.

(a) Unauthorized Teaching Activities, in School and out of School
Teaching of unauthorized material, in school and contrary to the explicit instructions of school authorities, is insubordination and grounds for dismissal. Unauthorized teaching activities outside school are permitted if

they comply with the general law and do not contravene the Criminal Code. They are ordinarily protected by the Charter of Rights and Freedoms. If they upset a vociferous section of the community, social pressures on the school board and the teacher may still make the teacher's position difficult, and the controversy may lead the school board to dismiss or suspend the teacher in such a way that the teacher has very little recourse but to leave.

(b) Contentious Conduct as Citizens
The question here is whether the teacher's conduct (or the school board's conduct, for that matter) is such that it destroys the confidence that ought to exist between employer and employee. If that confidence is lost, the relationship must cease. The only question that remains is who pays how much to whom.

(c) Denominational Cause
Denominational cause is secured by the Charter of Rights and Freedoms. A teacher in a denominational school is expected to uphold the values of the school. If he or she validly exercises legal rights in a way that contradicts those values (such as criticizing beliefs and normative practices of the denomination), the denominational school has the right to dismiss the teacher. The employee is acting in a way detrimental to the reputation of the school in its community or denominational constituency, and the confidence between employer and employee has been diminished or lost.

In Summary

The 'invisible centre' that we proposed would be present is indeed present. Most evident of all is the concern to maintain or correct the employer-employee relationship. The notions of 'employee misconduct' and 'reasonable cause' for dismissal or other penalty clearly aim to defend an ideal for the employer-employee relationship. This ideal corresponds to the set of inherent necessities suggested earlier in this chapter.

The inherent necessities that we discerned for teaching, as such, are not as clearly evident. They are, however, present. The fiduciary duty or duty of care that the teacher must have concerning the immature student is recognized by the cases in one way or another. The necessity of trustworthiness and the maintenance of the authority of the teacher are also recognized. The distinction between the authority inherent in the teacher as one who knows and the positional authority of the teacher in the school organization, however, is not clearly made.

Some of the cases assert that the teacher is supposed to be a 'role model' for pupils (and perhaps for the general community as well), both in school and out of school. This modelling goes beyond the inherent necessities of teaching in general and of public school teaching in particular. The teacher as a role model becomes a general exemplar of the community's, state's, or denomination's official values and is thus set up on a sort of pedestal for all to see. Whether the schoolteacher should be regarded as such a role model is another question. The answer depends on the ideals of the entire educational system and will vary from school to school, from community to community, and from society to society.

APPENDIX A

Methodological Note

The Beginning Questions

This inquiry revolves around two themes: (a) the responsibility of school-teachers for their 'out-of-school' activities; and (b) the legal means whereby local and district school boards can become agencies enabling the community to impose upon teachers some degree of conformity to community standards. These themes are held together by the rubrics of 'employee misconduct' and (more precisely) 'disreputable outside conduct.' To what extent, we wondered, did school boards act as such agencies controlling unconventional behaviour? And would board of reference decisions, which reviewed school boards' decisions to suspend or dismiss teachers, reveal interesting examples? We had before us the Shewan case in British Columbia, but what was happening in the rest of Canada? Since the answers to these questions were not readily available, we proposed a Canada-wide inquiry.

A division of labour was set up between the two primary researchers. Romulo Magsino was then teaching at Memorial University in Newfoundland and would later move to Manitoba. He therefore took responsibility for the Atlantic provinces and Manitoba. Stuart Piddocke was teaching part-time at universities and colleges in Vancouver and Burnaby, B.C. He took responsibility for British Columbia, Alberta, Saskatchewan, and Ontario. By a curious coincidence, these were the four provinces with a clear board of reference procedure similar to that in British Columbia. Quebec had to wait until we could find a researcher familiar with French (eventually this turned out to be Elizabeth Grace). Michael Manley-Casimir, whose brainchild the entire project was, would coordinate the inquiry and arrange for the publication of the final results.

Data Collection

Our first problem, as we saw it, was to try to make a complete inventory of the board of reference decisions for each province. From this collection, we would select those cases which (a) concerned out-of-school misconduct and (b) involved the community as a player in the dispute. While making this inventory, of course, we would also ascertain the provincial legislation setting up boards of reference and try to get some idea of the administrative processes involved. As it transpired, Magsino and Piddocke took somewhat different approaches in their data collection.

Thanks especially to Mr Earl Cherrington of the B.C. Ministry of Education, we were able to get a complete list of B.C. board of reference cases from 1974, when this procedure first came to British Columbia, to 1989, which was both the time when our study began and when British Columbia changed its procedures, with the effect of making the board of reference procedure largely obsolete. In consequence of this, Piddocke chose to try to cover especially this same time period in the other provinces.

Stuart Piddocke visited the ministries of education for Alberta, Saskatchewan, and Ontario, and was given the opportunity to inspect and read the board of reference records which the ministries had on file. This access was granted him on his undertaking to respect the privacies of the teachers involved. He learned about the administrative procedures then being followed, and was able to gather statistics on the numbers of applications per year and the various outcomes which resulted. For various reasons, however, he was not able to gather a complete inventory of *all* board of reference cases for these provinces, and he therefore concentrated on the period 1974–89. *Within that period*, he was able to get a complete listing of all board of reference cases, including those not directly relevant to our inquiry. From this range, he especially examined those cases which involved the interaction between teacher, school board, and community, and which shed light on the principle that a teacher should act outside the school in a manner which upholds the reputation of the school in the community. The cases varied a great deal in the degree to which they met these criteria.

In Ontario, he encountered the fact that board of reference procedures were currently an alternative to grievance procedures under collective bargaining, and that these grievance procedures were rapidly replacing board of reference procedures and relegating the latter to a supplementary role. The Ontario Ministry of Labour published a regular series of lists briefly summarizing labour arbitration decisions. Piddocke searched these lists for the period 1975–89 looking for cases involving the disreputable outside conduct of public school teachers and found none. He therefore decided to concentrate on the board of reference decisions (which were well documented) and to reserve labour arbitration cases for a later examination. The board of reference decisions were much more comparable to the board of reference decisions in British Columbia, Alberta, and Saskatchewan. At the same time, Piddocke was prepared to include any labour arbitration cases which might come his way that promised to shed light on teacher/school-board/community interactions.

Of course, finding no schoolteachers in the labour case lists did not mean that there were no grievance arbitrations involving schoolteachers. Case 32, 'Gross Indecency in a Public Building,' was one such: we learned about it from one of our early interviews and not through the regular search aids. However, Krashinsky and Sack's (1989) collection of representative Canadian labour arbitration decisions also has none involving the disreputable outside conduct of public school teachers.

Romulo Magsino took a somewhat different approach, which was more purely qualitative than quantitative. Faced with a diversity of procedures and boards – variously labelled 'boards of reference,' 'boards of appeal,' and 'boards of arbitration' – he concentrated on collecting cases which involved contentious conduct by teachers and which also in some way involved the expression of community standards. The time span of his collection was particularly the later 1970s and the 1980s.

In making our searches, we were variously helped or hindered by the different provisions for publication of board of reference or arbitration decisions, or for reporting these to the various ministries of education.

(a) In British Columbia, board of reference decisions were regarded as private arbitrations and were not usually reported in law reports. However, the process was administered by the ministry, and a copy of the decision went into the teacher's professional file. The same file recorded the ministry's administration of the board of reference procedure.

(b) In Alberta, the board of reference process was administered by a special branch of the ministry. This branch received a copy of the decision but did not include it as part of the teacher's professional file, which was the concern of a different branch. (Copies of these decisions, however, were also filed at the court-house where the hearing took place – and were therefore distributed throughout Alberta, if one knew where to look.)

(c) In Saskatchewan, the ministry received copies of the decisions and duly filed them. Little background material was included with these files.

(d) In Manitoba, by contrast, the equivalent tribunal was a board of arbitration which did not have to report its results to the ministry. Romulo Magsino was therefore not able to make a complete inventory of these decisions.[1]

(e) In Ontario, board of reference hearings were administered by the Ministry of Education. The decisions were reported to the ministry and filed under the teacher's name. Like the B.C. cases, these files included a good deal of background material. They included the preliminary reports which had to be made before the minister could decide whether or not to grant a board of reference. A complete inventory therefore existed of the Ontario cases. Piddocke closely inspected those files for the period 1975–89, especially those containing evidence of some community action.

(f) In Quebec, the equivalent procedure followed the labour arbitration model, and these cases were formally reported. Elizabeth Grace examined the complete collection of reports, and the results of her enquiry are given in Grace 1993.

(g) For the Atlantic provinces, the diversity of procedures prevented Romulo Magsino from making a complete inventory. He was able, however, to collect cases from all four provinces revealing interactions among teacher, school, and community. Some of these cases might be called the 'board of reference type,' others 'board of arbitration,' and still others 'labour arbitration' or 'grievance arbitration,' no matter what the labels actually used in the provinces.

When all these difficulties and differences are taken into account, we think that, apart from disputes falling under the grievance procedures of collective agreements, we have managed to achieve a nearly complete survey of board of reference hearings, and hearings before equivalent tribunals, for the years 1974–89. The setting aside of grievance arbitrations means that our study is not a total picture. There must be cases of grievance arbitrations under collective agreements involving 'disreputable outside conduct' of teachers which we have left out of account. But our study nevertheless shows, for the first time and on a national scale, the approximate shape of the iceberg, so to speak, above water.[2]

The Historical Epoch

The inquiry concentrated on the cases for the years 1975–89. These were years of change in Canada. In 1982 the Constitution Act, 1982, introduced the Charter of Rights and Freedoms. For the first five years or so after its introduction, the Charter does not seem to have much influenced the decisions of boards of reference or equivalent tribunals. The most important Charter provision affecting teachers in this first decade, indeed, seems to have been the clause protecting denominational rights in education.

Nor do there seem to have been any board of reference cases during this time involving offences against human rights codes. The Ross case, which is not a board of reference case, is an exception in many ways. David Attis brought in the human rights tribunal precisely because the school board would not suspend or dismiss Ross.

The time, however, was one of change. Grievance arbitration under collective agreements became progressively more important for teachers in all parts of the country, except perhaps Alberta. The language of Charter rights would also become increasingly important. Our study describes the lull before the storm.

Selecting the Cases

The present collection includes all the board of reference cases during the years 1974–89 which expressly illustrate one or more of the types of misconduct listed in chapter 1, together with some involvement by the community. They are not necessarily typical cases – sometimes they are the *only* cases of their kind. If there were no board of reference cases illustrating the particular kind of misconduct plus community involvement, then we still sought to present at least one case showing the relevant kind of conduct (even though lacking any evidence of community involvement).

The selection tries to present cases from all across Canada. Hence we have amplified the board of reference cases with relevant court cases and labour arbitration cases, and others, which we encountered. The selection aims to display the *principles* at work in these various disputes – to show types – rather than to give a statistical overview. As we made this selection, one thing became increasingly evident to us. Most of the interesting disputes never reach a board of reference. They are settled before any hearings are convened. The disputes which come before boards of reference, and equivalent tribunals, are only the tip of an iceberg.

Or at least, that was the situation in 1990, when our research rested.

A Question of Definition

Our use of the labels 'board of reference' and 'board of arbitration' has given one anonymous reviewer some trouble. Perhaps some explanation is therefore due.

The labels 'board of reference,' 'board of arbitration,' and 'board of appeal' are used differently from province to province (see Appendix B). In describing the particular cases, we use the term which was used in the province where the case occurred. But in our more general discussion in chapter 2, 'A System of Control,' we apply the term 'board of reference' to tribunals set up under ministerial authority and supervision, subject to special legislation, to solve disputes between teachers and school boards. This class may be subdivided according to whether the minister has the discretion to deny a properly made application for a board of reference, or not. The term 'board of arbitration' is in that chapter applied to arbitration tribunals set up by the disputing parties themselves, albeit necessarily subject to special enabling legislation, without ministerial intervention (apart perhaps from the arbitrators' duty to inform the ministry of the results). This second type resembles boards of arbitration set up by general labour legislation, and may or may not (depending on the province) be subsumed under the latter.

Bias

The anonymous reviewer who raised the question of definition also thought that our selection is biased and therefore not a true reflection of the real state of affairs in Canada. He (or she) especially noted our omission of labour arbitration cases. This reviewer was partly right. Our study is biased towards board of reference cases and away from grievance cases arising under collective agreement, which we did not examine. As a result of this bias in our collection, our study also has perhaps a greater representation from Western than from Eastern Canada. But within this constraint, and within our time-frame of 1974–89, we believe that our selection includes all the board of reference decisions which concerned the conduct of teachers outside the classroom and the school. Our selection is therefore probably as representative as any selection can be. How, by the way, do you infer the shape of the whole iceberg from that portion above the water, unless you already know what's beneath the water? – and we don't.

APPENDIX B

Statutory Background for Boards of Reference or Equivalent Tribunals

Note that the following account describes the statutes up to the year 1989, by which time the bulk of our research was done. For this reason, this account is written in the past tense. Much of what follows has also appeared in the articles by Piddocke, Magsino, and Grace in *Education and Law Journal* 5/1 (April 1993).

British Columbia

The statutory foundation for boards of reference in British Columbia is to be found in the School Act in its various forms. Before 1973, boards of reference did not exist in British Columbia, and disputes over dismissals and suspensions had to be referred to the courts and the common law of master and servant. In 1972 changes to the School Act gave greater job security to teachers by instituting boards of reference and the corollary right to reinstatement if the dismissal was held to be unjustified. These changes were part of the labour legislation of the then recently elected NDP government, which also introduced the new B.C. Labour Code. After the NDP lost the next election, the Social Credit government amended the Labour Code but left the lesser changes of the School Act alone. Some years later, in 1988, Bill 20 introduced a new Teaching Profession Act (which is now law) and also amended the School Act. These amendments retained boards of reference, but reduced them to a remedy available if no grievance procedures existed in the collective agreement between the school board and the local association of teachers. Given the prevalence of collective agreements by this time, however, this amendment abolished boards of reference for all practical purposes. The Teaching Profession Act created a new College of Teachers, which would police the professional conduct of teachers and was enabled to recommend that teachers be decertified or otherwise penalized for professional misconduct. Prior to that time, decertification was purely the responsibility of the minister of education, and the B.C. Teachers' Federation occupied an uncertain position in between a trade union and a self-policing professional association.

The former School Act, R.S.B.C. 1979, c. 375, provided that teachers might be suspended by their school boards (a) for misconduct, neglect of duty, or refusal to obey a lawful order of the school board; or (b) if charged with a criminal offence (section 122[1]). Section 122(3) then allowed the school board to dismiss the teacher if the teacher was convicted of the criminal charge. Section 122(2)(b) allowed the school board, after suspending a teacher for misconduct, etc., subsequently to dismiss the teacher for that same reason. After a teacher was formally notified in writing of the suspension, he or she had to be given a chance within one week of the date of the notice to present her or his side of the story to the school board (sec. 122[2][a]). After this hearing by the school board, and not until, the board might then resolve to dismiss the teacher or to extend the suspension with or without pay. If the board chose to dismiss the teacher, or to suspend the teacher for more than ten days, on grounds of misconduct, etc., or criminal charge or conviction, the teacher then had ten days in which to appeal the decision of the school board (sec. 129[1]).[1]

To appeal for a board of reference, the teacher, or his/her legal representative, wrote a letter to the minister of education requesting that the minister appoint a board of reference to review the decision of the school board.[2] This right to appeal to a board of reference was given to the teacher by the statute (sec. 129[2]), and the minister had no discretion to refuse the appeal if it were made within the ten days provided by the statute.

The minister next appointed the board of reference. This board had three members: (i) the chair, appointed from a list of nominees provided by the chief justice of the Supreme Court of British Columbia; (ii) a member nominated by the B.C. School Trustees' Association; and (iii) a member nominated by the B.C. Teachers' Federation (sec. 129[2]). The board heard the teacher and the school board and whatever witnesses these wished to present. Each side might have, and usually had, legal counsel present. After the hearing was over, the board had thirty days to bring down its decision, but this thirty days might be extended by the minister, and in most cases was thus extended.

Until 1980 the boards of reference could only allow or dismiss the appeal by the teacher. In 1980 they were granted the power also to vary the decision of the school board, 'and make any order [they considered] appropriate in the circumstances' (sec. 129[6]). Before then, if a board of reference decided that a teacher had committed misconduct but that the suspension or dismissal by the school board was excessively severe, the board could only allow the appeal.

If either the teacher or the school board was unhappy with the decision of the board of reference, they might appeal this decision to the county court or the Supreme Court of British Columbia (sec. 129[7]). This appeal was usually formulated by saying that the board of reference erred in some manner 'in law.' This appeal was subject to the rules of the respective courts.

The legislation under section 122 did not limit its effect to any particular class of teachers.

The changes to the School Act coming into force as a result of Bill 20 deleted the former section 122 and replaced it with a new section 122. Section 122(1) now allowed a school board to 'dismiss or discipline a teacher for just and reasonable cause.' Section 122(2) provided that if the teacher's employment was the subject of a collective agreement, the appropriate grievance procedure shall apply. Section 122.1 permitted unsatisfactory performance as grounds for dismissal, and section 122.2 permitted suspension of the teacher with or without pay if the teacher should be charged with a criminal offence. Section 122.6(1) still required the minister to appoint a board of reference if one was properly applied for, but changed the composition. The board was now to consist of (i) one person nominated by the teacher; (ii) a nominee of the school board; and (iii) a chair nominated jointly by the other two nominees or, if they could not agree quickly enough, chosen by the minister. This change made the composition of boards of reference more like that of Manitoba's boards of arbitration.

Alberta

In Alberta in 1989, teachers were subject to three distinct but interlocking systems which acted to keep the behaviours of teachers up to a certain standard, and to nudge out of the profession those persons who could not or would not abide by this standard. The first and third systems go back to the mid-1930s and the legislation of William Aberhard's Social Credit government. The second is much more recent, but is a reform of the practice of certification by the Ministry of Education, which is oldest of all. These systems were (a) the discipline procedure of the Alberta Teachers' Association, which penalized 'unprofessional conduct'; (b) the practice review procedure of the Council on Alberta Teaching Standards, which, subject to ministerial approval, penalized 'incompetence'; and (c) the power given by the School Acts to school boards to terminate a contract or a designation for 'reasonable' grounds. The penalties imposed by the A.T.A. ranged from expulsion or suspension from the Association to fines to recommending to the minister of education that an offender's teaching certificate be cancelled. Membership in the Association was required for a teacher to teach in Alberta or, more exactly, to be employed by a school board as a teacher (Teaching Profession Act, R.S.A. 1980, c. T-3, s. 5). Possession of a valid teaching certificate was also required for employment by a school board (School Act, S.A. 1988, c. S-3.1, s. 74). The penalties imposed by the minister ranged from cancellation or suspension of the teacher's certificate to remedial studies and training. Since a teacher could not legally teach in Alberta without the certificate, cancellation stopped both the occupation and employment of the teacher. The penalties which a school board could impose were dismissal or suspension, with or without pay or damages in lieu of notice. These penalties affected directly the employment of the teacher, and might entail his or her leaving the school district in order to find further employment as a teacher. It was also legally open to the minister to cancel or suspend a teacher's certificate if (in the minister's view) the cause for the dismissal or suspension by the school board should warrant it: this legal possibility, however, seems not to have been used by the minister unless the A.T.A. had also recommended the cancellation or suspension of the certificate.

The decisions of the A.T.A. were open to review by the Teaching Profession Appeal Board, and the decisions of the school boards were open to review by boards of reference. Each of these boards consisted of a judge from the Alberta Court of Queen's Bench.[3] They served not only to correct teachers, but also to correct the discipline procedure of the A.T.A. and the actions of school boards when these went awry. Generally, school boards seem to have required and to have received more correction than did the A.T.A. But the A.T.A. was very conscious that its procedures must satisfy the scrutiny of the T.P.A.B. and the higher courts.

In 1988 (when the data behind this summary were collected) there were two School Acts to be taken into account. One was assented to 6 July 1988 but was yet to be proclaimed in force (Statutes of Alberta 1988,

c. S-3.1). The second was the older School Act, R.S.A. 1980, c. S-3, with amendments in force as of 1 July 1985.

In the older version, a public school board could employ as a teacher only someone who held a qualifying certificate issued by the Department of Education (School Act, R.S.A. 1980, c. S-3, s. 80). A teacher's contract with the school board terminated if the certificate was suspended or cancelled or simply allowed to expire (ibid., s. 88). The school board was also allowed to terminate a contract of employment with a teacher, or to terminate a designation of a teacher as a principal or other administrator,[4] provided that termination gave the teacher at least thirty days written notice (ibid., s. 89[1]). In making this termination, the board was required to specify the reasons for the termination, 'and in each case the board shall act reasonably' (ibid., s. 89[2]).

The School Act allowed a school board, on reasonable grounds, to suspend a teacher for 'gross misconduct, neglect of duty or neglect to obey a lawful order of the board' (s. 90[1]). The notice of this suspension had to be sent to the teacher in writing and also be communicated to the minister of education (s. 90[2]). The teacher might then within fourteen days appeal to the minister, who was then obliged to refer the appeal to a board of reference. The board of reference was given the power to investigate the matter and to confirm or reject the decision of the school board (ss. 90[3] and 90[4]). If the board of reference confirmed the suspension, the school board was allowed to terminate the teacher's contract (s. 90[7]).

Section 96 of the School Act provided that if a disagreement arose between a teacher and a school board concerning a termination of a contract of employment, or a termination of a designation, then the school board or the teacher might appeal to the minister, who shall then refer the appeal to a board of reference. The board of reference was allowed to 'make any order it considers just with respect to the appeal' (s. 98[3]).

The School Act did not state whether or not the decision of the board of reference might be appealed.[5] Section 98.1(1) provided that 'a copy of an order of the Board of Reference may be filed with the clerk of the Court of Queen's Bench in the judicial district in which the cause of the proceedings before the Board of Reference arose.' The new School Act retained these various provisions. Section 124 of the new act, however, provided that a copy of the board of reference decision shall be filed with the clerk of the Court of Queen's Bench. The setting-up and arranging of board of reference hearings was the administrative responsibility of the registrar of the Teacher Certification and Development Branch.

Saskatchewan

The legislation governing the termination of teachers' contracts, the appealing of such terminations, and the powers of boards of reference was in 1989 set out in sections 206 to 226 of the Education Act, Statutes of Saskatchewan, 1978, c. 17;[6] amended 1979–80, c. 92, s. 24; 1980–1, c. 52, ss. 16–22; 1982–3, c. 16, s. 15; 1983, c. 17, ss. 21–2; 1984–5, c. 30, s. 10.

Concerning teachers' contracts and dismissals, section 206(a) of the Education Act[7] gave the school board, or 'board of education,' the power to suspend or dismiss a teacher, and terminate the teacher's contract, without notice for 'gross misconduct, neglect of duty or refusing to obey any lawful order of the the board,' but required the board to give to the teacher written reasons for such termination within five days of the termination.

Section 206(b) empowered a board of education to terminate a teacher's contract, with not less than thirty days notice in writing, when the 'teacher is employed in a teaching position that is no longer considered by the board to be necessary for the teaching requirements or educational programs of the division.' The reasons for this termination had to be set out in the notice. The reason for termination which this section thus gave the school board may be summed up under the rubric of 'redundancy.' This section also applied 'notwithstanding any other provision of this Act.'

Sections 206(c) and (d) together empowered a school board simply to terminate a teacher's contract at any time provided the teacher was given not less than thirty days notice in writing setting out the 'reason or reasons' for the termination.

Section 210 amplified sections 206(c) and (d). It stated:

Where a notice of termination is given pursuant to clause 206(c) or (d), the reasons for the termination required by those clauses to be stated in the notice may include professional incompetency, unprofessional conduct, immorality, neglect of duty, physical or mental disability, or any other cause which in the opinion of the school board renders the teacher unsuitable for the position then held by him, and the notice shall state that in the opinion of the board the teacher is, for the reasons so stated, unsuitable for continued teaching service in that position.

Both 'redundancy' and 'unsuitablity' turn out to be major concerns for the board of reference decisions.

Section 209 provided that the school board 'shall' give the teacher an opportunity, if the teacher requested such an opportunity, to appear before the school board to show cause why the contract should not be terminated. Section 207 allowed a teacher to terminate his or her contract with the school board by giving thirty days notice in writing. Section 208 allowed the teacher and the school board to terminate the contract by mutual agreement in writing.

Both the teacher and the school board might appeal the termination of the contract and apply to the minister of education for 'an investigation of the termination by a board of reference.' The school board was empowered by section 213 to apply if the teacher gave notice that the contract would terminate before 30 June. The teacher was empowered by section 212(1) to appeal all terminations made by the school board under section 206. The appeal by the teacher had to be made within twenty days, that by the school board within fifteen days, of receipt of the notice of termination.

But not all teachers might apply for a board of reference. Section 212(2) stated:

Where a notice of termination is given pursuant to clause 206(c), subsection (1) shall not apply in the case of a teacher:
(a) who has attained, or will attain, the full age of 65 years on or before June 30 of the school year in which the notice of termination is given; or
(b) who has not been employed as a teacher by the board of education:
   (i)   for at least two complete school years;
   (ii) for at least four complete and consecutive terms; or
   (iii) during a period in respect of which he has received the equivalent of two years' salary in accordance with this Act.

This clause has been understood by the minister of education to permit the minister to reject an application for a board of reference if the teacher falls into any one of the four classes described in the subsection. This subsection denies the minister the jurisdiction to grant boards of reference to teachers in these circumstances, and the minister has in fact refused boards of reference on these grounds.

Section 214(1) required the minister ('the minister shall appoint') to appoint a board of reference upon the receipt of the application from the teacher or the school board. The board of reference was to consist of (a) a person nominated by the teacher; (b) a nominee of the school board; and (c) the chair of the board. The chair was either a person jointly nominated by the other two nominees, or, if these two could not agree on a chair within ten days after the receipt by the minister of the application, a person nominated by a judge of the Court of Queen's Bench (subsec. 3). Furthermore, by subsection (4), if either the teacher or the school board failed to nominate a representative within that ten days, the minister 'may' also appoint a representative for either.

The sections which follow in the Act set out the powers and procedures of the board of reference. We may especially note that the board 'shall' investigate and decide the issue within thirty days after the appointment of the chair (s. 215[1]). Section 217 limited the 'scope of the investigation and the findings of the Board of Reference' to 'the reasons given in the written notice of termination of the contract of employment.' Section 220 provided that the decision of the board of reference is by majority vote of all the members, with the chair also having a casting vote. The powers of decision of the board of reference were set out by section 221:

The board of reference may:
  (a) confirm the termination of the contract of employment;
  (b) order the continuation of the contract of employment;
  (c) make any additional order or recommendation with respect to a matter incidental to an order under clause (a) or (b); or
  (d) where the board of education and the teacher, at any time prior to or during the investigation, agree in writing to a mutually acceptable disposition of the matter, make an order confirming that settlement;
and the chairman of the board of reference shall forward a copy of its findings and decision to the minister and to the parties to the investigation.

Section 221(c), in effect, allowed the board to vary the decision of the school board. Thus the board might uphold a termination of contract but also require the school board to pay substantial damages to the teacher. In 1982 to 1988, for example, there were nineteen board of reference decisions in Saskatchewan, consisting of eight decisions in which the board confirmed the dismissal by the school board, nine in which the board reinstated the teacher, and two in which other decisions were arrived at. But the confirmations, for the most part, included orders by the board for damages to be paid to the teacher, so that these awards were by no means unambiguous victories for the school board. Stuart Piddocke was told, both by officials in the ministry of education and by legal counsel for the Saskatchewan Public School Trustees' Association, that indeed school boards perceived that the board of reference procedure was loaded in favour of the teacher and therefore that they preferred to 'settle out of court' rather than risk a board of reference.

Section 222(1) provided that the decision of the board of reference was final and binding, but section 222(3) provided that the decision might be appealed to the Court of Queen's Bench on the grounds that

(a) there is an error of law on the face of the record;
(b) the board of reference lacked jurisdiction to hear the matter; or
(c) the board of reference exceeded its jurisdiction.

These are, of course, standard grounds in administrative law for appealing the decision of any administrative tribunal.

Besides sending copies of the decision to the minister and to the parties (sec. 221), the chair of the board was required by section 223 to file a certified copy of the decision 'in the office of a local registrar of the Court of Queen's Bench within 14 days after the decision is made.'

Manitoba

In Manitoba, the idea of a board of reference goes back at least as far as 1919, when the Manitoba Teachers' Federation was formed.[8] Following representations by the Federation, the Manitoba government in 1920 set up a board of reference to decide disputes between teachers and school boards. However, after a promising beginning, two school boards refused to abide by the board of reference's decisions and found that its decisions did not have the force of law. Later, appeal to the board of reference was provided for in a standard form of contract, but the contract form itself was not made obligatory for school boards. School boards apparently continued to flout inconvenient board of reference decisions. Teachers relied primarily on the Manitoba Teachers' Federation for help. They had many occasions to do so. 'Thus,' says Magsino, 'disgruntled teachers went to the Federation for assistance in 948 tenure cases in 1937 and 701 tenure cases from Easter to September of 1939' (Magsino 1990: 3)

In 1948 the Manitoba Labour Relations Act provided a legal mechanism for collective bargaining and for conciliation of disputes. The definition of 'employee' in the Act allowed the Act to be construed to cover teachers. In 1956 the Public Schools Act (1954) was revised to transfer the provisions regarding collective bargaining and dispute settlement, where teachers were concerned, from the Labour Relations Act to the Public Schools Act. However, 'dispute' was carefully defined to *exclude* any 'controversy or difference arising out of the termination or threatened termination of the contract of a teacher by reason of alleged conduct unbecoming a teacher on the part of the teacher' (quoted in Magsino 1990: 4).

This unsatisfactory state of affairs was eventually remedied in 1963 by An Act to Amend the Public Schools Act. This Act provided for boards of arbitration whose decisions had the force of law but could be appealed to the Manitoba Court of Appeal. So finally there existed in Manitoba a legal mechanism equivalent to the boards of reference which have been reviewed for British Columbia, Alberta, and Saskatchewan.

The Manitoba Public Schools Act, R.S.M. 1970, c. P250, sec. 281(3)(a) (or, more recently, S.M. 1980, c. 33, s. 92[5][a]) permitted a teacher, after receiving notice of his or her dismissal by the school, to

... require that the matter of the termination of the agreement be submitted to an arbitration board composed of one representative appointed by the teacher and one representative appointed by the board, and a third person, who shall be chairman of the board of arbitration ... and chosen by ... the two persons so appointed, none of whom shall be a member or employee of the board ...[9]

The Act went on to prescribe that

the issue before the arbitration board shall be whether or not the reason given by the board for terminating the agreement constitutes cause for terminating the agreement ... (sec. 281[3][d] [S.M. 1980, c. 33, s. 92(5)(d)])

If the arbitration board found that the reason given did not constitute cause for terminating the agreement, the arbitration board was empowered to order the continuation of the agreement (sec. 281[3][e] [S.M. 1980, c. 33, s. 92(5)(e)]). Copies of the arbitration decision were to be sent to the parties and to the minister (sec. 281[3][f] [S.M. 1980, c. 33, s. 92(5)(f)]).[10] Some of the duties of a teacher were set out in section 283.

Comparing this legislation with that from the other provinces, we may note that the boards of arbitration were set up by the parties to the dispute, and did not require any action, whether obligatory or discretionary, by the minister. The board had only the power to confirm the termination or reinstate the teacher, and it might decide only whether or not the reasons given by the school board were good 'cause' for termination. The board was not allowed to vary the school board's decision nor impose its own resolution of the dispute. Nevertheless, the reference to 'cause' allowed the entire law of employee discipline to be applied in deciding whether or not such cause had been given in the proferred reasons.

Boards of arbitration have tried, in one case at least, to vary a school board's decision. In *Marcoux v. Fort Garry School Division No. 5*, the board changed a dismissal into a reinstatement (as the board was empowered to do) but imposed a penalty upon the teacher of suspension without pay. Upon appeal (by the school board) to the Manitoba Court of Appeal, the appeal judge upheld the reinstatement but removed the suspension without pay, and said that imposing such a penalty was beyond the jurisdiction of the board of arbitration (see Czuboka 1985: 157–65, 300).

Teachers were also made subject to discipline committees set up by the minister of education. These committees were provided by the Department of Education Act (1941–3) in order to investigate and report to the minister 'in any case where a teacher's certificate is suspended for any cause other than incompetency' (Magsino 1990: 7, quoting from *Revised Statutes of Manitoba* [1954]). In 1980 the Education Administration Act changed the name from 'discipline committee' to 'certificate review committee,' and made the procedures of such committees more explicit. Teachers under review had the right to legal counsel.

Furthermore, the rights of school boards to dismiss or suspend teachers, and of teachers to appeal such dismissals or suspensions to boards of arbitration, were usually treated in the collective agreements between teachers and school boards.

Ontario

Ontario presents us with still another variation on the board of reference. A hearing before a board of reference was not a right of the teacher (or, for that matter, of the school board). The minister had the discretion to refuse to grant a board of reference. Boards of reference had only the power to continue or discontinue the contract; they did not have the power to vary a dismissal by the school board or to order the payment of damages. The application for a board of reference might be made only following the termination of a contract, and was not available for suspensions. There was no *explicit* mention of 'reasonable' or any other grounds for termination, nor of 'misconduct' as grounds. The absence of such mention left the board of reference free to fall back on standard master-and-servant law in order to determine whether the termination of the contract was fair in the circumstances.

Boards of reference in Ontario go back to 1938, when the Teachers'

Board of Reference Act was enacted (see Waters 1991). The purpose of this legislation was to provide a clear procedure for resolving a difference of opinion concerning the dismissal, or termination of contract, of a permanent teacher. Until that date, teachers had only the right under common law to sue for wrongful dismissal, whereby they could receive payment for damages but not gain back their positions. The board of reference legislation gave teachers the right of reinstatement. Until the passage in 1975 of the School Boards and Teachers Collective Negotiations Act (also known as Bill 100), boards of reference were the only such procedure available to teachers. Bill 100 introduced the possibility of grievance arbitration under collective agreements (sec. 52 of the School Boards and Teachers Collective Negotiations Act), when the collective agreements contained clauses which gave teachers the right to grieve what they considered unjust dismissal and to proceed to a board of arbitration. In consequence, grievance procedures have emerged as an alternative to appeals to boards of reference. Grievance appeals fall under the law of labour arbitration, which is not quite the same as either the jurisprudence concerning boards of reference or the master-and-servant law which preceded both labour law and boards of reference. Since 1975 these grievance procedures have increasingly replaced board of reference applications, which have in recent years fallen noticeably in number. There are still occasions outside the purview of collective agreements, however, when the board of reference procedure is required in order to ensure fairness.

The legislation regarding boards of reference in Ontario was in 1989 given as part of the Education Act, R.S.O. 1980, c. 129.[11] Section 150 of the Education Act defined the powers of school boards in Ontario. In that section, subsection (1), sub-subsection (2), stated that a school board may

... subject to Part X, appoint and remove such officers and servants and, subject to Part IX, appoint and remove such teachers, as it considers expedient, determine the terms on which such officers, servants and teachers are to be employed, prescribe their duties and fix their salaries ...

Part IX (sec. 230–48) concerned teachers. Within this part, sections 238–48 provided for boards of reference. The following describes the sections in Part IX that we should note in particular.

Section 230 provided that full- or part-time teachers who are not occasional teachers shall be either probationary or permanent. The contract between the school board and the teacher shall be in writing, but if such a memorandum in writing of the contract has not been made, the contract shall be deemed to follow the form of contract prescribed for a permanent teacher. One effect of this provision was to open the way for a teacher who has been hired on a probationary basis and then is rehired hastily without a written memorandum of contract to be considered as hired on a permanent contract and therefore to be eligible to apply for a board of reference. Section 238, which begins the legislation concerning boards of reference, defined a 'teacher' for the purposes of that legislation as being 'a person qualified to teach in an elementary or secondary school and employed by a school board on the terms and conditions contained in the form of contract prescribed for a permanent teacher.'

Section 234 allowed a school board, with the consent of the minister, to terminate the teacher's contract either immediately or with thirty days' notice, when 'a matter arises that in the opinion of the Minister adversely affects the welfare of the school in which the teacher is employed ...'

Section 235 prescribed the duties of a teacher. Most of this section referred to activities in the classroom or in the school. It did not exclude, however, duties outside the school which might be held to be incumbent on the teacher as a necessarily implied part of the teacher's role. Subsection (c) went further. It stated that the duty of a teacher is

to inculcate by precept and example respect for religion and the principles of Judaeo-Christian morality and the highest regard for truth, justice, loyalty, love of country, humanity, benevolence, sobriety, industry, frugality, purity, temperance and all other virtues ...

This provision certainly makes the off-the-job conduct and the lifestyle of the teacher a proper concern of the school board, especially when the teacher falls noticeably short of one of these virtues. It is a two-edged sword, however, and possibly could be used to justify the conduct of a teacher at odds with the community and the school board when the conduct of these latter also falls noticeably below the standard of behaviour proclaimed in this subsection (although we have not yet encountered any examples of this possibility actually occurring).

Section 239 required that termination of the contract by either the school board or the teacher be by notice in writing. Section 239(3) then gave the teacher the right to appeal the termination or the dismissal to the minister, within twenty-one days after receiving the notice of termination.

Section 241(1) then stated:

Upon receipt of an application for a Board of Reference, the Minister shall cause notice of the application to be sent by registered mail to the other party to the disagreement and shall within thirty days of sending the notice inquire into the disagreement and shall, within the same time,

(a) refuse to grant the Board of Reference; or

(b) grant the Board of Reference and appoint a judge to act as chairman thereof.

The minister must, that is to say, conduct a preliminary inquiry, but then has the discretion to refuse or grant a board of reference. Hence a board of reference was not, in Ontario, a statutorily granted right. The teacher had the right to a ministerial inquiry, but the granting of the board of reference was very much at the discretion of the minister.

Section 241(3) required the teacher and the school board to each nominate a representative to the board of reference within twelve days of being sent a notice to this effect by the minister. If the applicant (namely, the teacher) failed to nominate a representative within this time, the minister was instructed to deem the application abandoned (subsec.[4]). If the respondent (namely, the school board) did not appoint a representative in time, the minister was instructed to order the continuation of the contract (subsec.[5]).

Section 244(1) gave the board of reference the power to direct that the contract be continued or discontinued. This direction was, according to section 246(1), binding upon both school board and the teacher. These are the only powers to order which the Act gave to the board of reference.

Section 244(2) instructed the chair of the board of reference to report to the minister and the parties the disposition of the application which came before the board of reference.

The Act made no provision for appealing the board of reference decision to the courts, but neither did it forbid either party to appeal to the courts for judicial review of the board of reference decision. Such a judicial review would consider whether or not the board had erred in its application of the law.

The impact of the minister's discretion can be clearly seen in the fact that of a total of 321 applications received by the ministry during 1973–88, 123 were granted and 101 were refused boards of reference. Boards of reference were not granted when, in the minister's opinion (after the ministry had made a preliminary inquiry and some recommendations), the issue at stake concerned the interpretation of a collective agreement. They were granted when the minister considered that there was some issue or question of fact or of law which needed to be decided.

Quebec

Quebec's procedure resembles that of Manitoba rather than those of the 'board of reference' provinces.[12] In brief, when a school board suspended or dismissed a teacher on the grounds of incapacity, negligence in the performance of his or her duties, insubordination, misconduct, or immorality ('pour cause d'incapacité, de negligence à remplir leurs devoirs, d'insubordination, d'inconduite, ou d'immoralité ...'), the school board was required, upon the teacher's request, to provide him or her with the reasons for its decision. The teacher was then entitled to appeal the decision to a 'conseil d'arbitrage,' subject to the grievance provisions of the collective agreement. The council of arbitration comprised a representative of the teachers' union, a representative of the school board, and a 'president' or chair chosen by the other two members.

The council of arbitration was required to determine whether proper procedure for the dismissal, etc., had been followed, and whether the reasons alleged by the school board were among the causes listed, namely incapacity, neglect of duty, insubordination, misconduct, or immorality. The powers of the council were limited to setting aside the decision of the school board if the prescribed procedure was not followed or if the reasons alleged were not well founded, ordering the reinstatement ('reintegration') of the teacher, and determining compensation to which the teacher might be entitled. Some tribunals have viewed this last provision as allowing them to order suspension without pay in preference to outright dismissal. The decisions of these councils of arbitration might be appealed to the Quebec Superior Court.

This procedure has remained much the same from 1964 to 1988. Up to 1977, the dismissal or suspension of teachers by school boards was governed by the Loi de l'Instruction Publique, or Education Act, R.S.Q. 1964, c. 235. This Act was modified slightly in 1969, and then revised further in 1977 (Education Act, R.S.Q. 1977, c. I-14). The changes did not affect the powers of the school board to dismiss, suspend, or fail to reengage teachers. The regulations under the revised Act of 1977 did specify in more detail, however, the procedures of the council of arbitration, and allowed the council to award damages to the teacher in lieu of reinstatement. In 1982 the Act was amended to give greater weight to the collective agreements between teachers and school boards. The previous arbitration procedure remained as the 'default' procedure, if the collective agreement failed to specify a procedure. During 1988–9, the former Education Act was repealed and replaced by a new one. This new Act appeared to leave out all reference to criteria for the dismissal and non–re-engagement of teachers by school boards, and to concentrate on the circumstances under which the minister of education can revoke or suspend a teaching licence.

The minister's powers deserve some mention. Section 18 of the 1964 Education Act (R.S.Q. 1964, c. 235, s. 18) provided that upon receipt of a complaint accusing a teacher of 'bad conduct, immorality, drunkenness, or grave neglect of duty,' the minister was to cause the substance of the complaint to be served on the teacher by a bailiff, and to require the teacher to declare whether she or he admitted or denied the charge. If the teacher denied the charge, the minister would set up a special committee to hear the complaint and to report to the minister (Grace 1991: 1). In 1984, An Act Respecting Public Elementary and Secondary Education, S.Q. 1984, c. 39, restated this procedure and provided for an investigating committee to recommend that a teacher's certificate be suspended, revoked, or maintained subject to conditions 'for exceptional cause such as misconduct or immorality or for any serious offence in the performance of his duties.' The 1989 Education Act repeated these provisions.

The Atlantic Provinces[13]

Nova Scotia

The 1947 Education Act, section 45, allowed the summary suspension or dismissal of any teacher for incompetence, persistent neglect of duty, or immoral conduct. The school trustees, however, could do this only by unanimous resolution and subject to the approval of the school inspector. The trustees were also required to give a written statement of their action, its grounds, and the evidence for the grounds to the school inspector and the superintendent of schools. There was no requirement that the teacher be heard by the school trustees, nor that the trustees give a reason or report to the teacher. The teacher was allowed to appeal the suspension or dismissal to the governor-in-council, who might vary or reverse the action of the trustees. This procedure was affirmed by the Education Act, R.S.N.S. 1954, c. 78, s. 100, which merely replaced 'trustees' by 'school board' and 'superintendent' by 'minister.'

In 1965 amendments to the Education Act required school boards to give the teacher 'reasonable notice of the complaints against him and an opportunity to be heard in person or by counsel before the board.' The amendments also required the school board to send a copy of the suspension or dismissal report to the teacher, who was then given thirty days in which to appeal to the governor-in-council.

In 1969 the Act to Amend the Education Act 1967, R.S.N.S. 1969, c. 38, set out procedures for suspending and dismissing permanent and probationary teachers. Among other provisions, it granted the teacher the right to a board of appeal comprised of a member appointed by the teacher, a member appointed by the school board, and a chair appointed by the two other members or by the minister if these could not agree. The board of appeal had the power 'to make an order confirming, varying, or revoking the suspension or dismissal or confirming or revoking the cancellation of contract.' The board of appeal's order was to be final and binding upon school board and teacher, and copies of the order, reasons, and report were to be sent to the school board and the teacher. This board of appeal thus resembles the Manitoba board of arbitration rather than the original B.C. board of reference.

In 1972 further amendments to the Education Act dropped incompetence, persistent neglect of duty, immoral conduct, or unsatisfactory performance of contract as grounds for suspension or dismissal, and replaced them by the ground of 'just cause.'

In 1974 the Teachers' Collective Bargaining Act, S.N.S. 1974, c. 32, ss. 11, 12, required every teacher in Nova Scotia to belong to the Nova Scotia Teachers' Union and declared the Union to be the exclusive bargaining agent for the teachers vis-à-vis their employer. In 1987 the Union finally reached an agreement with the minister concerning grievance procedures. The grievance procedures concern alleged violations of, or differences of interpretation concerning, the collective agreement. Also in 1987 the board of appeal procedure was incorporated by law into the collective agreement.

New Brunswick

New Brunswick's Education Act (1973, ss. 42[2], 47) declared that a school board 'shall' not dismiss a teacher employed by it for three consecutive years, except *for cause* and provided that the teacher is given a notice of dismissal. The teacher might then appeal to a board of reference whose decision was final. The Act, at section 56, also stipulated that though the terms and conditions of the teacher's employment are those set out in the Act, these terms might be altered by a collective agreement made under the Public Service Labour Relations Act; and that the terms of the collective agreement would prevail over the Education Act in this matter. The Public Service Labour Relations Act, and the agreement between the Board of Management (i.e., the Province as employer) and the New Brunswick Teachers' Federation, provided for grievance procedures and for boards of adjudication to decide disputes.

The New Brunswick board of reference procedure seems thereby to have been largely superseded by general labour legislation.[14]

Newfoundland

Newfoundland teachers gained collective bargaining rights in 1973 after a bitter fight, lasting several years, with the provincial government. Collective agreements made between the Newfoundland Teachers' Association, on the one side, and the Newfoundland Association of School Trustees and the provincial Treasury Board, on the other, specified grievance procedures and the arbitration of disputes.[15] Either the teachers, the Newfoundland Teachers' Association, or the employer might request an arbitration. Arbitration boards consisted of a member appointed by the teacher, a member appointed by the school board, and a chair chosen by the first two (or, if they could not agree, by the minister of labour and manpower).[16] The board of arbitration had

... full power to direct payment of compensation, vary the penalty, or to direct reinstatement of a benefit or privilege, or to affirm the taking away of such benefit or privilege as the board may determine appropriate to settle the issues between the parties, and may give retroactive effect to its decision.[17]

Prince Edward Island

In Prince Edward Island as of 1988, the collective agreement between the government and the Prince Edward Island Teachers' Federation prescribed no grievance procedure for either party. However, the School Act (R.S.P.E.I. 1974, cap. s-2) did prescribe a procedure. The Act stated that a teacher's contract shall continue in force from school year to school year, and may be terminated only at the end of a school year by notice in writing given by one party to the other. The Act permitted a regional school board to dismiss a teacher at any time for cause or for unsatisfactory service (sec. 43). It stated that this dismissal was to be done in the manner provided by regulation.

The regulations[18] allowed for a board of reference both when a school board suspended or dismissed a teacher and when the minister suspended or cancelled a teacher's licence.

When a regional school board decided to suspend or dismiss a teacher, the board was required to notify the teacher in writing and give the precise reasons, which had to fall within the general category of 'for cause or unsatisfactory service.' Before the board thus suspended or dismissed the teacher, the board had to give the teacher an opportunity to meet with the school board and present his or her own side of the story. But the initiative for this meeting was left up to the teacher.

After the teacher had received notice of the suspension or dismissal, the teacher had thirty days in which to request the minister to establish a board of reference. The minister was required to establish the board of reference within ten days after receiving the teacher's written application. This board was to consist of a nominee of the teacher, a nominee of the regional school board, and a chair chosen by the other two. If the first two could not agree on a chair, the regulations authorized the minister to appoint one. After the board of reference had been established, the teacher had five days in which to appeal to the board. The board had the power to administer oaths and to compel the attendance of witnesses. A majority decision, with the chair having the casting vote if necessary, was the board's decision. Copies of the decision were to be sent to the teacher, the regional school board, and the minister. The regulations did not indicate whether the board had the power to vary the suspension or dismissal, or to assign damages. They did state that when the board decided to reinstate the teacher, the teacher was to be reinstated 'without loss of any benefit which would have accrued to him had he not been suspended or dismissed.' The decision of the board was final and binding on both parties.

When the minister decided to suspend or cancel a teacher's licence 'for cause,' the minister was required to send a written notice to the teacher and set out the precise reasons invoked against the teacher. The teacher then had ten days in which to request that a board of reference be established, and the minister was then obliged to establish one. The board of reference was to comprise a nominee of the teacher, a nominee of the minister, and a chair chosen by the other two. If the two could not agree on a chair, the lieutenant-governor-in-council was empowered to appoint one. The rest of the procedure was the same as in boards of reference arbitrating disputes between teachers and school boards.

APPENDIX C

Statistical Summary for British Columbia, Alberta, Saskatchewan, Manitoba, and Ontario

Note that the differences of procedure among the provinces have the result that only British Columbia, Alberta, Saskatchewan, and Ontario are strictly commensurable. The filtering of cases may be readily appreciated from tables 1 (B.C.), 2 (Alberta), 3 (more Alberta), 4 (Saskatchewan), and 5 (Ontario). Table 6 makes some percentage comparisons between these four provinces.

Table 7 tells how many board of arbitration hearings regarding the dismissal of tenured teachers were held in Manitoba during the years 1965–84. The data are taken from Michael Czuboka's useful book, *Why It's Hard to Fire Johnny's Teacher* (1985). This book gives summaries and discussions of both arbitration hearings and other relevant court cases, including appeals to the Manitoba Court of Appeal. Czuboka has tried to be complete; but the possibility remains that he may not have covered all the board of arbitration hearings in Manitoba.[1]

Table 8 compares the outcomes of boards of reference and boards of arbitration for British Columbia, Alberta, Saskatchewan, Manitoba, and Ontario.

Tables 6 and 8 thus suggest that there are differences between provinces in the ways in which disputes over teachers' dismissals and suspensions are dealt with by boards of reference. But to understand the meaning of these statistics, we must look more closely at the particular procedures in the various provinces (see Appendix B).

Table 9 compares the average yearly crop of applications and decisions for these five provinces. One might expect a positive correlation between the number of applications and decisions per year, one the one hand, and the number of people and thus of teachers in the province, on the other; but no clear correlation seems to emerge. This lack of correlation itself hints at provincial differences.

TABLE 1
Outcomes of applications for boards of reference, British Columbia, 1973–87

(a)	(b)	(c)	(d)	(e)	(f)	(g)	(h)	(i)	(j)
1973	2	–	–	–	–	2	–	–	–
1974	2	–	–	–	–	2	–	–	1
1975	1	1	–	–	–	–	–	–	–
1976	1	--	–	–	–	–	1	–	–
1977	4	–	–	–	–	2	2	–	1
1978	6[a]	1	–	–	–	3	2	–	3
1979	6	–	–	–	2	3	–	1[b]	–
1980	1	–	–	–	–	1	–	–	–
1981[c]	4	1	–	–	–	1	1	1	–
1982	4	2	–	–	–	2	–	–	–
1983	7	–	–	–	–	3	2	2	–
1984[d]	0								
1985	6	4	–	–	–	1	1	–	1 [1]
1986	10	4	1	2	–	2	1	–	1
1987	3	2	–	1	–	–	–	–	–
Total	57	15	1	3	2	22	10	4	7 [1]

Key to columns
(a) Year
(b) No. of applications made in the year
(c) No. of applications withdrawn or abandoned before the board of reference convened
(d) No. of applications withdrawn or abandoned during the hearing by the board of reference
(e) No. of board of reference hearings deferred or adjourned, pending decisions in the courts
(f) No. of cases for which the disposition is not clear from the list
(g) No. of decisions made by board of reference in which the board dismissed the teacher's appeal
(h) No. of decisions made by board of reference in which the board allowed the teacher's appeal
(i) No. of decisions made by board of reference in which the board varied the decision of the school board
(j) No. of appeals by school board or by teacher to the B.C. Supreme Court and, in brackets, from Supreme Court to B.C. Court of Appeal

Source
These figures are based on a 'List of Teacher Discipline Appeals' made by Mr Earl Cherrington of the B.C. Ministry of Education, who kindly permitted the present authors to inspect the list. The list is believed to be complete to 1987.

Notes
The acts by the school boards which provoked the applications were the dismissal or suspensions (usually without pay) of teachers.
Total no. of applications withdrawn or abandoned: 16
Total no. of board of reference decisions: 36
Column (b) = columns (c) + (d) + (e) + (f) + (g) + (h) + (i)
[a]Though there were six applications this year, only five teachers were involved. In one case, the board of reference allowed the teacher's appeal because of procedural failings by the school board. The school board then amended these failings, dismissed the teacher again, and a second, new board of reference dismissed the teacher's second appeal.
[b]In 1980 boards of reference became able to vary the decision of the school board. An appeal beginning in 1979 therefore became eligible for variation if the actual hearing took place in 1980.
[c]In October of this year, the deposit of $150 required to be made by applicants was abolished.
[d]No boards of reference this year.

TABLE 2
Outcomes of applications for boards of reference, Alberta, 1959–83

(a)	(b)	(c)	(d)	(e)	(f)	(g)	(h)	(i)
1959	2	2	–	2	–	–	–	–
1960	–	–	–	–	–	–	–	–
1961	2	2	–	2	–	–	–	–
1962	3	3	–	2	–	1	–	–
1963	3	3	–	3	–	–	–	–
1964	2	2	–	–	1	1	–	–
1965	3	3	–	2	–	1	–	–
1966	1	1	–	1	–	–	–	–
1967	2	2	–	1	–	–	–	1
1968	2	2	1	1	–	–	–	–
1969	1	1	1	–	–	–	–	–
1970	9	9	1	6	2	–	–	–
1971	26	24	–	10	7	5	1	1
1972	19	20	–	12	4	2	–	2
1973	17	18	–	6	7	2	3	–
1974	10	10	1	7	–	1	–	1
1975	7	5	–	4	–	–	–	1
1976	7	8	–	6	1	1	–	–
1977	25	21	1	14	3	2	–	1
1978	18	16	–	13	1	1	–	1
1979	10	11	1	6	3	–	1	–
1980	7	10	–	6	4	–	–	–
1981	9	8	–	4	3	–	–	1
1982	11	14	–	10	1	3	–	–
1983	–	1	–	–	1	–	–	–
Total	196	196	6	118	38	20	5	9

Key to columns
(a) Year
(b) No. of applications made in the year
(c) No. of appeals 'settled' in the year
(d) No. of appeals withdrawn with teacher reinstated
(e) No. of appeals withdrawn with teacher status indeterminate (teacher probably resigned from position or designation)
(f) No. of board of reference hearings in which the board dismissed the teacher's appeal
(g) No. of board of reference hearings in which the board allowed the teacher's appeal
(h) No. of board of reference hearings in which a settlement was arrived at (whether out of court is not indicated)
(i) Indeterminate

Source
These figures are compiled from a set of summary files kept in the Alberta Ministry of Education. The purpose of these files is to record and trace the process of the administration of boards of reference.

Notes
The events which provoked the applications for boards of reference were terminations of contract of employment (161), terminations of designations as principals of schools (30), and suspensions (5).
The figures given in column (c) are for the years in which cases were settled, either by being withdrawn or abandoned or by being decided by a board of reference. Column (b) gives the number of applications for the year. Particularly in the later years, when the number and complexity of cases increased, some applications may have been made in one year but settled in the next.
Column (c) = columns (d) + (e) + (f) + (g) + (h) + (i)

TABLE 3
Outcomes of applications for boards of reference, Alberta, 1983–8

(a)	(b)	(c)	(d)	(e)	(f)	(g)
1983 (Nov., Dec.)	1	–	–	–	1	–
1984	15	5	4	4	2	–
1985	19	16	1	–	2	–
1986	8	6	1	1	–	–
1987	30	22	3	2	2	1
1988	8	8	–	–	–	–
Total	81	57	9	7	7	1

Key to columns
(a) Year
(b) No. of applications for the year
(c) No. of appeals withdrawn (includes those settled out of court, whether or not a hearing was commenced)
(d) No. of board of reference hearings in which the board dismissed the teacher's appeal
(e) No. of board of reference hearings in which the board allowed the teacher's appeal
(f) No. of board of reference hearings in which the board of reference substantially varied the school board's decision (includes cases in which the termination was upheld, but more than nominal pay or damages were awarded to the teacher)
(g) No. of board of reference hearings in which the outcome was indeterminate

Notes
These figures summarize a collection of more recent applications (1983 to 1988) filed in the Alberta Ministry of Education for the administration of boards of reference. The applications were *completed* either by a withdrawal or a board of reference decision. The collection did not include applications whose outcomes were still pending. The collection numbered 82 cases, but one case from the collection, concerning a rather subtle issue of jurisdiction, has been excluded from the table.
Total of columns (d) + (e) + (f) + (g): 24

TABLE 4

Outcomes of applications for boards of reference, Saskatchewan, 1979–81 and 1982–8

(a)	(b)	(c)	(d)	(e)	(f)	(g)	(h)	(i)
1979	?			1		1		
1980	?			5	2	2	1	
1981	?		2	2				
1982	10	2	4	4	1	3		
1983	3	1	1	1	1			
1984	5	2	–	3	1	1	1	
1985	11	1	5	5	2	2	1	
1986	5	–	2	2+1*	1	1+1*		
1987	5	–	2	3	2	1		
1988	4	–	3	–	–	–	–	1
Total '82–'88	43	6	17	19	8	9	2	1

Key to columns
(a) Year
(b) No. of applications made in the year
(c) No. of applications refused
(d) No. of appeals withdrawn
(e) No. of board of reference decisions
(f) No. of board of reference decisions in which the termination of the contract was confirmed (includes cases in which the board ordered compensation to be paid)
(g) No. of board of reference decisions in which the board ordered reinstatement of the teacher or continuance of the contract
(h) No. of other board of reference decisions (includes cases in which the board confirmed a settlement reached by the parties)
(i) No. of appeals not yet concluded or of uncertain outcome

Source
The figures in this table are compiled from a collection of recent cases kept in box binders in the Ministry of Education, Regina, Saskatchewan, for the years 1982–8. They were inspected by Stuart Piddocke on 30 March 1989. The collection comprised records of successful and unsuccessful applications for those years and also included summaries of thirteen board of reference decisions for the years 1979–81. Because of a recent administrative reorganization, files and summaries for the years before 1982 were not available at the time the collection was inspected.

Notes
Column (b) = columns (c) + (d) + (e) + (i)
Column (e) = columns (f) + (g) + (h)
*Indicates a case whose full outcome is uncertain since the board of reference decision is not on file, and it is uncertain whether or not the teacher's reinstatement followed the board of reference decision.

TABLE 5
Outcomes of applications for boards of reference, Ontario, 1973–88 (after J. Berryman)

(a)	(b)	(c)	(d)	(e)	(f)	(g)	(h)	(i)
1973	24	6	14	4	5	5	4	–
1974	23	5	14	4	5	6	3	–
1975	26	21	4	1	2	2	0	–
1976	10	3	5	2	2	2	1	–
1977	23	4	14	5	6	5	3	–
1978	45	3	13	29	7	–	6	–
1979	19	4	6	9	2	2	2	–
1980	62	23	16	23	11	3	2	–
1981	17	0	13	4	6	3	3	1
1982	10	5	5	0	2	2	1	–
1983	12	6	6	1	4	2	0	–
1984	9	4	2	3	0	1	1	–
1985	15	6	3	6	2	0	1	–
1986	18	6	5	7	1	1	0	3
1987	4+{1}*	1	1	2	0	0	0	1
1988	3	0	2	1	0	0	0	2
Total	321	97	123	101	55	34	27	7

Key to columns
(a) Year
(b) No. of applications made in the year
(c) No. of applications withdrawn before a board of reference hearing was granted
(d) No. of board of reference hearings granted
(e) No. of applications refused by the minister of education
(f) No. of applications abandoned after a board of reference hearing was granted
(g) No. of decisions made by board of reference in which the board ordered that the
    teacher's contract be continued
(h) No. of decisions made by board of reference in which the board ordered that the
    teacher's contract be discontinued
(i) No. of board of reference hearings in progress

Source
These figures reproduce a table given in Dr Jack Berryman, 'Boards of Reference: Are
They Needed? A Position Paper,' unpublished manuscript, revised version, January 1989.
Dr Berryman, who is with the Ontario Ministry of Education, has kindly granted permission
to quote this table.

Notes
The occasions provoking the applications for a board of reference were dismissals or discon-
tinuations by school boards of teachers' contracts.
As of 25 April 1989, three applications had been received in 1989.
Column (b) = columns (c) + (d) + (e)
Column (d) = columns (f) + (g) + (h) + (i)
*In this case, the preliminary inquiry which precedes the minister's decision to grant (or
not to grant) a board of reference is still being conducted

TABLE 6
Ratios of outcomes to applications for the provinces of British Columbia, Alberta,
Saskatchewan, and Ontario

(a)	(b)	(c)	(d)	(e)	(f)
British Columbia 1973–87	100% (57)	63.1% (36)	17.5% (10)	38.6% (22)	7.0% (4)
Alberta 1959–83	100% (196)	29.6% (58)	10.2% (20)	19.4% (38)	
Alberta 1983–8	100% (81)	28.4% (23)	8.6% (7)	11.1% (9)	8.6% (7)
Saskatchewan 1982–8	100% (43)	39.5% (17)	20.9% (9)	18.6% (8)	
Ontario 1973–88	100% (321)	19.0% (61)	10.6% (34)	8.4% (27)	

Key to columns
(a) Province and period
(b) Total percentage (and number) of applications
(c) Percentage (and number) of applications decided by boards of reference
(d) Percentage (and number) of appeals allowed by the board (i.e., decisions in favour of
    the teacher)
(e) Percentage (and number) of appeals dismissed by the board (i.e., decisions in favour of
    the school board)
(f) Percentage (and number) of appeals varied by the board (i.e., decisions partly for the
    teacher and partly for the school board)

Note
These figures are not strictly comparable. 'Varied,' for British Columbia, means decisions in
which the board of reference allowed the teacher's dismissal or suspension, but changed
the duration, or changed a dismissal to a suspension, and so on. For Alberta (1983–8), 'varied' means that the school board's decision was substantially changed, and includes cases in
which the termination was upheld but more-than-nominal pay or damages were awarded to
the teacher. Also, the occasions provoking an application for a board of reference differ
from province to province. In Saskatchewan and Ontario, termination of the teacher's
teaching contract was at issue; in British Columbia and Alberta, suspensions were also
appealable; and in Alberta, further, the termination of a teacher's designation as principal
could give rise to a proper application for a board of reference. Finally, the three categories
of 'appeal dismissed,' 'appeal allowed,' and 'school board's decision substantially varied' do
not cover all the occasions when boards of reference were granted, as J. Berryman's category of 'appeal abandoned' indicates. These comparisons should therefore be treated with
caution. But, even so, we find them interesting.

TABLE 7
Outcomes of board of arbitration hearings, Manitoba, 1965–84 (after M. Czuboka, 1985)

(a)	(b)	(c)	(d)	(e)	(f)	(g)
1965	0					
1966	0					
1967	0					
1968	0					
1969	1	1	–	–		
1970	1		1	–		
1971	0					
1972	4	3	1	–	–	2
1973	1	1	–	–	1	
1974	0					
1975	1	1	–	–	1	
1976	0					
1977	2	1	1	–	1	
1978	1	1	1	–		
1979	1	1	1	–	–	1
1980	1	1	–	–	1	
1981	2	1	–	1*	–	1*
1982	0					
1983	1	–	1	–	–	1
1984	1	1	–	–	1	
Total	17	12	6	1	5	5

Key to columns
(a) Year
(b) No. of arbitration awards or decisions given in the year
(c) No. of decisions in which the teacher's dismissal was reversed (i.e., appeal allowed)
(d) No. of decisions in which the teacher's dismissal was confirmed (i.e., appeal dismissed)
(e) No. of decisions in which the original dismissal was neither confirmed nor reversed, but was varied
(f) No. of decisions appealed to the Manitoba Court of Appeal, and the court allowed the appeal
(g) No. of decisions appealed to the Manitoba Court of Appeal, and the court dismissed the appeal

Source
M. Czuboka, *Why It's Hard to Fire Johnny's Teacher: The Status of Tenured Teachers in Manitoba and Canada*, 3rd ed. (Winnipeg: Communigraphics / Printer's Aid Group, 1985).

Note
*In this case, the board of arbitration changed the dismissal to a suspension without pay. The Court of Appeal agreed with the board of arbitration that the school board had not shown cause sufficient for termination, but ruled that the board of arbitration erred in imposing a penalty. The court therefore ordered a full reinstatement of the teacher. The school division was the applicant in the Court of Appeal. See Czuboka 1985: 157–65, 300.

TABLE 8

Outcomes of decisions by boards of reference or boards of arbitration, for the provinces of
British Columbia, Alberta, Saskatchewan, Manitoba, and Ontario

(a)	(b)	(c)	(d)	(e)	(f)
British Columbia 1973–87	36 100%	10 27.8%	22 61.1%	4 11.1%	–
Alberta 1959–83	58 100%	20 34.5%	38 65.5%	–	–
Alberta 1983–8	23 100%	7 30.4%	9 39.1%	7 30.4%	–
Saskatchewan 1982–8	19 100%	9 47.4%	8 42.1%	–	2 10.5%
Manitoba 1965–84	17 100%	12 70.6%	4 23.5%	1 5.9%	–
Ontario 1973–88	61 100%	34 55.7%	27 44.3%	–	–

Key to columns

(a) Province and period

(b) Total no. of decisions

(c) No. and percentage of appeals allowed (i.e., decision for the teacher)

(d) No. and percentage of appeals dismissed (i.e., decision for the school board)

(e) No. and percentage of appeals varied by the board

(f) No. and percentage of other decisions by the board

Notes

Column (b) = columns (c) + (d) + (e) + (f)

'Decisions' excludes hearings in progress, adjourned, deferred, abandoned, or settled 'out
of court.'

TABLE 9
Average yearly number of applications for boards of reference and of decisions of boards
of reference or arbitration for the provinces of British Columbia, Alberta, Saskatchewan,
Manitoba, and Ontario

Province and Years	Applications	Decisions
British Columbia 1973–87	57/15 = 3.8	36/15 = 2.4
Alberta 1959–83	196/25 = 7.8	58/25 = 2.3
Alberta 1983–8	81/6 = 13.5	23/6 = 3.8
Saskatchewan 1982–8	43/7 = 6.1	19/7 = 2.7
Manitoba 1965–84	–	17/20 = 0.85*
Ontario 1973–88	321/16 = 20.1	61/16 = 3.8

Note
*If we ignore the first four years, 1965–8, when no hearings were held or decided, this average becomes 1.1.

APPENDIX D

List of Cases Cited

A. Cases Cited in the General Text and Notes Thereto

Abbotsford School District 34 v. Shewan (28 June 1985), board of reference, unreported decision.

Abbotsford School District 34 Board of School Trustees v. Shewan (1987), 2 B.C.L.R. (2d) 93 (B.C.C.A).

Attis v. Board of Education of District 15 (1991), 121 N.B.R. (2d) 1, (*sub nom Attis v. New Brunswick School District No. 15*, 15 C.H.R.R.D./339) (Human Rights Board of Inquiry)

Attis v. Board of Education District 15 (1991), 121 N.B.R. (2d) 361 (Q.B.).

Attis v. Board of School Trustees, District No. 15 et al., etc. etc., [1996] S.C.J. No. 40 (S.C.C.). Indexed as *Ross v. New Brunswick School District No. 15.*

Re Board of School Trustees, School District No. 34 (Abbotsford) and Shewan (1986), 26 D.L.R. (4th) 54 (B.C.S.C.).

The Board of Trustees of the Edmonton School District v. Malati (1970), 74 W.W.R. 435.

Caldwell et al. v. Stuart et al. (1985), 1 D.L.R. (4th) 1 (S.C.C.); [1984] 2 S.C.R. 603 (S.C.C.). This case is cited in the board of reference decision and the subsequent court decision in case 29, 'The Teacher Who Pursued an Incompatible Lifestyle.'

Canadian Broadcasting Corporation v. Keegstra (1986), 35 D.L.R. (4th) 641 (B.C.C.A.).

Re Cromer and British Columbia Teachers' Federation (1986), 29 D.L.R. (4th) 641 (B.C.C.A.).

The Essex County Roman Catholic School Board v. Denise Tremblay-Webster and Ron W. Ianni, Rejean Belanger and Leonard P. Kavanaugh, in the Supreme

Court of Ontario, Divisional Court; heard 8 and 9 December 1982; judgment released 17 January 1983, per Southey J.

The Essex County Roman Catholic Separate School Board v. Denise Tremblay-Webster and Ron W. Ianni, Rejean Belanger and Leonard P. Kavanaugh, in the Supreme Court of Ontario, Court of Appeal; heard 13 February 1984; judgment released 23 February 1984, per Zuber J. A. Cited as *Essex County Roman Catholic Separate School Board and Trembly-Webster et al., Re* (1984), 5 D.L.R. (4th) 665 (Ont. C.A.).

Re Essex County Roman Catholic School Board v. Porter et al. (1977), 16 O.R. (2d) 433.

Re Essex County Roman Catholic School Board v. Porter et al. (1979), 21 O.R. (2d) 255. (Ont. C.A.).

Keegstra v. One Yellow Rabbit Theatre Association (1992), 91 D.L.R. (4th) 532 (Alta C.A.).

Margaret Temple Gordon v. The Board of the Moosomin School Unit No. 9, (Saskatchewan) board of reference decision dated 10 April 1973. Source for case 37, 'The Teacher Who Brought *Georgia Strait* to Class.'

R. v. Keegstra (1988), 43 C.C.C. (3d) 150 (Alta C.A.).

R. v. Keegstra et al. (1990), 61 C.C.C. (3d) 1 (S.C.C.).

R. v. Keegstra (1991), 63 C.C.C. (3d) 110.

R. v. Keegstra, 19 C.C.C. (3d) 254 (Alta Q.B.).

Riabov v. Lac La Biche School Division #51 (1985), 62 Alberta Reports, 241 (Board of Reference).

Ross v. Moncton Board of School Trustees, District No. 15, 110 D.L.R. (4th) 241 (N.B.C.A.).

Ross v. New Brunswick School Dist. No. 15 (No. 1), 11 C.H.R.R. (1990), decision 56. Affirmed Re Ross and Board of School Trustees, District No. 15 et al., 78 D.L.R. (4th) 392 (N.B.C.A.).

Ross v. New Brunswick School Dist. No. 15 (No. 2), 11 C.H.H.R. (1990), decision 57. Affirmed *Re Ross and Board of School Trustees, District No. 15 et al.,* 78 D.L.R. (4th) 392 (N.B.C.A.).

Shewan v. Abbotsford School District No. 34 (1987), 47 D.L.R. (4th) 107 (B.C.C.A.).

Stack v. St. John's (Roman Catholic School Board) (1979), 99 D.L.R. (3d) 278 (Nfld. T.D.).

Syndicat des Professeurs de la Ville de Laval c. Commission Scolaire Chomedy de Laval, S.A. 2529 (1982). Affirmed *Commission Scolaire Chomedy de Laval c. Jacques Sylvestre* (1983), S.A.E. 2529 (C.S.).

B. Cases Cited on Master-and-Servant Law (Chapter 2)

Cases Cited by Diamond (1946) Concerning Misconduct

For the general idea of employee misconduct: *Clouston v. Corry* [1906]
A.C. *per* Lord James of Hereford at p. 129; *Pearce v. Foster* (1886), 17
Q.B.D. 536; 55 L.J.Q.B. 306; 54 L.T. 664; *Procter v. Bacon* (1886), 2 T.L.R.
845; *Jupiter General Insurance Co. v. Schroff*, [1937] 3 A.E.R. 67; *Tomlinson
v. L.M.S.Rly*, [1944] 1 A.E.R. 537.

For immorality: *R. v. Marlborough* (1700), 12 Mod. Rep. 402; 88 E.R. 1409;
R. v. Brampton (1777), Cald. Mag. Cas. 11; *Atkin v. Acton* (1830), 4 C. &
P. 208; *R. v. Welford* (1778), Cald. Mag. Cas. 57; *McPherson v. City of Toronto* (1918), 43 O.L.R. 326; 43 D.L.R. 604; *Denham v. Patrick* (1910), 15
O.W.R. 349; 20 O.L.R. 347.

For drunkenness: *Clouston v. Corry* (supra); *Speck v. Phillips* (1839), 5 M. &
W. 279, at p. 281; *Wise v. Wilson* (1845), 1 C. & K. 662; *Edwards v. Mackie*
(1848), 11 D. (2nd series) 67; *McKellar v. Macfarlane* (1852), 15 D. (2nd
series) 246.

For insolence: *Shaw v. Chairitie* (1850), 3 C. & K. 21; *Edwards v. Levy*
(1860), 2 F. & F. 94; *Smith v. Allen* (1862), 3 F. & F. 157; *Selby v. Baldry*
(1867), 5 S.L.R. 64.

For criminal conduct: *Cunningham v. Fonblanque* (1833), 6 C. & P. 44;
Baillie v. Kell (1838), 4 Bing.N.C. 638; 7 L.J.C.P. 249.

For other conduct inconsistent: *Amor v. Fearon* (1839), 9 A. & E. 548;
8 L.J.Q.B. 95; *Ridgway v. Hungerford Market Co.* (1835), 3 A. & E. 171;
4 L.J.K.B. 157; *Hands v. Simpson, Fawcett and Co.* (1928), 72 S.J. 138;
44 T.L.R. 295.

Cases Cited by Avins (1968) at the Pages Noted

Abrams v. Anglican Schools, (1960) 2 West Indies Rep. 187. Avins, at p. 649.
Biron v. Fournier, 1955 Que. Q. B. 588. Avins, at p. 641.
Chaldaean Syrian Church v. Francis, ILR 1953 Trav.-Coch. 482, AIR 1954
Trav. Coch. 104. Avins, at p. 633.
Clouston and Co. v. Corry, [1906] A.C. 122 (P.C.), at. p. 129 (*per* Lord James
of Hereford). Avins, at pp. 639–40.
Dean v. Bennett, (1870) 6 Ch. App. 489; Avins, at p. 639.
Denham v. Patrick, (1910) 15 Ont. W.R. 349, 20 Ont. L.R. 347. Avins, at
p. 643.

Durga Singh v. State, AIR 1957, Punjab 97. Avins, at p. 639

Gaudry v. Marcotte, 11 Lower Can. R. 486 (Que. S.C. 1861). Avins, at p. 641.

Hague v. St. Boniface Hospital, 44 Man. R. 129, [1936] 3 Dom. L. R. 363, [1936] 2 W.W.R. 230 (Man Q.B.). Avins, at p. 534.

In re Fremington School (1847) 11 Jur. 421, 9 L.T. (o.s.) 333. Avins, at pp. 634–5, 650.

In re S., 9 N. Z. Mag. Ct. Dec. 216 (Teachers' Ct. of App. 1957). Avins, at pp. 649–50.

Mortimer v. Freeman, (1611) 1 Brownl. & Golds 70, 123 Eng. rep. 671; Avins, at p. 639.

Murray v. Donaldson, 13 S. 128, 10 F. 90 (Scot. Ct. of Sess. 1834). Avins, at p. 634.

National Union of Public Service Emp. v. City of Sudbury, (1963) 13 Can. Lab. Arb. Cas. 431. Avins, at p. 653.

Orr v. University of Tasmania, [1956] Tas. S. R., aff'd 10 Comm. L. R. 526 (Aust. H. C.). Avins, at p. 636.

Pearce v. Foster, (1886) 17 Q.B.D. 536 (C.A.). Avins, at p. 642.

Phillips v. Meiring, 1955 (1) So. Afr. L.R. 626 (C.P.D.) (at church social). Avins, at p. 639

Priestman v. Bradstreet, (1888) 15 Ont. R. 558 (O.H.C.). Avins, at p. 643.

Re Federal Meat Industry Award, 16 Aust. Ind. Info. Bull. 251 (Bd. of Ref. 1961). Avins, at p. 637.

Re Walsh and Jordan, [1962] Ont. R. 88, 132 Can. Cri. C. 1, 31 D.L.R. 2d 88. Avins, at p. 637.

United Elec. Rod. and Mach. W. v. Phillips Elec. Works Ltd., (1951) 3 Can. Lab. Arb. Cas. 829. Avins, at p. 653.

Wakeford v. Bishop of Lincoln, [1921] 1 A.C. 813 (P.C.). Avins, at pp. 636, 639.

Notes

1: Contentious Behaviours

1 The hypothetical cases in this first chapter are given capital letters in order to distinguish them from the actual cases given in chapters 3 to 5, which are given numerals.
2 See *Education and Law Journal* 5/1 (April 1993)
3 This classification follows, with some revision, the scheme proposed by Romulo Magsino and previously published in Manley-Casimir and Piddocke 1991: 136–8.

2: A System of Control

1 This section summarizes the various possibilities for controlling schools, public, denominational, or private. We can observe variations on these possibilities in the society about us.

A useful brief summary of the history, development, and structure of Canadian public education, including the tension between centralized and local control, and between secular and denominational education, is given in Giles and Proudfoot 1990, chapters 1 to 5. English and American patterns of state control and local control, and the tension between centralization and decentralization, are thoughtfully summarized in Banks 1971, chapter 6.

The tension between parental and state control of education in Canada is discussed in Wilson and Lazerson 1982. Private schools are discussed in Garner and Hannaway 1981, and various aspects of the tension between local and state control are explored in Bowers, Housego, and Dyke 1970.

The growth of state control of public elementary education in Ontario from the late 1830s to 1871 is explored in Curtis 1988. A worldwide perspective is given in Kazamias and Massiales 1965.

2 By 'institution' we mean any complex of human activities guided by a set of rules or norms in order to achieve or carry out some purpose. In this complex, a group of persons (the personnel) act out a number of partly prescribed parts (the roles), using a variety of skills and instruments, to achieve the purposes of the activities. Some of these purposes are explicitly set out for the personnel and define the type of institution. But people bring other purposes, not always spelled out, to these activities, and these purposes also become woven into the institution. An institution is thus both something intended and something actually done. It may be described as a set of rules, norms, or expectations, and also as a set of behaviours and their consequences: *both* sides, normative and behavioural, are essential to it. The rules or norms, as well as the purposes, which guide the institution may in addition be partly imposed on it from outside. An institution governed by rules set from outside may be labelled 'heteronomous,' and one governed by rules made by itself 'autonomous.' Public school systems are necessarily heteronomous since the school is responsible to a society, community, state, or constituency outside itself.

3 Or some equivalent group of persons.

4 Also known as public school acts and education acts.

5 The following are the cases cited by Diamond as authority for his summary.

For the general proposition: *Clouston v. Corry* [1906] A.C. *per* Lord James of Hereford at p. 129; *Pearce v. Foster* (1886), 17 Q.B.D. 536; 55 L.J.Q.B. 306; 54 L.T. 664; *Procter v. Bacon* (1886), 2 T.L.R. 845; *Jupiter General Insurance Co. v. Schroff*, [1937] 3 A.E.R. 67; *Tomlinson v. L.M.S.Rly*, [1944] 1 A.E.R. 537.

For immorality: *R. v. Marlborough* (1700), 12 Mod. Rep. 402; 88 E.R. 1409; *R. v. Brampton* (1777), Cald. Mag. Cas. 11; *Atkin v. Acton* (1830), 4 C. & P. 208; *R. v. Welford* (1778), Cald. Mag. Cas. 57; *McPherson v. City of Toronto* (1918), 43 O.L.R. 326; 43 D.L.R. 604; *Denham v. Patrick* (1910), 15 O.W.R. 349; 20 O.L.R. 347.

For drunkenness: *Clouston v. Corry* (supra); *Speck v. Phillips* (1839), 5 M. & W. 279, at p. 281; *Wise v. Wilson* (1845), 1 C. & K. 662; *Edwards v. Mackie* (1848), 11 D. (2nd series) 67; *McKellar v. Macfarlane* (1852), 15 D. (2nd series) 246.

For insolence: *Shaw v. Chairitie* (1850), 3 C. & K. 21; *Edwards v. Levy* (1860), 2 F. & F. 94; *Smith v. Allen* (1862), 3 F. & F. 157; *Selby v. Baldry* (1867), 5 S.L.R. 64.

For criminal conduct: *Cunningham v. Fonblanque* (1833), 6 C. & P. 44; *Baillie v. Kell* (1838), 4 Bing.N.C. 638; 7 L.J.C.P. 249.

For other conduct inconsistent: *Amor v. Fearon* (1839), 9 A. & E. 548; 8

L.J.Q.B. 95; *Ridgway v. Hungerford Market Co.* (1835), 3 A. & E. 171; 4 L.J.K.B. 157; *Hands v. Simpson, Fawcett and Co.* (1928), 72 S.J. 138; 44 T.L.R. 295.

6 *Chaldaean Syrian Church v. Francis*, ILR 1953 Trav.-Coch. 482, AIR 1954 Trav. Coch. 104. Avins, at p. 633.

7 *Hague v. St. Boniface Hospital*, 44 Man. R. 129, [1936] 3 Dom. L. R. 363, [1936] 2 W.W.R. 230 (Man Q.B.). Avins, at p. 534.

8 *Murray v. Donaldson*, 13 S. 128, 10 F. 90 (Scot. Ct. of Sess. 1834). Avins, at p. 634.

9 *In re Fremington School* (1847) 11 Jur. 421, 9 L.T. (o.s.) 33. Avins, at pp. 634–5.

10 *Wakeford v. Bishop of Lincoln*, [1921] 1 A.C. 813 (P.C.). Avins, at p. 636.

11 *Orr v. University of Tasmania*, [1956] Tas. S. R., aff'd 10 Comm. L. R. 526 (Aust. H. C.). Avins, at p. 636.

12 *Re Walsh and Jordan*, [1962] Ont. R. 88, 132 Can. Cri. C. 1, 31 D.L.R. 2d 88. Avins, at p. 637.

13 *Re Federal Meat Industry Award*, 16 Aust. Ind. Info. Bull. 251 (Bd. of Ref. 1961). Avins, at p. 637.

14 The following are the cases cited by Avins (at p. 639). Clergymen: *Mortimer v. Freeman*, (1611) 1 Brownl. & Golds 70, 123 Eng. rep. 671; *Dean v. Bennett*, (1870) 6 Ch. App. 489; *Wakeford v. Bishop of Lincoln*, [1921] 1 A.C. 813 (P.C.). School principal: *Phillips v. Meiring*, 1955 (1) So. Afr. L.R. 626 (C.P.D.) (at church social). Policeman: *Durga Singh v. State*, AIR 1957, Punjab 97.

15 *Clouston and Co. v. Corry*, [1906] A.C. 122 (P.C.), at. p. 129 (per Lord James of Hereford). Avins, at pp. 639–40.

16 *Biron v. Fournier*, 1955 Que. Q. B. 588. Avins, at p. 641.

17 *Gaudry v. Marcotte*, 11 Lower Can. R. 486 (Que. S.C. 1861). Avins, at p. 641.

18 *Pearce v. Foster*, (1886) 17 Q.B.D. 536 (C.A.). Avins, at p. 643.

19 *Priestman v. Bradstreet*, (1888) 15 Ont. R. 558 (O.H.C.). Avins, at p. 643.

20 *Denham v. Patrick*, (1910) 15 Ont. W.R. 349, 20 Ont. L.R. 347. Avins, at p. 643.

21 *Abrams v. Anglican Schools*, (1960) 2 West Indies Rep. 187. Avins, at p. 649.

22 *In re S.*, 9 N. Z. Mag. Ct. Dec. 216 (Teachers' Ct. of App. 1957). Avins, at pp. 649–50.

23 *In re Fremington School* (1847), 11 Jur. 421, 9 L.T. (o.s.) 333. Avins, at pp. 650, 634.

24 Here Avins, at p. 652, refers to some modern Indian cases: *Union of India v. Akbar Sheriff*, ILR 1961 Madras 747, AIR 1961 Mad. 486; *Dilbacgh P. Jarry v. Divisional Supt.*, AIR 1959 Punjab 401, 60 Pun. L.R. 597; *Dass v. Divisional Supt.*, AIR 1960 Allahabad 538, aff'd AIR 1961 All. 336, 1960 All. W.R. (H.C.) 654, 1960 All.L.J. 852.

25 Two Canadian cases are cited by Avins, at p. 653, namely: *United Elec. Rod. and*

Mach. W. v. Phillips Elec. Works Ltd., (1951) 3 Can. Lab. Arb. Cas. 829; *National Union of Public Service Emp. v. City of Sudbury*, (1963) 13 Can. Lab. Arb. Cas. 431.

26 Or 'superego,' if one prefers the Freudian term. This conscience may be based on a well-learned tradition, on ideals imprinted in early childhood, or on anxious sensitivity to the ideals and opinions of one's 'peers.' Compare David Riesman's discussion of 'tradition directed,' 'inner directed,' and 'other directed' personalities. Riesman also proposes a fourth alternative, the 'autonomous' personality – but this is a dangerous possibility in all but the most ethical and liberal of states.

27 Compare Egerton Ryerson's concerns as recounted in Curtis 1988.

28 The union will have to take notice, however, of any off-the-job activities of its members which would threaten the solidarity of the union, such as undue hob-nobbing with persons known to be opposed to the union.

29 Or we could put it the other way: the school board, representing the community.

30 'Control' includes trying to accommodate to or to reconcile the differing demands made by these powers upon the teacher. But if one can turn these demands to one's own benefit, that is even better.

31 The brief summary which follows of the forms of boards of reference has appeared in a slightly different version in Piddocke 1993b: 25–30.

32 This statement applies particularly to the years 1987–90, when the research for this study was carried out.

33 This is a very crude, though basic, division. For an example of a finer-grained approach, see LaNoue and Lee 1987: 43–8. In describing their cases, LaNoue and Lee distinguish the following 'stages': (1) triggering incident; (2) perception of alleged discrimination; (3) problem evaluation and informal consultation; (4) use of internal remedies; (5) settlement or litigation decision; (6) litigation preparation; (7) pretrial impacts; (8) trial impacts; (9) decision impacts; (10) post-trial impacts. *Mutatis mutandis,* a similar set of stages applies to the contenders in board of reference hearings. Other schemata are also possible.

34 Variants of this type are found in British Columbia, Alberta, Saskatchewan, and Ontario.

35 The statutes commonly require that the application be made within a certain time period after the original dismissal. Some applications may therefore be made by the teachers in order to keep open the possibility of a board of reference hearing rather than earnestly to pursue this remedy.

36 According to the provisions of the relevant statutes.

37 Variants of this type are found in Manitoba and Quebec.

38 When teachers were in demand and scarce, as in the early 1960s, the

requirement that teachers be certified could be considerably relaxed (for example, by granting temporary certificates easily or by waiving some requirements for permanent ones). But in the 1970s requirements began again to tighten.

39 See also the criticism of Bohannan's article by Veena Mong, and Bohannan's answer thereto, in *American Anthropologist* 69/2 (April 1967): 227–9. Double institutionalization is a special case of the interaction between what some students of society have called the 'little traditions' of local communities and the 'great tradition' of the whole society and its ruling elites. Public school education is another form of this interaction.

3: Misconducts of 'Character'

1 The present-day attack on smoking points to this possibility. The present rationale for forbidding smoking is, however, other than the chief one for forbidding the use of alcohol and the rest: smoking causes lung cancer in people who inhale the smoke; as cancer is an expensive medical problem, there is an incentive to reduce medical costs and lost labour-time by curbing smoking. It is true that for some people smoking is addictive; but smoking is not currently opposed on this ground, although there are plenty of advertisements for aids to stop smoking.

2 One can, of course, envisage an 'educational' system in which teaching cruelty is one of its expressed purposes, and which uses cruel methods accordingly. Some kinds of training for warfare include such cruelties, and these can become dominant cultural themes. Some systems of 'education' also rationalize cruelty under the names of 'discipline' and 'good teaching methods.' But in our view such systems are thereby poisoned at their very root.

3 Was it Oscar Wilde, punning on the more conventional statement, 'A gentleman is never intentionally cruel'?

4 Vulgar language is not the same as obscene language, although the words 'vulgar' and 'obscene' are often used as synonyms.

5 We also need, for instance, courage, love, justice, integrity, and exploration.

6 At this point, Curtis cites Ryerson 1847: 20. Curtis also refers to his own article (1983).

7 Or, in some jurisdictions, board of arbitration cases.

8 It is not clear from the records of this case whether or not these were different students or the same.

9 This letter is not quoted in the board of reference decision.

10 So the judge phrased it in his letter, dated 14 September 1982, withdrawing from the board of reference. We think the 'board' to which he refers is the

board of reference, but the phrasing in the letter allows the possibility that he may have meant the county board of education (in which case, the county board soon changed its view).

11 Interview with Stuart Piddocke, 14 October 1988.

12 This account is a paraphrase of a ruling handed down on 3 January 1977 and reported in Public Service Labour Relations Board, *New Brunswick Labour Law Cases* (Part II), p. 22135.

13 The case summary does not particularize which agent of the employer, or the school board, made the decision.

14 This account is a paraphrase of a ruling handed down on 3 September 1980 and reported in Public Service Labour Relations Board, *New Brunswick Labour Law Cases (Part III)*, pp. 22233–4.

15 This section gives a court the power to grant an absolute or a conditional discharge, the result of which is that the person is deemed not to be guilty of the offence. An absolute or a conditional discharge is therefore deemed not to be a conviction for the offence charged.

16 The teachers in both these cases happened to be women.

4: Sexual Misconducts

1 See chapter 6, 'The Normative Character of Teaching,' below.

2 We'd say it is never totally irrelevant, but the relevance may well be minor.

3 We're not saying here that this principle is true, although we do think that it is. What we're saying here is that this principle is presupposed in the expectation that a teacher's off-the-job conduct be consistent with the lessons which the teacher is supposed to teach.

4 Of course, sexual activities can be a distraction from teaching, just as ill health, family troubles, excessive debts, or worrying about the state of the world can be. But such distractions are not an inherently *necessary* interference in the meaning here intended.

5 This is because the teacher, besides to the students, is in fact responsible to the school, the community, the profession, the state, and so on, to ensure that the student gets a certain training and that examination results reflect the actual attainments of the student. If the teacher/student relationship was between only the teacher and the student, and both were consenting adults, an exchange of sexual favours in return for the teacher's skill and knowledge would be a fair bargain. But this situation does not happen in the public schools, or in any institution which issues certificates that are to be respected in the general society.

6 Our material is not clear on this point.

7 This section has already appeared, in slightly different form, as Piddocke 1993a.
8 'Consentual' is so spelled in the board of reference decision.
9 Of the B.C. cases, only one involved a relationship between a teacher and a student, and the student in that case was not in the teacher's school at all. See case 24 below.
10 This comment could be interpreted as conceding Miss F.'s maturity. On the other hand, it raises doubts about Mr T.'s belief in that maturity, since he thought he could determine her direction.
11 This case could therefore also be classifed under category (4), extramarital heterosexual relationships.
12 Portions of this account have previously appeared in Manley-Casimir and Piddocke 1991. It is taken particularly from the following documents, supplemented by the further knowledge of Michael Manley-Casimir as one of the expert witnesses at the hearing before the board of reference:
   a) 'Statement of Dr Dante Lupini,' written opinion prepared for the board of reference
   b) 'Statement of Dr Michael Manley-Casimir,' written opinion prepared for the board of reference
   c) *Abbotsford School District 34 v. Shewan* (28 June 1985; board of reference; unreported)
   d) Ibid., dissenting opinion of Marvin R.V. Storrow, Q.C., Chair
   e) *Board of School Trustees, School District No. 34 (Abbotsford)* and *Shewan*, Re (1986), 26 D.L.R. (4th) 54 (B.C.S.C.)
   f) *Shewan v. Abbotsford School District No. 34* (1987), 47 D.L.R. (4th) 107 (B.C.C.A.)
   We have also made some use of material collected in Siracusa 1991. In addition, Stuart Piddocke lived in Abbotsford in the 1950s and had a family connection there until the mid-1970s.
13 For example, see Dickinson and MacKay 1989: 594–610; and Proudfoot and Hutchings 1988: 358–62.
14 The two municipalities of Matsqui and Abbotsford amalgamated on 1 January 1995 to become the City of Abbotsford.
15 Above, note 12(b)
16 Above, note 12(d)
17 Ibid., at p. 16.
18 Ibid.
19 D.J.M. Brown and D.M. Beatty, *Canadian Labour Arbitration*, 2d ed. (Aurora, Ont.: Canadian Law Book, 1984).
20 Above, note 12(c).

21 Above, note 12(e), at pp. 78–9.

22 Ibid., at pp. 64–5.

23 Quoting R.S. Vasan, ed., *The Canadian Law Dictionary* (Don Mills, Ont: Law and Business Publications [Canada], 1980).

24 This definition is reproduced in the sixth edition of *Black's Law Dictionary* (Saint Paul, Minn.: West Publishing Co., 1990), p. 999.

25 Above, note 12(e), at p. 67.

26 Ibid., at pp. 70–1.

27 Ibid., at p. 71.

28 Ibid., at pp. 75–6.

29 Ibid., at p. 78.

30 Above, note 12(f), at p. 110.

31 Ibid., at p. 111.

32 Ibid., at pp. 111–12.

33 Ibid., at p. 112.

34 Ibid.

35 The case reference is *Syndicat des Professeurs de la Ville de Laval c. Commission Scolaire Chomedy de Laval*, S.A. 2529 (1982) [affirmed *Commission Scolaire Chomedy de Laval c. Jacques Sylvestre* (1983), S.A.E. 2529 (C.S.)]. We follow Grace 1991, a summary made for our research that includes a preliminary report on procedure and a list of cases.

36 The message of this comment is perhaps that a teacher can do anything off the job so long as it doesn't upset the parents!

37 (1985), 1 D.L.R. (4th), 1, S.C.C.

38 How the school board learned this was not revealed in the records.

39 It is worth observing that the hearing was held on 12 April 1985 and that the judgment of the board of arbitration was given 30 April 1985. The 'discipline' thus administered to Mr X. amounted to a year without employment and without pay.

40 The third member did not sign the chairman's judgment. The chairman also signed on behalf of the second member of the board of arbitration. We do not have a copy of the minority judgment, if there was one.

41 Then section 122(1)(a), School Act, R.S.B.C. 1979 c. 375, which provided that a school board may suspend a teacher for misconduct, neglect of duty, or refusal to obey a lawful order of the school board. Subsection (1)(b) permitted the school board to suspend the teacher for a criminal charge. This section has been replaced by section 15(3), School Act, S.B.C. 1989 c. 61, which allows a school board to dismiss an employee for 'just and reasonable cause.'

42 The College had been instituted by the government only the previous year to supervise the professional qualifications of B.C. teachers.

43 In view of the fact that previous boards of reference in British Columbia had enjoyed the power to vary the decisions of school boards, we find this ruling peculiar.

44 Having closed its hearing and rendered its decision, the board of reference was thus far *functus*. It had no jurisdiction to reopen the hearing. It could only do as the judge directed, and reconsider its decision on the basis of the evidence already presented to it. It did not have the power to, as it were, retry the case.

45 The new School Act, S.B.C. 1987, c. 19, sec. 122(1), allowed a school board to dismiss or discipline a teacher 'for just and reasonable cause.' This phrase has been continued by section 15(3), School Act, S.B.C. 1989, c. 61.

46 See Feinbloom 1977, a study of transvestism and transsexuality in Boston, Massachusetts.

47 Though the board of reference does not say so, the person assaulted, and who also had laid the complaint, was the assailant's foster son. The case was later the subject of a judicial decision in which a newspaper sought to get the names of the persons involved made public; in order to protect the complainant, the judge denied the newspaper access to this information.

48 Indeed, after reviewing a wide range of board of reference cases, we have come to the conclusion that it is inexact to describe a given board of reference case as 'average.' There are recurrent situations and issues, but these are combined differently and distinctively in each case. Each case also has its own unique features, and these may be decisive. Cases can be classified as of one type or another, as this study implies, but such classification certainly does not exhaust the diversity.

49 Since there is usually a limited time within which a teacher may apply for a board of reference, teachers may apply just to keep their options open and to tell the school board that they're prepared to fight the dismissal. Then the matter may be settled one way or another even before a hearing is arranged. Then the application appears in the records as 'abandoned' or 'withdrawn.' For the dispute to go to the actual hearing implies a certain intransigence by both parties.

50 But not in those pornographic materials in which the human body, most especially the female body, is demeaned and degraded. Such publications *are* harmful.

5: Unorthodox Teachings and Unquiet Citizens

1 If the criticism is *true* and the employee has been dismissed without due notice, we think that justice should require that the employee would have

some claim against the employer for damages in lieu of notice. The employer should not get off scot-free if the criticism is true, and therefore justified.

2 Except, of course, where the employer has a *de facto* monopoly and is, therefore, no longer an ordinary employer. This monopoly may also be created by a cartel or other working agreement among a group of ostensibly separate employers, who could agree together not to employ a blacklisted former employee of one of them. We have to look at the *actual* power relations.

3 *R. v. Keegstra* (1988), 43 C.C.C. (3d) 150 (Alta C.A.).

4 *R. v. Keegstra et al.* (1990), 61 C.C.C. (3d) 1 (S.C.C.).

5 *R. v. Keegstra* (1991), 63 C.C.C. (3d) 110. Some other events of Keegstra's legal tribulations are reflected in *R. v. Keegstra*, 19 C.C.C. (3d) 254 (Alta Q.B.) (pre-trial application, which was rejected, to have charge quashed on grounds that section 281.2 of the Criminal Code violated the Charter); *Canadian Broadcasting Corporation v. Keegstra* (1986), 35 D.L.R. (4th) 76 (Alta C.A.) (appeal, which was allowed, against injunction to CBC not to broadcast TV play based on the Keegstra affair); *Keegstra v. One Yellow Rabbit Theatre Association* (1992), 91 D.L.R. (4th) 532 (Alta C.A.) (appeal, which was rejected, by producer of a play based on the Keegstra affair against an injunction forbidding the producer to present the play while Keegstra was being tried in Red Deer).

6 With the exception that if these views are presented in a way which openly and overtly promotes malice and hatred, then there may be a justification for suppressing them. But open and public criticism is a much better way of countering them than suppressing them and forcing them underground to fester – and spread – in secret.

7 Which was at that time still a counter-cultural and relatively radical newspaper produced in Vancouver, B.C. (though the board of reference decision does not mention this fact).

8 Including denominational, 'separate,' and 'independent' schools.

9 This expectation that the teacher be a role model is normative or prescriptive. It would hold whether or not schoolteachers were actually followed as role models by anybody.

10 The following account of the events of the Ross case is collated chiefly from the special issue of the *University of New Brunswick Law Journal* 41 (1992), which was published after the New Brunswick Court of Queen's Bench had modified the decision of the board of inquiry but before the case was appealed to the New Brunswick Court of Appeal. Note particularly the descriptions in Mackenzie 1992: 348–51; Medjuck 1992: 286; and Gochnauer 1992: 317.

In addition, Stuart Piddocke has inspected Malcolm Ross's own publications: *Web of Deceit; The Real Holocaust – the Attack on Unborn Children and Life Itself; Christianity versus Judaeo-Christianity: The Battle for Truth;* and *Spectre of*

Power. Ross's errors and slimy innuendoes have been exposed in detail in Beverley 1990.

Most recently, the Ross case has been reviewed by Paul T. Clarke (1994). Clarke finds the majority opinion of the Court of Appeal in the Ross case to be seriously flawed.

Finally, we should like to acknowledge with appreciation the assistance of Mr David Hunnings, who recently completed (1994) a thesis on the Ross case and its moral and pedagogical significance.

11 These various sources are cited, for instance, in Ross's *Spectre of Power.*
12 Let Ross himself reveal his opinions at their most temperate in his own words at the beginning of *Spectre of Power:*

> I believe what they fear is an idea. To write about this idea is to provide citizens of our lands with an opportunity to find freedom from the increasingly heavy yoke of spiritual, moral, and economic slavery. It would replace our progressively decadent, decaying, and guilt-ridden society with one based on honour, truth, and justice. It would lead to the healing of our land, happiness, and laughing children instead of pollution, the AIDS terror, and the silent screams of unborn babies. This idea would bring true peace to the nations instead of that uneasy truce we now face. It would destroy the power of the Money Lenders and deliver the nations from crushing debt. It would defeat the plans of those who would subject us all to an international socialist world dictatorship where personal freedom and national traits would be mercilessly suppressed. This idea is the ancient Christian hope of the Kingship of Jesus in Society. (Ross 1987: 2)

13 *Ross v. New Brunswick School Dist. No. 15 (No. 1),* 11 C.H.R.R. (1990), decision 56. *Ross v. New Brunswick School Dist. No. 15 (No. 2),* 11 C.H.H.R. (1990), decision 57. Both affirmed *Re Ross and Board of School Trustees, District No. 15 et al.,* 78 D.L.R. (4th) 392 (N.B.C.A.).
14 *Attis v. Board of Education of District 15* (1991), 121 N.B.R. (2d) 1, (*sub nom Attis v. New Brunswick School District No. 15* 15 C.H.R. R.D./339) (Human Rights Board of Inquiry).
15 *Attis v. Board of Education District 15* (1991), 121 N.B.R. (2d) 361 (Q.B.).
16 *Ross v. Moncton Board of School Trustees, District No. 15,* 110 D.L.R. (4th) 241 (N.B.C.A.).
17 Ibid., 248–9.
18 [1986] 1 S.C.R. 103.
19 *Ross v. Moncton Board of School Trustees, District No. 15,* 110 D.L.R. (4th) 241, at p. 250.
20 Ibid.
21 Ibid., 251.

22 Ibid., 255–60.

23 *Attis v. Board of School Trustees, District No. 15 et al., etc. etc.*, [1996] S.C.J. No. 40. (indexed as *Ross v. New Brunswick School District No. 15*).

24 Here the court cites *Re Cromer and British Columbia Teachers' Federation* (1986), 29 D.L.R. (4th) 641 (B.C.C.A.) at p. 660, and then *Abbotsford School District 34 Board of School Trustees v. Shewan* (1987), 2 B.C.L.R. (2d) 93 (B.C.C.A.), at p. 97. The court also quotes from Allison Reyes, 'Freedom of Expression and Public School Teachers' *Dal. J. Leg. Stud.* 4 (1995): 35, at pp. 37 and 42.

25 But even one person killed because of anti-Semitism would be one person too many.

26 Integrity would require Ross not to teach evolutionary biology in school, and a certain courtesy would require the school board to accept his refusal to do so.

27 Should the school board continue to employ Ross in a *non-teaching* position? Would, for instance, the reasoning of the above paragraphs apply to a janitor employed by the school board who published on his own time books, such as Ross has published, so contrary to the basic values which the school system is obliged to uphold? Or should the Charter provision guaranteeing freedom of expression override a school board's dismissing the non-teaching employee? Since the janitor is not a member of the teaching profession, the question of professional qualification would not emerge: the janitor's employment would be governed by the law of 'master and servant,' and by collective agreements and labour law. But that law still allows the school board to dismiss an employee whose off-the-job actions threaten the reputation of the employer. So the question remains.

Stuart Ryan considers that Ross should be dismissed by the school board on the grounds 'that his continued employment in any *capacity* suggests that his publications enjoy a measure of support by members of the school board' (Ryan 1992: 315; emphasis added). But perhaps this goes too far. Much depends on whether or not the school board is prepared to state clearly and publicly just what values it does stand for.

28 This terminated his designation as principal, not his contract as a teacher. As a teacher, he would be given leave without pay for the duration of his stint as M.L.A., with no prejudice to his occupational security. But for some reason, Mr P. wanted to retain his designation as a principal.

29 This case is reported in *Riabov v. Lac La Biche School Division #51* (1985), 62 Alberta Reports, 241 (board of reference).

30 This, of course, was the reason duly entered in the records of the Teacher Certification and Qualification Branch in Edmonton when Mr Riabov applied for an appeal to a board of reference.

31 This case is from Magsino 1988. See also 'Ill Health, Threats End Teacher's Fight,' *Winnipeg Free Press*, 9 May 1991, p. 27.

32 Reported as *Re Essex County Roman Catholic School Board v. Porter et al.* (1979), 21 O.R. (2d) 255. (Ont. C. A.).

33 *The Essex County Roman Catholic Separate School Board v. Susan Porter and Patricia Podgorski*, Supreme Court of Ontario, Divisional Court, heard 4 May 1977, judgment released 17 June 1977. Reported as *Re Essex County Roman Catholic School Board v. Porter et al.*, 16 O.R. (2d) 433.

34 We would question this assertion. As employees of church-run schools, teachers would reasonably be expected to uphold the values of those schools; otherwise, they would cast the schools into disrepute in the esteem of the (religious) community to whom the schools appealed. The common law of master and servant would apply, and its principles antedated the time of Union.

35 Our source for the following account is *The Essex County Roman Catholic Separate School Board v. Denise Tremblay-Webster and Ron W. Ianni, Rejean Belanger and Leonard P. Kavanaugh,* in the Supreme Court of Ontario, Court of Appeal, heard 13 February 1984, judgment released 23 February 1984, *per* Zuber J. A. The case is cited as *Essex County Roman Catholic Separate School Board and Tremblay-Webster et al.*, Re (1984), 5 D.L.R. (4th) 665 (Ont. C.A.).

36 *The Essex County Roman Catholic School Board v. Denise Tremblay-Webster and Ron W. Ianni, Rejean Belanger and Leonard P. Kavanaugh,* in the Supreme Court of Ontario, Divisional Court, heard 8 and 9 December 1982, judgment released 17 January 1983, *per* Southey J.

37 This summary is taken from Magsino 1993: 159–65. Magsino cites the following sources: (a) 'Report of a Board of Arbitration. Between the Newfoundland Teachers Association and the Roman Catholic School Board for St. John's' (manuscript); (b) (1986), 59 Nfld. & P.E.I. R. 129 (Nfld. T.D.); (c) (1988), 7 Nfld. & P.E.I.R. 21 (Nfld. C.A.).

38 Namely *Stack v. St. John's (Roman Catholic School Board)* (1979), 99 D.L.R. (3d) 278 (Nfld. T.D.).

39 *Caldwell v. Stuart*, [1984] 2 S.C.R. 603.

6: The Normative Character of Teaching

1 But suppose we saw the garbage collector as the Scavenger or, as in India, for example, the Sweeper? Then the role would become invested with powerful meanings, becoming a symbol of rules of purity and impurity. In ancient Egypt, too, the stenographer was filling more than just an occupational role: he became a Scribe, a servant of the government and the gods, a keeper of the

sacred (and difficult) art of writing, and an exemplar of a certain kind of
morality expressed, for example, in the maxims which apprentice scribes were
expected to copy while learning to write.

2 Functionalist social analysis makes other distinctions: (a) 'eufunctions' are
consequences which favour the preservation of the social system of which the
institution is a part, while 'dysfunctions' are the consequences which favour
the change or even the destruction of the social system; (b) 'manifest functions' are those perceived by the actors themselves, while 'latent functions' are
those perceived only by the sociological observer. In Malinowskian terms, we
would also distinguish between those functions corresponding to the purpose
expressed in the Charter, and other functions corresponding to other purposes held by the various personnel.

3 Or possibly 'disheartened.'

Appendix A: Methodological Note

1 He was able, though, to make a complete list of the ministry's suspensions and
cancellations of teachers' certificates. But this was not quite within our sphere
of inquiry.

2 'Above water': think of all the disputes which must have occurred which were
not taken to a board of reference or other hearing. These latter represent the
great mass of disputes, like that nine-tenths of an iceberg which is hidden
under water.

Appendix B: Statutory Background

1 On occasion, teachers have been allowed to appeal even after this ten-day
period has expired.

2 Until 27 October 1981 the teacher had to enclose a deposit of $150, which
would be forfeited if the teacher lost the appeal. The school board whose decision was being appealed likewise had to submit a deposit of $150 which would
be forfeited if the teacher won the appeal. On 27 October 1981 the deposit
requirement was repealed. Abolishing the deposit requirement seems to have
made no difference to the frequency of appeals.

3 Teachers and school boards, for the board of reference, and teachers and the
A.T.A., for the T.P.A.B., might be represented by legal counsel at the hearings
of these boards.

4 Terminating the appointment of a teacher as a principal was not one of the
occasions permitting a board of reference in British Columbia.

5 The absence of such instruction did not prevent an appellant dissatisfied with

the result of a board of reference from appealing the decision to the higher
courts on the grounds that the board had erred in law or had exceeded or
otherwise improperly exercised its jurisdiction.

6 Or see Education Act, R.S.S. 1978 (suppl.), c. E-0.1, ss. 206–26.

7 The Education Act of 1978 replaced, among others, the former School Act,
   R.S.S. 1978, c. S-36, and the Teacher Tenure Act, R.S.S. 1978, c. T-6. The
   Teacher Tenure Act, s. 4(1), allowed the reasons for a school board's terminating a teacher's contract to include 'professional incompetence, neglect of
   duty, unprofessional conduct, immorality, physical or mental disability, and
   such other cause as in the opinion of the school board renders the teacher
   unsuitable for teaching service in the position then held by him.' It is continued in section 210 of the present Education Act. Section 244 of the School Act
   allowed a school board to terminate its agreement with a teacher 'subject to
   The Teacher Tenure Act.'

8 The following history of boards of reference and boards of arbitration in Manitoba is taken from Magsino 1990.

9 Public Schools Act, 1987, sec. 92(4)(a), according to Magsino 1990: 8–9. The
   other sub-subsections of 92(5) in the 1980 statute likewise become sub-subsections in section 92(4) of the 1987 Act.

10 'Board of arbitration,' not 'board of reference,' is the correct term for this tribunal. In Manitoba, 'board of reference' has another meaning. Sections 486
   and 487 of the Public Schools Act, among other matters, empower the lieutenant-governor-in-council to establish 'boards of reference' for particular districts or areas (sec. 486[1]), in order to settle matters concerning the transfer
   of districts from one school division to another, or to determine boundaries
   between divisions and wards of divisions, and related matters (sec. 487[9]).
       Czuboka (1985: 59–62) quotes section 92 of the Manitoba Public Schools
   Act, S.M. 1980, c. 33; am. S.M. 1982–83–84, c. c5, ss. 5 & 6.

11 As amended by S.O. 1981, c. 47, ss. 17–21; 1982, c. 20, s. 2; 1982, c. 32; 1984, c.
   48, s. 21; 1984, c. 55, s. 216; 1984, c. 60; 1986, c. 19, s. 2; 1986, c. 21; 1986, c. 29;
   1986, c. 64, s. 12; and 1987, c. 17, s. 3; but none of these amendments applies
   to the sections discussed in the text.

12 This information about procedures in Quebec is taken from Grace 1991,
   which gives a preliminary report on procedure and a list of cases. Quebec's
   procedures are also described briefly in Czuboka 1985: 223–9.

13 The information concerning the Atlantic Provinces is based on Magsino 1988.
   Procedures for the Atlantic Provinces are also described briefly in Czuboka
   1985: 229–51.

14 So much so, indeed, that Czuboka (1985: 229–34), in his quick review of New
   Brunswick procedures, mentions the board of reference not at all and

describes only the adjudication procedure under the province-wide collective agreement.

15 Provincial Collective Agreement between School Boards and the Government of Newfoundland and Labrador and the Newfoundland Teachers' Association, 1984–8, articles 31 and 32; quoted in Magsino 1988.

16 The minister may also appoint an arbitrator on behalf of a party to the dispute if the party itself fails to do so.

17 Provincial Collective Agreement, article 32.12.

18 Regulations under the School Act, 1974, division D and division F; cited in Magsino 1988.

Appendix C: Statistical Summary

1 Czuboka admits (at page 172) to missing one early hearing for the second (1980) edition of his book, and learning about its existence only in 1985, just in time for the third edition. He may possibly have missed others, ones which were not further appealed to the courts.

In table 9, the noticeable difference between the average number of decisions per year for Manitoba and those for the other provinces might be the result of Czuboka's not having found all of the decisions; however, it might also have other causes.

Bibliography

Anderman, Steven D. 1978. *The Law of Unfair Dismissal*. London: Butterworths

Arons, S. 1986. *Compelling Belief: The Culture of American Schooling*. Amherst, Mass.: University of Massachusetts Press

Avins, A. 1968. *Employees' Misconduct as Cause for Discipline and Dismissal in India and the Commonwealth*. Allahabad (U.P.), India: Law Book Co.

Badgley Committee Report. 1984. *Sexual Offences against Children*. Ottawa: Ministry of Supply and Services Canada

Banks, Olive. 1971. *The Sociology of Education*. London: B.T. Batsford Ltd.

Beale, H.K. 1936. *Are American Teachers Free?* New York: Charles Scribner's Sons. (American Historical Association, *Report of the Commission on the Social Studies in the Schools*, part 12.) Especially chapter 13, 'Conduct of Teachers,' pp. 374–409

Bercuson, D., and D. Wertheimer. 1987. *A Trust Betrayed: The Keegstra Affair*. Toronto: McClelland-Bantam Inc. Originally published by Doubleday Canada Ltd. in 1985

Beverley, James R. 1990. *Web of Error*. Sackville, N.B.: Department of Religious Studies, Mount Allison University

Blumer, H. 1986. *Symbolic Interactionism: Perspective and Method*. Berkeley: University of California Press

Bohannan, Paul. 1965. 'The Differing Realms of the Law' (part 2). *American Anthropologist* 67/6: 33–42

Bowers, C.A., Ian Housego, and Doris Dyke, eds. 1970. *Education and Social Policy: Local Control of Education*. New York: Random House

Brown, A.F., and M. Zuker. 1994. *Education Law*. Toronto: Carswell

Brown, D.J.M., and D.M. Beatty. 1984. *Canadian Labour Arbitration*. Aurora, Ont.: Canadian Law Book

Clarke, Paul T. 1994. 'Public School Teachers and Racist Speech: Why the "In-Class" / "Out-of-Class" Distinction Is Not Valid.' *Education and Law Journal* 6/1: 1–26

Cohn, N. 1967. *Warrant for Genocide: The Myth of the Jewish World Conspiracy and the Protocols of the Elders of Zion.* London: Eyre and Spottiswoode

Curtis, B. 1983. 'Preconditions of the Canadian State: Educational Reform and the Construction of a Public in Upper Canada, 1837–1846.' *Studies in Political Economy* 10: 99–121

– 1988. *Building the Educational State: Canada West, 1836–71.* London, Ont.: The Althouse Press

Czuboka, M. 1985. *Why It's Hard to Fire Johnny's Teacher: The Status of Tenured Teachers in Manitoba and Canada.* 3rd ed. Winnipeg: Communigraphics / Printer's Aid Group

Diamond, A.S. 1946. *The Law of Master and Servant.* 2nd ed. London: Stevens and Sons, Ltd; and Sweet and Maxwell, Ltd.

Dick, J. 1982. *Not in our Schools?!!!* Ottawa: Canadian Library Association

Dickinson, Gregory M., and A. Wayne MacKay, eds. 1989. *Rights, Freedoms and the Educational System in Canada: Cases and Materials.* Toronto: Edmond Montgomery Publications Ltd.

Durkheim, Emile. 1964 *The Division of Labour in Society.* New York: Collier-Macmillan (The Free Press of Glencoe). Originally published in 1933

Epstein, A.L. 1967. 'The Case Method in the Field of Law.' In *The Craft of Social Anthropolgy.* Ed. A.L. Epstein. London: Tavistock

Ewens, P. 1991. 'The Gordon Ledinski Case.' Unpublished research project in partial fulfilment of Master of Education degree, Simon Fraser University

Feinbloom, D.H. 1977. *Transvestites and Transsexuals.* New York: Dell Publishing Co., Inc.

Friedenberg, Edgar Z. 1980. *Deference to Authority: The Case of Canada.* White Plains, N.Y.: Sharpe

Garner, William T., and Jane Hannaway. 1982. 'Private Schools: The Client Connection.' In *Family Choice in Schooling: Issues and Dilemmas.* Ed. Michael E. Manley-Casimir. Lexington, Mass.: D.C. Heath and Co. 119–33

Giles, T.E., and A.J. Proudfoot. 1990. *Educational Administration in Canada.* 4th ed. Calgary: Detselig Enterprises Ltd.

Givan, D. 1992. 'The Ross Decision and Control in Professional Employment.' *University of New Brunswick Law Journal* 41: 333–44

Gluckman, M. 1964. *Custom and Conflict in Africa.* New York: Barnes & Noble

Gochauer, Myron. 1992. 'Of Liberty and Social Practices: The Case of Malcolm Ross.' *University of New Brunswick Law Journal* 41: 317–26

Gorer, G. 1956. 'Modification of National Character: The Role of the Police in

England.' In *Personal Character and Cultural Milieu*. Ed. D.G. Haring. 3rd ed. rev. Syracuse, N.Y.: Syracuse University Press. Originally published in *Journal of Social Issues* 11/2 (1955): 24–32

Grace, E. 1991. 'Findings on Misconduct – Quebec.' A preliminary report on procedure and list of cases (unpublished)

– 1993. 'Professional Misconduct or Moral Pronouncement: A Study of "Contentious" Teacher Behaviour in Quebec.' *Education and Law Journal* 5/1: 99–142

Hepple, B.A., ed. 1981. *Hepple and O'Higgins on Employment Law*. 4th ed. London: Sweet and Maxwell

Hill, L.E. 1992. 'Malcolm Ross' Influence in School District 15.' *University of New Brunswick Law Journal* 41: 277–84

Hoebel, E.A. 1954. *The Law of Primitive Man*. Cambridge, Mass.: Harvard University Press

Holdsworth, W.A. 1907. *The Law of Master and Servant*. New ed., revised and enlarged by John R. McIlwraith. London: George Routledge and Sons, Ltd.

Hoyle, E. 1969. *The Role of the Teacher*. London: Routledge and Kegan Paul

Hunnings, D. 1994. 'Malcolm Ross: Truth, Hatred, and the Teacher.' M.A. Thesis, Simon Fraser University

Hurlbert, E.L., and M.A. Hurlbert. 1992. *School Law under the Charter of Rights and Freedoms*. Calgary: University of Calgary Press

Kazamias, Andreas M., and Byron G. Massiales. 1965. *Tradition and Change in Education : A Comparative Study*. Englewood Cliffs, N.J.: Prentice Hall

Krashinsky, Stephen, and Jeffrey Sack. 1989. *Discharge and Discipline*. Toronto: Lancaster House

LaNoue, G.R., and B.A. Lee. 1987. *Academics in Court: The Consequences of Faculty Discrimination Legislation*. Ann Arbor: University of Michigan Press

Llewellyn, K.N., and E.A. Hoebel. 1941. *The Cheyenne Way*. Norman: University of Oklahoma Press

Lortie, D.C. 1969. 'The Balance of Control and Autonomy in Elementary School Teaching.' In *The Semi-Professions and Their Organization*. Ed. Amitai Etzioni. New York: Macmillan. 9–53

Macintyre, A. 1984. *After Virtue: A Study in Moral Theory*. 2nd ed. Notre Dame, Indiana: University of Notre Dame Press

Mackay, A.W. 1984. *Education Law in Canada*. Toronto: Emond-Montgomery

Mackenzie, E.D. 1992. 'You Be the Judge.' *University of New Brunswick Law Journal* 41: 345–53

Magsino, R.F. 1986. 'Denominational Rights in Education.' In *Courts in the Classroom: Education and the Charter of Rights and Freedoms*. Ed. M.E. Manley-Casimir and T.A. Sussel. Calgary: Detselig Enterprises Ltd. 77–94

– 1988. 'Compelling Teacher Behaviour: A Study of Conflicts and Resolution Mechanisms in the Atlantic Provinces.' Unpublished manuscript
– 1990. 'Compelling Teacher Behaviour: A Study of Conflicts and Resolution Mechanisms in Manitoba.' Unpublished manuscript
– 1993. 'Institutional Responses to Teacher Misconduct in the Atlantic Provinces.' *Education and Law Journal* 5/1: 143–65
Malinowski, B. 1944. *A Scientific Theory of Culture and Other Essays.* Chapel Hill, N.C.: North Carolina University Press
Manley-Casimir, M.E. 1982. 'Canadian and U.S. Legal Traditions – Implications for Administrative Practice.' *Canadian School Executive* 2/5: 18–21
Manley-Casimir, M.E., and S. Piddocke. 1991. 'Teachers in a Goldfish Bowl: A Case of "Misconduct."' *Education and Law Journal* 3/2: 115–48
Manley-Casimir, M.E., and T.A. Sussel, eds. 1986. *Courts in the Classroom: Education and the Charter of Rights and Freedoms.* Calgary: Detselig Enterprises Ltd.
Mead, M. 1965. *And Keep Your Powder Dry.* New York: William Morrow and Co. Expanded edition of work originally published in 1942
Medjuck, Sheva. 1992. 'Rethinking Canadian Justice: Hate Must Not Define Democracy.' *University of New Brunswick Law Journal* 41: 285–94
Merton, R. 1967. *Social Theory and Social Structure.* Rev. and enlarged ed. Glencoe, Ill.: The Free Press
Nicholas, R. 1968. 'Rules, Resources, and Political Activity.' In *Local Level Politics: Social and Cultural Perspectives.* Ed. M.J. Swartz. Chicago: Aldine. 295–332
Parker-Jenkins, M., and J.A. Osborne. 1985. 'Rights in Conflict: The Case of Margaret Caldwell.' *Canadian Journal of Education* 10/1: 66–76
Piddocke, S. 1986. 'Social Sanctions.' *Anthropologica* 10/1: 261–85
– 1993a. 'Sexual Liaisons between Teachers and Students: Four Board of Reference Cases.' *Education and Law Journal* 5/1: 53–69
– 1993b, 'Settling Disputes between School Boards and Teachers: A Review of Formal Procedures and Some Provincial Variations.' *Education and Law Journal* 5/1: 23–51
Pitsula, Pat, and Michael E. Manley-Casimir. 1989. 'The Charter, Educational Administration and U.S. Case Law: Contrasting Legal Norms and Traditions.' *Education Law* 2/1: 49–72
Proudfoot, A.J., and L. Hutchings. 1988. *Teacher Beware: A Legal Primer for the Classroom Teacher.* Calgary: Detselig Enterprises Ltd.
Riesman, David, Nathan Galzer, and Reuel Denney. 1954. *The Lonely Crowd: A Study of the Changing American Character.* New York: Doubleday
Ross, M. 1978. *Web of Deceit.* Moncton, N.B.: Stronghold
– 1987. *Spectre of Power.* Moncton, N.B.: Stronghold

Ryan, Stuart. 1992. 'Malcolm Ross and Free Speech.' *University of New Brunswick Law Journal* 41: 311–16

Ryerson, Egerton. 1847. *A Report on a System of Public Elementary Instruction for Upper Canada.* Montreal: Lovell and Gibson

Siracusa, Gabriella S. 1991. 'The John and Ilze Shewan Case: Unconventional Teacher Behaviour: Private Life in Public Conflict.' Unpublished research project in partial fulfilment of Master of Education degree, Simon Fraser University

Steele, Rev. William. 1992. 'Ross, Rights, and Justice.' *University of New Brunswick Law Journal* 41: 295–310

Turner, V.W. 1957. *Schism and Continuity in an African Tribe.* Manchester: Manchester University Press

Waller, W. 1965. *The Sociology of Teaching.* New York: John Wiley

Waters, Joseph St Clair. 1991. 'Boards of Reference in Ontario: Resolving Teacher-Board Contract Termination Disputes.' D.Ed. diss., University of Toronto

Wigmore, J. 1940. *Evidence in Trials at Common Law.* 3rd ed. Boston: Little Brown

Wilson, J.D., and M. Lazerson. 1982. 'Historical and Constitutional Perspectives on Family Choice in Schooling: The Canadian Case.' In *Family Choice in Schooling.* Ed. Michael E. Manley-Casimir. Lexington, Mass.: D.C. Heath and Co. 1–22

Index